A Geo-Big Year

Pandemic Retirement is
for the Birds

A Geo-Big Year

Pandemic Retirement is for the Birds

Alan M. MacEachren

Osprey View
Press

ISBN: 979-8-9871158-5-5 (Paperback)

32 31 30 29 28 27 26 25 24 23   15 14 13 12 11 10 9 8 7 6 5 4

Library of Congress Control Number: 2022919830

DEDICATION

For Fran

Contents

Acknowledgments

This Geo-Big Year was primarily a solo quest. As will become clear, it did not start out that way. My wife Fran had planned to accompany me on many trips. As mentioned in the account of the year below, she was able to join only three short trips among the many that found me birding on approximately 50% of the days during 2021. So, I begin by thanking Fran for tolerating my quest and for supporting me in many ways from home throughout the year.

Next, due to the pandemic, I seldom birded with others. But I would like to acknowledge the birders who I did encounter out in the field. Several provided local knowledge that helped find species I might have missed. In many cases, we talked birds but did not even introduce ourselves. So, here I acknowledge all birders who I encountered in the field, however briefly – you may remember me if you read this – Thanks!

Beyond specific individual birders who I met, I want to acknowledge the Cornell Lab of Ornithology, the eBird Team, plus hundreds of contributors who submitted eBird lists for Pennsylvania in 2021 and before. Without eBird's tools to learn about what had been seen where, I would have been much less successful finding as many species in each county as I did. On the eBird Team, a special thanks goes to my former Graduate Student (from many years ago), Tom Auer, who helped with data that made my mapping efforts easier and who passed along input I had on eBird features to the rest of the team.

Finally, I want to acknowledge the eBird volunteer reviewers across Pennsylvania who devote substantial time to minimizing errors in the eBird data I used to plan my travels. In particular, I thank those reviewers who caught the entry mistakes I made and/or prompted me to provide better details about what I reported.

The book includes over 1000 photos and some maps. All photos were taken by the author. Some are of existing art, historical panels, or maps created by others. For these, credits are included at the end of the book in the **Figure Credits** section. The **Figure Credits** section also includes credits for maps I generated with OpenStreetMap as well as for data accessed from eBird to generate quest progress maps using QGIS.

Who is this book for?

This book recounts a year-long birding adventure, comprised of travel to a wide variety of natural and not so natural places, that was undertaken by a university geographer — a geographer who was in the process of retiring during the year in the midst of the COVID-19 pandemic.

Thus, this book is for a wide audience. Aspects of the account should resonate with you:

- if you're a birder, or want to be birder;
- if you like photos of birds;
- if you like to travel, particularly on back roads and to natural places that are off the beaten track;
- if you're an academic thinking about work life balance;
- if you have thought about camping or tried camping after not doing any for a long time;
- if you're retired or contemplating retirement;
- if you've experienced life changes or expect to encounter some soon;
- or if you've ever contemplated pursuing a birding big year or any other kind of year-long quest.

Guide to Reading this Book

This book is published in black-and-white but is accompanied by a full color web supplement found at https://ospreyviewpress.com. That color supplement contains all figures in the book. All through the November sub-chapter are open to anyone. To see figures for December and beyond, the password is the first bird seen in December (no space). In most cases, the color figures are less tightly cropped. For bird photos, this provides a better sense of the environments that the birds were seen in. For photos of landscape scenes, art, signs, buildings, and other artifacts in places I visited, more of the setting is visible. The web site also includes full captions for figures written as alt-text to be meaningful in place of the figures as well as descriptions of them. In many cases these captions provide details beyond those in the main text.

To make it easy to relate figures in the book to those in the web supplement, call-outs in the text are keyed to embedded numbers in each figure (or figure sets). Figures are numbered separately for the introduction (In.01, In.02, etc.), for each month of the quest (January – 01.01, 01.02, …; February – 02.01, 02.02 …; …; December –12.01, 12.02, …; etc.), the concluding Reflections (Re.01, Re.02, etc.), and the Epilogue (Ep.01, Ep.02, etc.). In most cases, two, three, or more photos are grouped into one figure set identified with a single figure number. When specific photos in a set are mentioned together, photos in a set are (in almost all cases) arranged in sequence to match the text. When mentioned in separate statements, the following shorthand is used: -L = left, -M = middle, -R = right, -T = top; -B = bottom with combinations of the above in some cases (e.g., -BML = the middle left of 4 photos in the bottom row of a photo set).

In addition to color figures, the web supplement contains an index to bird species named in the text, with page numbers for species mentioned (mostly ones seen and a few searched for unsuccessfully). A second index is provided to mentions of counties in Pennsylvania.

In the text, when I cite bird species seen (or heard), I use common names and in most cases stick with the singular name, even when I saw more than one. This simplified generating the index. In situations where I mention groups of birds that I have already named in the singular, I sometimes use the plural form when it helps with the flow.

Introducing the Geo-Big Year

What was I thinking?
Retire in a pandemic
Lets go see some birds

Birding "Big Years" are both the bane and the joy of addicted birders. For non-birders (and some birders) the idea of a Big Year is known (if at all) through the movie *The Big Year* (with Steve Martin, Owen Wilson, and Jack Black) — a movie my wife Fran and I have watched 3 times! *The Big Year* movie documents a quest to see the most bird species ever in North America. The movie, while a great comedy (in our opinion), was adapted from Mark Obmascik's book *The Big Year: A Tale of Man, Nature, and Fowl Obsession,* Free Press, 2004, which documented an actual Big Year by Sandy Komito, Al Levantin, and Greg Miller who were all going after the earlier record set by Komito.

The Big Year let the broader public know about the extremes to which some birders go for rarities. And, the book and film stimulated a lot of birders to do their own quests, not only for big years but for specific "lifers" (species seen for the first time in one's life). I've heard several birders mention Great Gray Owl as their most sought-after species (I'm included in that group); I'll not be the movie spoiler by explaining why. I also met one birder who told me he had watched *The Big Year* about a dozen times in 2021 with non-birder friends and family. It was a way to explain his personal quest for a state big year.

Big years have been undertaken at all geographic scales, from individual counties, through states, countries, continents, and designated birding regions, to the entire globe. For many birders, Noah Stryker's 2015 Global Big Year was the most captivating. He set off to break the 5000 species barrier globally (the prior global big year record was 4,342); he ended up seeing 6,042 species!

My wife Fran and I had the pleasure of attending a talk by Stryker at *Wings Over Water* on the North Carolina Outer Banks about 2 months before he started his quest. Many of us monitored his blog throughout the year and then read the more detailed account of the quest in his subsequent book (*Birding Without Borders: An Obsession, a Quest, and the Biggest Year in the World*, Houghton Mifflin Harcourt, 2017).

When Stryker completed that global big year, his record seemed (to me, at least) insurmountable. But, as he recounts at the end of that book, Dutch birder Arjan Dwarshuis was already closing in on the record the very next year as Stryker finished his book. By the end of that year (2016), perhaps in part due to learning from Stryker's quest, Dwarshuis broke Stryker's global big year record by a substantial margin, with 6852 species seen.

Birding Big Years are frequently competitive. Once a record is set, someone else will surely try to outdo it — and almost certainly someone will. This tendency for one-upmanship is clear in *The Big Year* movie (and the real quest it reflects) and in the global quests by Stryker and then Dwarshuis. The birder I mentioned above (who watched *The Big Year* movie many times) had just pushed beyond the state record he was chasing when I talked to him toward the end of December 2021. As with Stryker's global big year, the record he surpassed had been set just the prior year.

While records are made to be broken, for many birders (perhaps most), birding is more about seeing and hearing birds, being outdoors, and learning about bird behavior. Committed birders often devote considerable time and energy (and resources) to improving their own ability to find and recognize species. For them, Birding Big Years can be a personal challenge focused on individual goals rather than competition with others.

While traditional Big Years are fascinating to me, and even tempting to try, I'm not in the class of birder that sets records. I (and my wife Fran) have been birding since 1991. We got started on the Outer

Banks of North Carolina, where we spent my first sabbatical from Penn State during the 1991-92 academic year. My primary focus that year was writing. Mostly, I worked on 2 books (both about cartography, not birds). We lived in a small apartment right on the ocean that my in-laws loaned us, and there were lots of birds! We got hooked on the challenges of identifying what we saw. I quickly began using birding as a diversion to clear my mind during the intense year of writing (I finished one book and half of the other). A typical day, when the weather allowed, was a walk or run on the beach, breakfast, intense writing, time watching birds, lunch, intense writing, and more time watching birds. I bought a scope (a Nikon ED) that lasted me through the Geo-Big Year I recount here; and that I finally replaced in early 2022 when stripped threads caused the eyepiece to keep falling out.

That first year of birding was a long time ago. Still, starting birding at 40 was an impediment (along with a busy academic career that focused on cartography and data visualization rather than birds) to developing a good memory for bird songs and calls. One plus from my year-long quest was that it increased my audio birding skill. But there continue to be species that my birding friends (particularly those who started birding as kids) can distinguish by ear that I must see to ID.

Given my overall skill level and the fact that I'm a Geographer, I decided on a different kind of Big Year, focused on *place* more than on *species* — thus a **Geo-Big** Year. More specifically, I defined a *Geo-Big Year* as one focused on birding a predetermined set of places and reaching target totals in each place rather than achieving the highest possible total overall. My original plan for the set of places was to bird in every state of the U.S., setting a modest target of 50 species in each state. Fran and I began birding together, but she has never been into lists nor as enamored with bird-specific travel as I have been. So, the modest target in each state was intended to allow us to do a lot of the travel together while enjoying aspects of each state beyond birds. Fran's first degree (from Stanford) was in art with a focus on painting. While she had focused on fabric art during our years in Pennsylvania (check out: https://quiltedvisions.net), she was planning to switch back to painting and the U.S. travel would provide stimuli for those paintings.

The pandemic put the U.S. Geo-Big Year plan on hold. That much travel, some necessarily by air, seemed too risky. So, I opted for the set of all counties in Pennsylvania as the places to bird and set a target of 67 species per county. That arbitrary target matched the number of counties in the state. The higher target with more places (compared to 50 species in each of 50 states) seemed practical given the very much smaller territory to cover.

If I had pursued the U.S. Geo-Big Year, I might have retired in December 2020 to devote 2021 to that travel. Instead, I stuck with my intention to retire at the end of the 2020-2021 academic year. My spring 2021 teaching was scheduled to be completely online, and the continuing pandemic meant all Departmental and other meetings were online as well. So, with a more local focus on Pennsylvania where we live, I decided to pursue the Geo-Big Year in 2021, starting with counties close to home while still working.

As will become clear as the story of the year unfolds, the Pennsylvania Geo-Big Year turned out to be a more completely solo quest than initially planned. Fran (and dog Skoti) supported from the home base in Centre County, PA, joining me on fewer trips than we had envisioned.

+++

A starting point for Geo-Big Year planning was analysis of eBird sighting records for "hotspots" in Pennsylvania. As most birders know, eBird is a global, online bird sighting database created and run by the Cornell Lab of Ornithology (https://ebird.org/). It is one of the largest successful Citizen Science projects, with over 500 million records contributed by thousands of birders globally. Lists posted to eBird get anchored to places, with tools that encourage (but do not require) birders to link their sightings to preestablished *hotspots.* Hotspots in eBird are proposed by birders, typically places they bird regularly.

The map below (ln.01) depicts all eBird hotspot locations for Pennsylvania in early 2021 as I began the quest. The official guidelines for good hotspots are: (a) the location is open to the public (in practice, not all are), (b) the location encompasses a small enough area to be useful as a place that sighting data can be aggregated to (in practice, hotspots vary in size and can nest, with some such as state parks including smaller hotspots), and (c) are places for which the boundaries are defined and identified easily (in practice this varies, with places like parks having clearly marked boundaries but more localized hotspots within them typically having much fuzzier bounds).

Pennsylvania eBird Hotspots

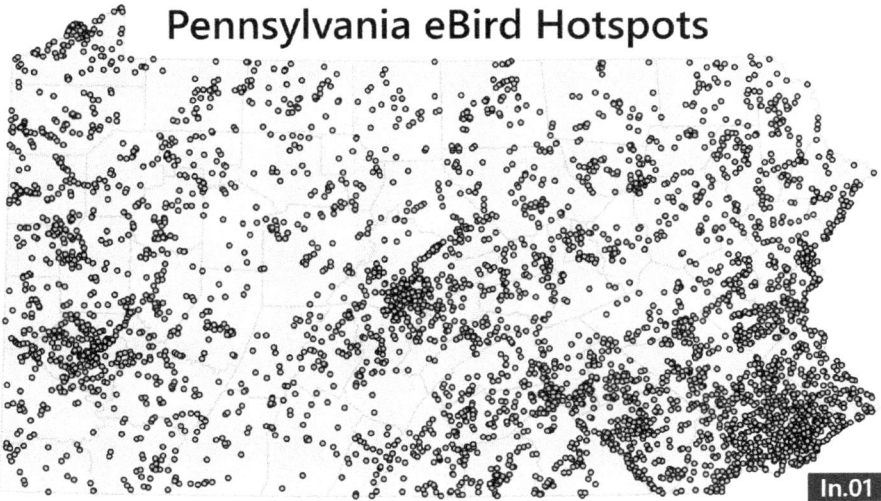

In.01

As is clear from the map, hotspots, are not evenly distributed. Because they reflect where birding happens, they cluster around populated places (e.g., Philadelphia and the southeast as well as Pittsburgh) and other places where active birding communities exist (e.g., Centre County where the main Penn State University campus is and where there is a very active bird club, which Fran and I are members of — https://www.scbirdcl.org).

eBird provides several tools that enable birders to leverage contributed data to determine when and where specific species might be seen and to learn what has been seen at specific places. Because of the population-bias, eBird data are less helpful for finding birds in rural counties than in urban counties. At the same time, lack of data in rural places makes it important for some of us to generate data in those empty places. That is a primary motivator for doing a Geo-Big Year.

While eBird's utility varied by county, I typically made use of the data summarization features to get a rough idea of what might be seen when and where. eBird makes it easy to generate a bar chart that depicts frequency of sightings by week of the year for all species ever recorded at any place within eBird. The degree to which the graphs match actual species abundance, of course, depends on the abundance of birders in the place/region represented. These bar charts can be generated for individual hotspots or for larger areas (e.g., whole counties or states). An example is shown below for the Hawk Mountain Sanctuary North Lookout hotspot in Schuylkill County (In.02).

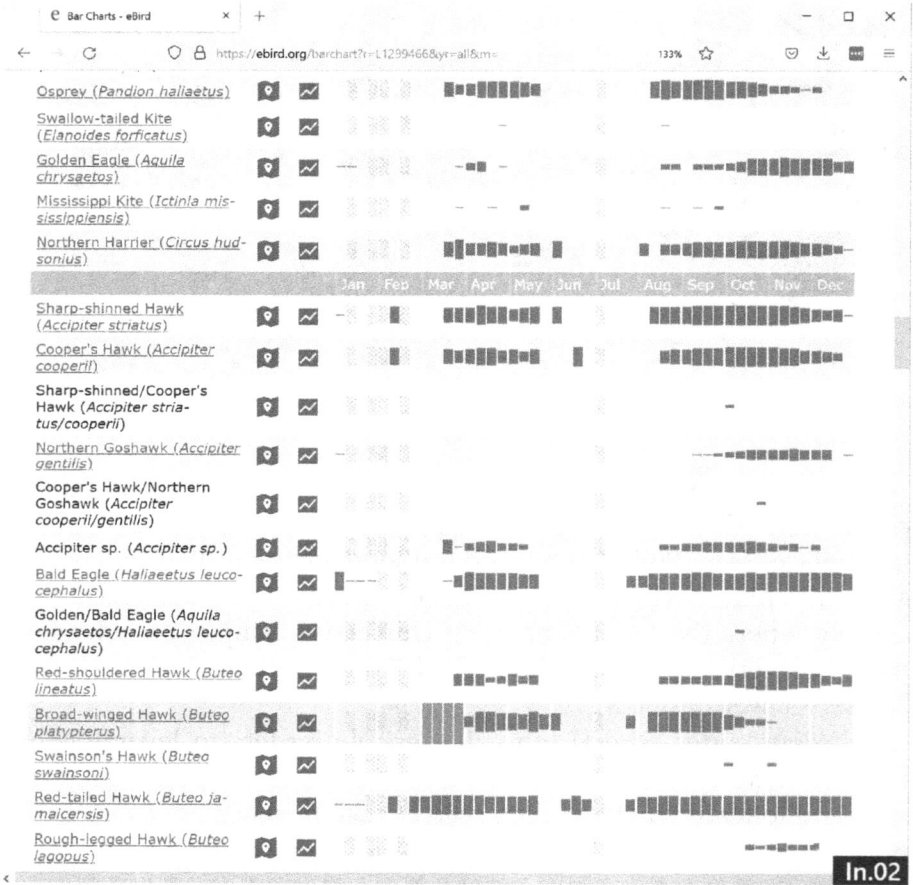

In.02

The eBird screen capture shows a subset of the much longer bar chart. I highlighted Broad-winged Hawk and March in its row. As shown, Broad-winged Hawks are unlikely in March, but Northern Harrier, and Osprey might be seen. Since it is impossible to visit all places at once, I needed to be strategic about when to visit each county. I tentatively picked the 3rd week in October to visit Hawk Mountain.

As I'll discuss later, some hotspots are quite easy to locate in the field and others are not. But, once located, the eBird mobile app makes it simple to select the hotspot as the location for any list created. My iPhone eBird screen below shows the interface to do this (In.03).

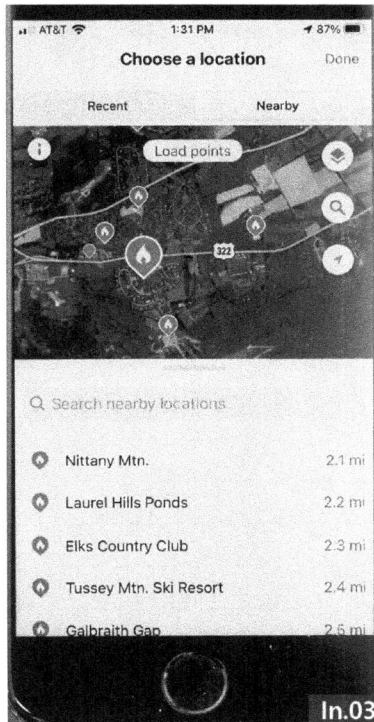

Once you start a list with the eBird mobile app, it records time spent and (unless you turn the feature off) records a track of your position while doing that list. When the track is stopped, the app calculates distance traveled. Guidelines for eBird ask users to adjust the distance traveled to avoid double-counting if they follow an out-and-back path. Some eBird reviewers prompt distance corrections when birders (like me) forget. If you chose not to have your path tracked (e.g., you are birding a sensitive or private site where tracking is not appropriate), eBird still requires a travel distance estimate for all non-stationary lists.

All individuals who use eBird can download their own data. The combination of eBird's list creation and recording policies meant that at the end of the year I could download my own records, complete with duration and distance for each list (distance, of course, is not included for stationary lists).

+++

My quest evolved during the year for many expected and unexpected reasons. The expected reasons relate to the seasons, Pennsylvania breeding birds, and bird migration. The unexpected reasons relate to life generally and the global pandemic.

Despite this being a book about a *Geo*-Big Year, I organize the core chapters temporally, by quarters of the year (roughly seasons) and within each quarter by month. This choice was prompted by strategies I developed to cover the state and life situations that changed as the year progressed. It also reflects the seasonal variations in birding experiences over time and across space.

First Quarter
Winter Toward Spring

It is cold outside
But a rarity to chase
Nowhere to be found

And, so it began — a Geo-Big Year. What were we in for? On January 11, 2021, Fran and I returned to Pennsylvania (PA) from our "vacation" house on the Outer Banks of North Carolina (OBX), the place where we have started every year since 2013. I had my best start to a birding year ever with 149 species in Dare County, NC from January 1-10. But that is the prequel to the story. Those birds don't count in my Pennsylvania Geo-Big Year.

JANUARY

On January 12, 2021, I started my Geo-Big Year quest. The year's goal was (at least) 67 species in each of Pennsylvania's 67 counties. The first PA bird of 2021 was a Dark-eyed Junco (5 of them to be precise), at Colyer Lake in Centre County. The individual below (01.01) is not one of the 5; they did not cooperate for a photo. This junco was seen under our feeders at home the next day. By then, it was my 23rd 2021 Junco for the county, but the first photogenic one. Check out color versions of this and all photos on the book's web page.

That partial morning of birding at Colyer Lake resulted in 20 species, a slow start compared to a typical January morning on the OBX. As I knew all too well when I began the quest, we have many fewer winter species in Central PA. Pileated Woodpecker and Horned Lark were the highlights of that first day.

As mentioned in Chapter 1, my planned retirement from Penn State was slated to start on July 1. That meant January-June would be a balancing act between birding and ongoing responsibilities as a Professor of Geography and Information Sciences & Technology at Penn State. My formal teaching responsibilities were scheduled to end in mid-March, as my last teaching as an active professor was in a compressed, 10-week class within our online Professional Master in GIS program. Other responsibilities (most done remotely due to COVID-19)) continued through June; these included collaboration on writing papers, faculty meetings, committee work, student advising, plus the major challenge of moving out of the office that I had occupied for 36 years!

So, the plan for the first two quarters of the year was organized around this gradual decrease in work responsibilities. While my employment was officially through June, like other tenure-line faculty at Penn State, my contract was for 36 weeks (ending with spring commencement in early May). Our salaries are spread across full academic years, but we only have formal summer responsibilities if we have external research funding or teach summer classes. I had neither for my final Penn State Year. Thus, I would be able to start ignoring most University emails on May 10 — the day after Spring Commencement!

As the year started, Fran still planned to join me for many of the overnight trips. For those trips, we intended to use our new Lance camping trailer that we bought in fall 2020 (a *model 1985*) … the best laid plans … But, I'm getting ahead of myself.

Let's start at the beginning. During the next few days of the quest, January 13-15, it was quite cold — a disincentive for birding. I worked on the course I was teaching and reviewed a dissertation for a January 15 defense. Birding was from my workspace, overlooking our patio — where I got the photo of the Junco above. I did chase after a Hoary Redpoll that had been visiting a local birder's house for a couple weeks. I had no luck. I saw my first 2021 Cooper's Hawk for Centre County near that house and hoped that the Redpoll had not become a meal.

Saturday (Jan. 16) I finally had time for a full morning of birding. I found the recurring Hoary Redpoll (a lifer) and a Common Redpoll in the same day! These species are tricky to distinguish. Many people had seen the Hoary before me. The very faint streaks and very small bill were good clues and another local birder managed to get audio as added confirmation. The Common Redpoll I found was somewhat whiter than typical, but the bolder flank streaking plus repeated nasal call were the clinchers. Both (01.02) were eBird rarities here for January and were accepted as valid reports by the local eBird reviewer.

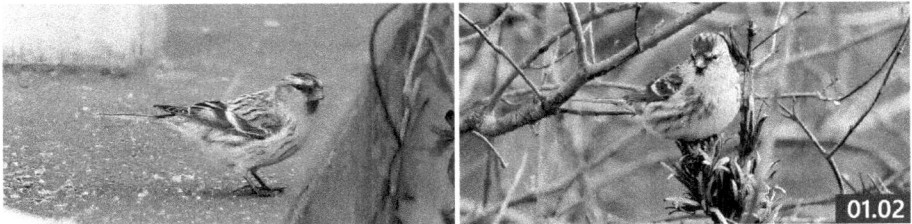
01.02

Sunday (Jan. 17) found me finally hitting 40 species in Centre County for the year — with a Northern Shrike (01.03) at Mid-State Airport, a place it had frequented for a couple weeks. The location of the Airport prompted me to make short detours into adjacent Clearfield and Blair Counties. Those netted only 7 and 4 species, respectively.

01.03

More than halfway through January, my Geo-Big Year was off to a very slow start. In addition to the time spent in North Carolina and my Penn State work, the weather was (not surprisingly) cold and windy. I quickly remembered why I seldom got out to bird in Pennsylvania in January. Given the small number of likely Year Birds for Centre County over the next week, I began branching out to surrounding counties. On Saturday, January 23, I decided to chase a Trumpeter Swan seen repeatedly at Prince Gallitzin State Park in Cambria County.

I got out of the house a bit later than planned, but by 8:00am was halfway there. The goal was to see the Trumpeter and get a good start on my Cambria County list. The route took me through a part of central Pennsylvania that I hadn't seen before. Tyrone, which I had driven by on I-99, but had never driven through looked a bit depressing on that gray January day, unsurprisingly for a shrinking central Pennsylvania town in winter. Tyrone's population peaked at just over 9,000, in 1930, then slowly fell to under 6,000 today. Its unemployment rate is about 1% higher than the national average, although this is still nearly 2 percentage points better than Pennsylvania overall.

Once through the edge of Tyrone, the countryside is typical rural central PA with farms, hills, and valleys. I got to the State Park, and it was cold (low 20s and windy). So, I birded partly from the car and partly on foot. After scanning the lake from the parking area at the marina, and seeing little at first, I found a cluster of water birds across the lake near the far shore. There were a lot of Canada Geese, many ducks (hard to identify from that distance, even with a scope) and one swan.

I presumed the swan was the Trumpeter, since the only recent swan reports from Prince Gallitzin State Park had been a lone Trumpeter. But the distance was too great for a confident ID. I decided to drive the few miles around the lake to the boat launch on the other side, closer to the Swan. I got there and walked through a bit of snow to the best vantage point. I could see a lot of Canada Geese, some Bufflehead, Mallard, Common Merganser, and Ring-billed Gull, but not the Swan — it was apparently around the bend in the next cove.

I was hoping for a trail to walk the roughly ½ mile distance to a better vantage point. But my *Pocket Earth* app showed no trail and I saw no sign of one on the ground, under the 6-8 inches of snow. So, I decided to return to the other side of the lake and try scoping again from various locations and to take photos with my Olympus OMD E-M1 Mark

III. I have the 300mm Pro lens (that on this 4/3 mirrorless camera acts like a 600mm) + a doubler that extends to a 1200mm equivalent.

I got some fuzzy photos, but not crisp enough to distinguish a Trumpeter from a Tundra Swan. I did find Canvasback (01.04), Ruddy Duck and Hooded Merganser (multiple of each), and two Ring-necked Duck, so the morning outing was not a complete waste.

I found out the next day that a couple hours after I left, another Centre County birder reported the Trumpeter and got a better photo — the swan apparently moved closer to the boat launch. While that birder's sighting was confirmed by eBird, I could not be sure I saw the same bird. Thus, I left my report as a *Swan Sp*.

Back in Centre County I ventured out in the cold the next day to try adding species to my home county list. During the previous week, I'd tried twice for Evening Grosbeak, seen by seemingly everyone else in Centre County. The Grosbeaks had been hanging around at houses with feeders in Penns Valley. But I missed them on both previous tries. This time (Sunday, Jan. 24) I got an early start and went straight to Penns Valley. I was rewarded with about 30 Evening Grosbeaks plus Common Raven flying overhead, both shown below (01.05), and my first Golden-crowned Kinglet of the year.

After that rather quick success, I decided to drive to Mifflin County to get a start there. I picked the wrong route, the back way over the mountain. The route started fine — a small paved and snow-free rural road. As I progressed, it switched from paved to semi-paved but still seemed fine, so I headed up the mountain. When I hit the State Forest, the road plowing stopped. I found packed snow and ice, with only a few cinders sprinkled on top. Still, it seemed passable, safely with the AWD in Fran's RAV4 I drove that day. But, as the road got steeper, I started to worry about sliding over the steep and quite close edge ... or into the ditch on the interior side. I also started to think about what the downhill might be like once I crossed the peak .... Many years back I would have forged on ahead. Fran still talks about one outing where we nearly slid down/off the mountain and another where we nearly got our Subaru Forester stuck in about 2 feet of snow that I decided to drive through (with her and our little dog of the time, Muffie, along for the exciting ride).

This time, I decided to not chance it. But that meant I was forced to do a rather precarious U-turn on the narrow road, with a lot of very careful back-and forth to get turned around without slipping over the edge. Ultimately, I did get turned around and heading back where I'd started from without mishap ... working my way down the mountain in first gear. Once on clear pavement, I picked a different route over the mountain on the main highway.

That route did not work out well either — the newly opened US-322 expansion, with its divided highway meant driving 8 miles past my planned destination, exiting the highway, crossing over, then heading back on the other side. As I went past my planned destination (a rest stop with a good list of possible species), I saw it was closed and blocked off. So, I skipped it and drove to Reed's Gap State Park. When I eventually got there it was the quietest place I'd visited all year — almost no birds at all! I left the park after about 30 min. with just 4 species — picking up two more for Mifflin County on the way home.

After lunch, I decided to try Huntingdon County. I did a quick drive over to Shaver's Creek Environmental Center (a Penn State Outreach facility in Stone Valley). Bird activity was only slightly better there; I managed 10 species in about 1 hour, but nothing unusual. I took a short side trip to try for Evening Grosbeak in Huntingdon County. They had been reported in a nearby neighborhood — but I had no luck.

I quit for the day and generated a status table to gauge progress for the first two weeks of my quest. Progress was clearly slow. To see 67 species in each of 67 counties would require a pace of about 86 new species per week across the year. My current pace was less than half that. Plus, I started about 2 weeks into the year and expected to miss some other weeks with trips back to our house on the OBX in North Carolina. So, my pace for weeks in Pennsylvania needed to be even faster. It was winter, of course. While not welcome, a slow start was expected. Migration months later in the year would clearly be critical.

SPECIES TOTALS AS OF JANUARY 24			
CENTRE	46	CLEARFIELD	7
CAMBRIA	12	MIFFLIN	6
HUNTINGDON	10	BLAIR	4

The Trumpeter Swan still beckoned. So, on January 25, I headed back to Prince Gallitzin State Park — stimulated by the sighting reported just after my last trip to the park. On my drive through parts of Tyrone, things looked less depressed than my prior time through — amazing what some sunshine will do.

I saw good birds on this trip, including Common Merganser and Redhead. There was one swan again. Reports had continued of a Trumpeter, and this bird resembled photos others had posted. I got lots of pictures, better than on my previous trip … but from views through my scope and a quick look at the photos, I was not sure if it was a trumpeter. The bill had a rounded edge with the head and there seemed to be a notch near the gape. So, in spite of the lack of yellow near the eyes, this looked (to me) more like a Tundra Swan than Trumpeter — I needed to review photos at home before deciding.

I got home, processed photos, and spent a long time reviewing them. I also explored online info about distinguishing Trumpeter and Tundra Swans. As much as I wanted this to be a Trumpeter, I could not 'turn it into one'. I ultimately decided it was a Tundra Swan posted that to eBird with photos and my explanation. That Tundra ID got confirmed by eBird review.

The end of January was near, so I tried to bird when I could fit it around work, despite the weather. On January 29, I headed out on a very cold morning, 18°F but feeling like 3°F according to the weather app. Although it was quite cold, I was well prepared for both cold (and

COVID-19 risk, should anyone else be foolish enough to be out birding), with my heavy coat, hat, and neck gaiter Covid facemask (01.06).

I decided to run up to Bald Eagle State Park, since I figured it might still have a bit of open water. I was pleasantly surprised by extensive ice-free areas. I saw many Common Merganser (150 at one stop), some Ring-Billed Gull, Belted Kingfisher (2), and my first Northern Pintail and American Black Duck of the year (a couple each).

The next day was yet another cold morning. I decided to chase a Snowy Owl and a different Trumpeter Swan, both reported in Cumberland County. This might not have been smart, since the site with the owl was about an hour and a half away. But I opted to try because the next day was predicted to be quite 'snowy' (of the precipitation kind). At least traffic was light when I headed out.

The car navigation system took me through Port Royal Pennsylvania, a place I'd never been. It looked like a town that time forgot. Houses were well kept up but there was little activity. The app then took me on State Route 74. That route goes zigzagging up and over the mountain (01.07). A slow drive, but with nice views.

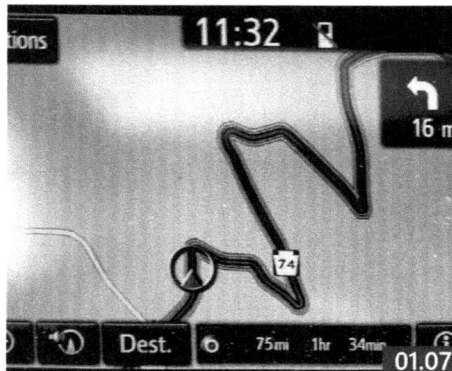

I did find the Snowy Owl, but like the dozen or so other birders there that day, only had a distant view of it partly hidden in a corn field. My brief foray into Cumberland County yielded 23 species, including a Red-Shouldered Hawk, Cooper's Hawk, Barred Owl, and Bald Eagle.

+++

I reached the end of January with nine counties visited, at least briefly. To track progress, I generated another table that depicts number of species in each of the nine counties birded.

SPECIES TOTALS AS OF JANUARY 31			
CENTRE (IN THE CENTER)	51	MIFFLIN	7
CUMBERLAND	23	BLAIR	4
CAMBRIA	22	JUNIATA	3
HUNTINGDON	10	PERRY	3
CLEARFIELD	7		

Since this was a Geo-Big Year, and I am a geographer, I opted (not surprisingly) to map my progress. I generated a choropleth map (01.08) with counties shaded from white (for zero) to black (for 67 species or more). The intervening four categories reflect percentiles between these extremes. Locations of the eBird lists I posted are indicated by the open circles. Obviously, I had stayed relatively local and had avoided the coldest counties to the north. *My first maps used online tools. Starting in late summer I generated more finished maps, which I include here.*

Pennsylvania Geo-Big Year - January

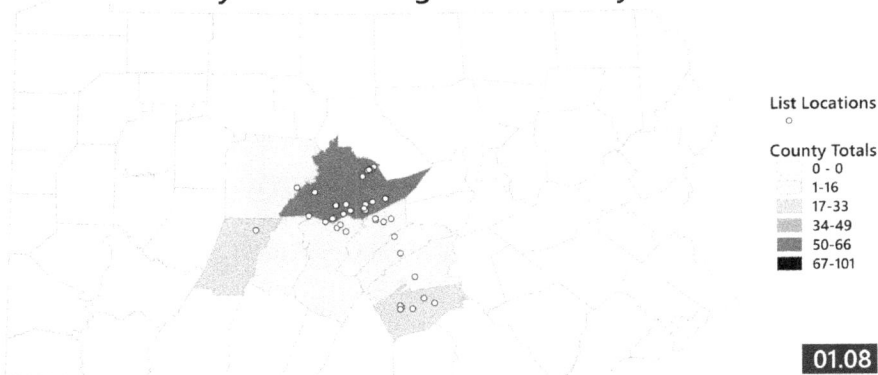

List Locations
∘

County Totals
0 - 0
1-16
17-33
34-49
50-66
67-101

01.08

+++++

FEBRUARY

February started slowly. Work restricted birding to home for a few days and I added no new species. On February 6, I decided to head to Bald Eagle State Park. It was the only place in Centre County with open water and a Pied-billed Grebe had been seen. After about 100 Common Merganser, I finally spotted the Pied-billed Grebe diving near the marina. As I was leaving, I got a bonus, my first-of-year Great Blue Heron in the county, flying over the marina and then off over the trees.

Local birders in Dare County, NC use *Group Me* to share bird sighting texts. Centre County, PA birders use *WhatsApp* instead. I am a "conscientious objector" to all things Facebook (who bought *WhatsApp* in 2014) so don't use it. The drawback of sticking to my ethics is that I wait for eBird to learn about sightings, later and with less precise locations.

By avoiding WhatsApp, I nearly missed Short-eared Owl seen near the airport. Once I learned of the sighting, I was in luck. I drove to the airport and two owls were still there flying around. They stayed at a distance, but close enough to ID (with both scope views and photos). After about a half hour of watching, I decided to settle for the views I'd gotten. As I was driving away, one of the owls started working the field closer to me so I stopped. It landed on a fence post. I turned around and drove slowly up to the post with the window down. The owl stayed, about 15 feet away from me (02.01). What an experience!

The day after the owls (Sunday, Feb. 7), snow was falling. I headed out Route 45 looking for Lapland Longspur and Snow Bunting. I tried a dirt road through some Penn State fields, but the snow was too much for my AWD. I tried to back up, but was impeded by my snow-covered backup camera. Eventually, I worked my way back out to the main road and decided to progress on into Huntingdon County.

Although it was snowing quite a bit, I did see a few good species. First was a group of six Wild Turkey. Then, I spotted a group of Horned Lark. Continuing toward the end of the county where I was going to turn around, I got to Warriors Mark and looked at the dashboard. I had forgotten to get gas and the car told me I had 9 miles left.

02.01

There were no nearby gas stations, the closest was a few miles back the way I had come in Centre County. I turned around and headed there. I was happy to reach the station with 6 miles of gas left (02.02).

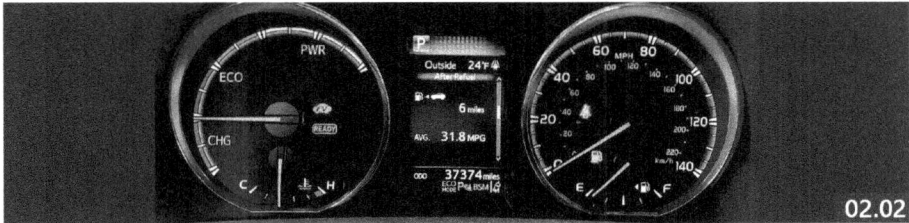

02.02

But I pulled in, inserted my credit card in the pump, and the pump's screen kept going blank. I backed up to the pump behind. It's screen said it would not take cards at all. I got back in the car and headed to the next likely station a couple miles down the road. I made it … they had gas and pumps that took cards!

The next day (Feb. 8) I went chasing a Cackling Goose seen at the Pennsylvania Furnace Pond. I arrived early, parked, and walked to the pond. It was full of Canada Geese; about 75. I stood in the cold scanning the geese multiple times carefully — no Cackling Goose. The only bird other than Canada Goose was one Common Merganser. On return to the car the temperature read 4°F. No wonder my hands were freezing.

I drove to the nearby Fairbrook Wetland to scan from the car — more Canada Geese, some Mallard, and little else. It remained at 4°F. I went looking for Snow Buntings, a species often best seen using the car as a blind. No luck with them either, so I headed home.

+++

I took a few days to recover from the cold and focus on teaching. On February 13, I ventured out on another cold morning; it was 18°F but felt like 9°F. So rather than going after the 21 year-species recently seen in Centre, County, I headed to Raystown Lake (where I had a chance to see some new species from the warm car). A particular target was a Common Loon reported there. Plus, the chance of other species was good since I only had a few species in Huntington County at that point.

Using eBird, I was directed to Seven Points Beach at the Lake. I saw a Common Loon almost immediately. There were also Bufflehead, Hooded Merganser, Common Merganser, a couple Ruddy Duck, a Mallard, and many Ring-Billed Gull — all were new for the county. I stuck around trying to get good photos of the Loon (they never got close enough for one to include here, but I did post a distant shot in eBird). While trying for photos, I saw a second loon and then eventually a third. I shifted to the other side of the lake where I noticed a picturesque stone house ruin, always a shame to see such an impressive structure abandoned — but it provides a nice photo opportunity (02.03). Near the ruin, I found a Yellow-bellied Sapsucker and a Winter Wren. All in all, a good morning.

02.03

I went home for lunch, then decided to try the Duck Pond here in State College. The normal entrance was closed indefinitely (due to construction at the water treatment facility). Thus, the route in is a trudge through the snow and down a steep hill from the street behind and above the pond. It was worth the trudge — I found Canvasback, a pair (02.04-L) that were enjoying the slightly heated water (a result of being at the outflow from the water treatment facility). I also saw Gadwall (02.04-R) and Mallard (many).

With these sightings, I was quickly closing in on 67 species for Centre County. It was on track to be my first "completed" county; no surprise there since I had 220 species in Centre County for 2020.

The morning of February 14, Valentine's Day, I got up early to dismal weather — freezing drizzle around the county and beyond. Still, I ate a quick breakfast and took Skoti (our dog) for a walk in the woods. Then, I decided to head to Mill Hall to start on Clinton County. One hotspot (Duck Run Rd.) had 25 species seen in the prior three days. It was foggy, so conditions were not ideal, but it seemed worth a try.

The site proved to be a good one — I got 25 species (including a couple Golden-crowned Kinglet, a Yellow-bellied Sapsucker, and some Green-winged Teal). My morning total at 3 sites in the county was 31, my most that far for the first day in any county.

A couple days later, I planned to head back to Bald Eagle State Park (Centre County) to look for a Long-tailed Duck seen the day before. The weather was uncooperative. A snowstorm prevented an early outing. After working at home in the morning, I tried for the Duck after lunch. I spent a lot of time looking, with no luck. I did get 5 Common Goldeneye, a year-bird for the County. So, it was worth the trip.

+++

I had been trying to get my first COVID-19 vaccine shot and finally had it scheduled for February 17. But while out birding, I got a text from Geisinger Health saying it was rescheduled to February 28. My plan was to wait at least until I had both shots before doing any overnight trips — so it would continue to be day trips for a while.

After a few days catching up on work, I decided to start on Union County, where Bucknell University is. I checked eBird for help but found few postings. Since the drive each way was over an hour, I hoped lack of postings meant few birders rather than few birds.

It was yet another cold morning, 17°F when I started out. The Union County birds turned out being as scarce as eBird suggested they might be. The best were Common Merganser and Pileated Woodpecker (at two different locations). On the way home I picked up a bunch of Horned Lark, Eastern Bluebird (several), and a couple other species, but reached just 20 for the day.

+++

Up to this point in the year, I had (mostly) resisted the urge to chase species very far from home. But a Clay-Colored Sparrow reported in Indiana County was intriguing since it would be a life bird that I'd tried for multiple times without success. So, I decided it was worth a chase. I headed for Indiana County on the morning of February 20 with the temperature at 8°F. I knew I had a really cold morning in store, and as I left town, the temperature dropped to 0°F. As I passed Penn State's football stadium, I looked around for a Peregrine Falcon reported around there repeatedly, but of course did not see it. I had tried for that Falcon at least a half dozen times with no luck.

The Clay-colored Sparrow was reported at a private residence. I found the right general location, but not the specific house because the map from eBird didn't match the real world. Since I'm a Geographer with a research and teaching focus on Cartography, this was no surprise! With no certain way to find the house, I refocused on a nearby county park. There, I had Black-capped Chickadee (several) come up to check me out, almost too close for my lens (02.05-L). A Red-bellied Woodpecker (02.05-R) also was curious and put on an impressive display with its tail. While a black & white image captures a lot of the Chickadee's charm, it does not do justice to a Red-Bellied Woodpecker (check out the web color supplement). While encounters with both Chickadees and Woodpeckers were nice, I found few other species. I decided to try again to find the Clay-colored Sparrow location.

On the drive back to the most likely street, I had an up-close and personal encounter with an immature Bald Eagle (02.06).

My second try was successful — at finding the right house. By then, the temperature was 23°F, a bit more tolerable. I staked out the dozen or so feeders from across the street. There were American Goldfinch, Dark-eyed Junco, Downy Woodpecker, Red-bellied Woodpecker, along with both Red-breasted Nuthatch and White-breasted Nuthatch. But I had no luck on Clay-colored Sparrow or even Chipping Sparrow. After about 45 minutes standing there in the cold, two Saint Bernards came into a nearby driveway. They began barking at me. I said *hi guys*! They seemed relatively friendly, but persisted in barking, and barking, and barking. I finally decided I better give up, get back in the car, and depart because the dogs might disturb the entire neighborhood (or already had).

From the stakeout, I headed to Yellow Creek State Park since I did not want to waste the trip. However, by the time I arrived, birds were scarce and quiet; I only found 5 species in 25 minutes. After standing out in the cold for an hour previously, the continuing cold seemed intense. So, I gave up and headed for home. The trip was disappointing, with no lifer and only 17 species total.

+++

With the start of a new workweek, and continuing cold temperatures, I stayed home for a few days to "coach" students in my online course, get assignments graded, and deal with other work responsibilities. Three days before my rescheduled vaccine shot, I got a message from Geisinger that my shot was again rescheduled, this time to March 20th! I got online and managed to get myself and Fran onto the waiting list for a shot at the hospital instead. I checked the box indicating that we could be available on short notice if a space opened up.

+++

By Friday (Feb. 26), I was caught up on grading. We had no word about the vaccine shot, so I decided to head out to bird in adjacent Huntingdon County. While still cold, it was sunny with very blue sky. On the way, I stopped within Centre County at Fairbrook Wetland to check it out. There was nothing at the wetland, or at the Johnson Rd. Pond, or the Pond at Pennsylvania Furnace. So, I continued on.

The first site I tried in Huntingdon County, where several species had been reported, turned out to be mostly inaccessible since the roads were private. This was my first hint of the troubles I'd have during the year using eBird to chase species at hotspots I was unfamiliar with — but that is a story for later. While trying to find access to the hotspot (which I did not), I picked up Cedar Waxwing, an adult Bald Eagle that flew by, then a lone Red-winged Blackbird calling from a tree.

In my attempt to find the hotspot, I wasted too much time to get to the next site I had intended to visit. So, I opted for Shavers' Creek again (with its Lake and trails). I had little time left because I wanted to get back home in case the hospital contacted us about the COVID-19 vaccine shots. I heard Common Raven when exiting the car on arrival and I took a quick 14-minute jaunt along one trail with no birds seen. On my way out, I saw a Hairy Woodpecker in the parking lot. Just before I arrived home, Fran got an email saying her vaccine shot was scheduled for March 1 (Mon.); but nothing on mine yet.

+++

The next morning (Saturday, Feb 27) was a bit warmer, 34°F. I decided to head over to Big Valley for Mifflin County species. As I drove over the mountain, it began to get foggy. On the downslope, I found thick fog hanging across the valley. There was still some visibility, so I pressed on — and was rewarded with an American Kestrel on the way into Belleville.

As I was birding a rural road, an Amish fellow (from the Peachey family who are prominent in the valley) stopped with his horse cart to chat about the Kestrel. He had knowledge of local birds and knew some local non-Amish birders. He also recognized good binoculars (he noticed my Swarovski 8.5x42 ELs) and knew Aden Troyer who owns The Lost Creek Shoe Shop where I bought the binoculars. Aden's Shoe Shop is also the top optics store in Central Pennsylvania. Aden is an expert birder who once visited our house when we had a rare (for Pennsylvania) Varied Thrush in the yard for a few days.

I had a nice chat with Mr. Peachey. He mentioned having Rough-legged Hawk around his place over the winter and having seen Snow Buntings within the past few days. That prompted me to stop frequently and scan the likely fields for the Buntings, but I had no luck.

The trip to Mifflin County was only marginally productive. I decided to return home for lunch after going to Victory Park in Lewistown and seeing virtually nothing. I found that my position on the COVID-19 vaccine list at Mount Nittany had disappeared. I may have accidently canceled the appointment when trying to check it with their clumsy phone interface. So, I wanted to get home to get myself back on that list. Fran still had her shots scheduled so at least one of us was on track.

I planned to head back out after grabbing lunch at home. I thought about Clinton County based on recent sightings. But the closest site was a 45-minute drive, so I changed my mind. I opted to just go to Bald Eagle in Centre County to look for waterfowl but got nothing new.

+++

It was predicted to rain most of February 28. I planned to stay home and work on the update of *Some Truth with Maps* that I'd intended to do for years. *Some Truth with Maps* is a small textbook I published through the Association of American Geographers in 1994. They returned the rights for the contents to me when the *Resource Publications* series it was published in ended. But, while still a full-time faculty member, I had no time to work on a new version. Now, about to become Emeritus, it seemed like the time to try. I had already started to create all new figures and planned to add a chapter on the ethics of mapping. ... but, I looked at recent Clinton County sightings. Several species I had not seen were reported. And the rain wasn't supposed to start seriously there until about 11:00am. So, I thought I would give Clinton County a try as the second month of my Geo-Big Year came to an end.

+++

The weather report was not accurate — as typical. It started to rain by the time I got to Clinton County. A first pass along farm fields near Avis turned up little. I found Greater Scaup in the river nearby and saw an immature Bald Eagle scare up the waterfowl (mostly American Black Duck and Mallard). I tried a second location where waterfowl were seen but had no luck — I just got wet. I then checked eBird. Someone else got 4 species I'd not seen back at my first stop, so I returned there. I found Wood Duck and Hooded Merganser (**02.07**), as well as Lesser Scaup and American Wigeon. I also saw my first Clinton County American Kestrel on the drive home; all-in-all an OK morning considering rain from steady to downpour the whole time.

This day trip brought month two in my quest to an end. It was time to check status again. I had visited 12 counties, but had not yet reached the target in any, not even Centre County.

SPECIES TOTALS AS OF FEBRUARY 28			
CENTRE	64	UNION	20
HUNTINGDON	38	INDIANA	17
CLINTON	38	CLEARFIELD	7
CUMBERLAND	23	BLAIR	7
CAMBRIA	23	JUNIATA	3
MIFFLIN	21	PERRY	3

+++

To track progress geographically, I created another choropleth map (02.08). As with the first, darker grays represent more species and open dots depict locations of my eBird reports. As the map shows, I still had a long way to go. Since I continued working at Penn State with teaching, committee, and other responsibilities, I had confined my birding to part-day trips from home.

Pennsylvania Geo-Big Year - February

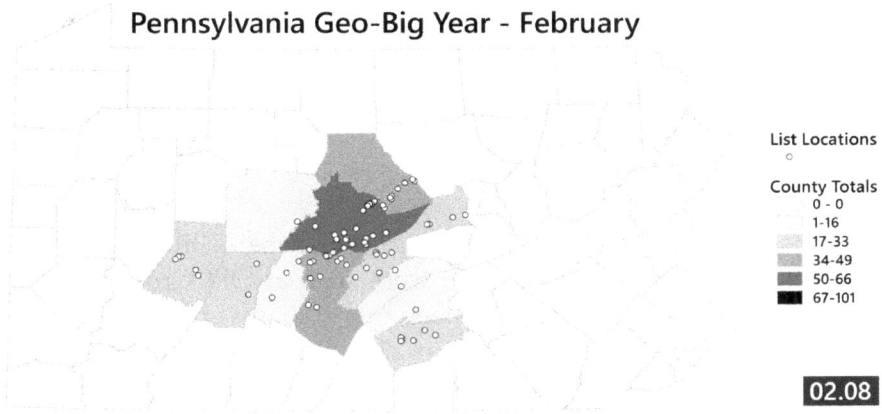

List Locations
○

County Totals
0 - 0
1-16
17-33
34-49
50-66
67-101

02.08

I was lucky that my final semester of teaching included only one online, asynchronous, 10-week compressed course. That meant I could do academic work at any time of the day or night, and any day of the week. Birding, then, could happen when the weather and birds were most promising. But, I would continue the strategy of part-day trips from home until at least late March after the course was completed.

+++++

MARCH

It had been a tough year for birding to this point, due to the pandemic. While birding solo keeps things safe, it meant little interaction with others. I missed running into the local birders to catch up on what they had seen and what they had been doing.

At that point, my typical morning or full day of birding included zero encounters with other birders. When I did run into anyone, since

I had not yet had my COVID-19 vaccine shots, I tended to keep my distance, saying hello, but not really talking. The encounter with Mr. Peachey in Mifflin County the day prior was a fun exception. I appreciated his knowledge of local birds and enjoyed the chance to recount the story of Aden Troyer's non-Amish friend driving him up to our house to see the Varied Thrush.

As February came to an end, I remained uncomfortable in any somewhat crowded birding spot like a boardwalk or observation platform when others showed up. I was looking forward to being vaccinated so that encounters with locals who know the sites and know about local birds would generate less anxiety.

+++

On March 2, I went off on a wild goose chase — literally. Several species, including Cackling Goose were seen at Old Crow Wetlands in Huntingdon County. I'd never been there, so, was not sure whether there was a chance for open water at 22°F. But the previous few days had been relatively warm, so I hoped to get lucky. It was quite a goose chase! I found Cackling Goose, not just one but two (03.01).

The real surprise was a Short-Eared Owl that I accidentally flushed. I watched it fly back and forth over the wetland and got a few passable photos (03.02). All in all. It was a great morning.

As I was in Huntingdon County, I also stopped at Raystown Lake and picked up a couple new species before heading home.

Geisinger emailed about open vaccine slots. When I got to the web site, the earliest was for 3/17, which I changed to. It was only 3 days sooner than the appointment I had, but every day might count.

+++

On March 3, I had assignments to grade, but got them done early. Temperatures were above freezing for a change. I needed 2 species to reach 67 in Centre County. I tried at Millbrook Marsh and initially had no luck. I was close to giving up for the day, but then saw one Red-winged Blackbird for number 66. My main target, then was American Coot. They are uncommon in early March. But one had been seen at the Marsh off-and-on. My first pass around the likely spots turned up nothing. But I decided to walk the boardwalk back to my car, retracing part of my route. As I turned a corner, I saw number 67, the American Coot, hidden in some reeds by the shore. It did me the favor of coming out into the open and I managed to snap a nice shot (03.03).

+++

The big event for the day was not birding. I got a phone call from Geisinger Health. They said they had a vaccine slot, that day, if I was free!! I jumped at the chance. It required driving to the Lewistown hospital, about 35 minutes away.

As detaild above, getting the vaccine was a quest of its own. My first appointment for February 17 at Geisinger was delayed until February 28, then delayed again to March 20. I got on a waiting list for Mt. Nittany Hospital, then accidently canceled my slot when trying to check its status on my phone. Then the Geisinger appointment moved up to March 17, and finally up again to March 3.

I drove to Lewistown and got in and out for my shot quickly; they were very organized in a big tent outside the main hospital entrance. After the jab, everyone was asked to sit in a waiting area (with chairs well-spaced) for 15 minutes in case there was a reaction. After that brief wait, I was happy to have no ill effects and to get on my way.

+++

Since I was in Lewistown, I decided to try Victory Park along the River to work on my Mifflin County list. I managed to add 12, with the highlight being a pair of Lesser Scaup. They were too distant for a good photo, but a Great Blue Heron (03.04) was close and quite cooperative.

+++

March 4 was again above freezing. I had not birded much in Blair County yet, so my list there was rather short. I decided to do a quick morning at a couple of sites where local birders posted reports the day before. I managed to progress from 7 to 23 species for Blair County. A few were cooperative for photos, including Killdeer, Eastern Bluebird, Carolina Wren, and Northern Cardinal (03.05). I spent the afternoon with email and collecting data on the new car we wanted.

We had decided to trade in our existing Toyota RAV4 hybrid on another Toyota RAV4 hybrid. The primary motivation to trade one RAV4 for another was the estimated 8 mpg better mileage of the new version. At least when I drive that car (which is primarily Fran's that she was not using much during the pandemic) the extra 8 mpg would lower my Geo-Big Year climate footprint.

+++

A couple days later (March 6 – at 32°F), I decided to head to Huntingdon County, attempting to "complete" a second county. It was a challenge since I was at 47 species, but it seemed within reach. I stopped first at the Evening Grosbeak site, just in case, but no luck. I did see Red-bellied Woodpecker, Hairy Woodpecker, Downy Woodpecker, Pileated Woodpecker, and Yellow-bellied Sapsucker. Not all were new, but it is always fun to see so many different woodpeckers in one place. I also picked up Purple Finch, House Finch, and Black Vulture.

From that stop, I headed to Raystown Lake hoping for waterfowl. That was a good choice. I added Common Goldeneye, Tundra Swan, Ring-necked Duck, and Pied-billed Grebe. I did not reach the 67 species target; I only made it to 59. But I figured one more morning or afternoon would be enough to hit 67, particularly if I waited until warblers came back.

It was a good morning, but I needed to get home to do some work. The 10-week intensive online class I was teaching in our Professional Master of GIS program was nearing its end. That meant lots of interactions with students and hours of grading.

+++

As I tried to spread out from Centre County, I was becoming frustrated with driving an hour or more for 2-4 hours birding at a time. As a life-long environmentalist, I also felt guilty about the miles driven. At least I was using a hybrid for most of it.

By this point in the year, I expected to be using the trailer mentioned above to do multi-day trips where Fran and I would set up camp and I (or we) would focus on nearby locations. That plan would cut down on my driving miles and hours in the car, but it might not help with the environmental impact. We had to buy a Ford Expedition as the "most efficient" vehicle I could find with the towing capability for the trailer.

At this point, in early March 2021, the camping trailer was back at the dealer we bought it from in West Virginia. It had been quite a saga. We custom ordered the trailer in June 2020. We picked a Lance 1985 (model number, not year) that seemed to be just the right size for the two of us and our dog. It had a queen-sized bed, a shower, and a slide-out dining area. The unit included large capacity tanks and we ordered two solar panels and lithium batteries. That meant it would be practical to camp in locations without any hookups if that proved best in relation to birding sites. The trailer (03.06) was delivered to the dealer in mid-August 2020, and we went down to pick it up. At first, it seemed great. We got it home and I started to learn how everything worked.

03.06

In fall, 2020, long before the Geo-Big Year start, we decided on a couple test runs with 2-night stays at State Parks in Centre County. The first (to Bald Eagle State Park) went well. The trailer seemed to be comfortable and functional (03.07). We were looking forward to more.

03.07

I took the trailer to a local RV place (in Milroy, PA) to get the state inspection. Being brand new, I assumed that would be quick. Instead, they found that the back-end top running lights were not working. I took the trailer home, called the dealer and then the manufacturer and tried several things. Nothing worked. So, the only option was to haul the trailer back to the dealer we bought it from in West Virginia.

We had booked a second trial outing, so went ahead with that (to Moshannon State Park, which was nice). Since we were not driving at night, the lights were not a safety issue. If we were stopped for not having an inspection sticker, I would explain that we had an appointment at the dealer in West Virginia to get the lights fixed. After the short trip, I drove the trailer to the dealer, hoping for a down and back trip. But they could not promise it would be done that day, so I did the 10-hour round trip, returning without the trailer.

I heard from the dealer in a couple days — with good news and bad. The good news was that they fixed the lights; some wires were crossed in construction. The bad news was that in doing so the technician broke a big piece of "trim" that was integral to a watertight trailer. Thus, they ordered a replacement part. It was October 2020, still well ahead of my Geo-Big Year start. So, we had a trailer parking pad installed during the wait. But, by early December 2020 I'd heard nothing, I was starting to worry. Then, we got a stove recall letter from the trailer's propane stove manufacturer. I called the dealer and was told they were waiting for the stove manufacturer to let them know when the repair kits would be ready. They were also still waiting for the trim part from Lance. The dealer promised to put us at the top of the repair list.

I checked repeatedly over the next couple months. The reply each time was "still waiting" with the delay attributed to pandemic *supply chain* issues. In February, the trim part came in, but Lance sent the wrong one — so the dealer reordered! Finally, in mid-March the correct piece came. But there was still no word on the stove repair kit. I declined the suggestion to do the 10-hour round trip to pick up the trailer as is, then bring it back to West Virginia when the stove kit came in.

+++

Given the trailer situation, continued COVID-19 risk (with having just one of two vaccine shots), my day trips would continue. March 7 found me driving out Route 45 on a cold but quite sunny day. My planned target was Clearfield County. But with the temperature at home hovering at 18°F, I decided to check weather in multiple nearby counties. Snyder County proved to be a bit warmer, so I opted to give it a try. Never having birded there, I was unsure what I might find or even the best place to try. I expected it's one small reservoir to be frozen. In eBird I found a birding trail with promising reports over the previous few days, so picked that as the place to start.

My route took me past the iconic round barn visible from Route 45 as one leaves State College heading east. The lighting was great, so I stopped for a quick photo (03.08) – the barn is red, and had been painted not long before, thus the color image online is worth a look.

03.08

As I drove along, I came up behind an Amish buggy. It would have been another great photo. I considered trying to take one while driving but thought better of it. I went around the buggy and traveled on.

I had my cruise control set at 50mph ... in a 45-mph zone. At that point, I looked in the mirror. I saw two state troopers, one right on my bumper and the other right behind. They stayed on my bumper for quite a while. I *eased* down to 45, figuring a quick slow-down might be judged as reckless driving. We approached a 35-mph zone and I (not surprisingly) slowed for that. The first trooper stayed right behind. We continued, and the speed limit increased back to 45-mph. I set my cruise control to 45-mph exactly and let the speed ease on up to that. Finally, both troopers passed me by, at well over the speed limit. A bit later, I found both cars parked in front of the local coffee shop in Millheim. Reflecting, I am surprised that I did not end up with a ticket ... for being an obstacle between the troopers and morning coffee!

+++

After all that, I reached Snyder County, but could not find the birding trail. The eBird location seemed to be on private property. I did find a nature trail through the trees (03.09). It was not the eBird hotspot, but it looked like a good place to try.

I parked and heard a Screech Owl, which was great. I then walked .8 miles along what was posted as a loop trail. I got to a point in sight of my car. But the trail was cut off by an overflowing stream (03.10). There was no bridge, no logs, no way across without wading. Temperature was near freezing, so I turned around and retraced my steps. That backtracking was a bit frustrating, but I ended with 34 species in the county before noon.

From those Snyder County sites, I moved over to Union County (where I had 20 species from a prior outing). Across 3 sites, I added another 10 to reach 30 before heading home about 2:30pm. The best was a Brown Creeper.

+++

Since starting the quest, I was concerned with environmental implications of my big year. The Ford Expedition we bought was (at the time) the *best* mileage vehicle able to tow our trailer with reasonable safety (considering I'd not towed a trailer since 1979). But when Ford came out with a hybrid F150 pickup I considered trading in the nearly new Expedition. I watched a video review and found that, although the empty, non-towing mileage of the F150 hybrid was very good for a truck, it would be worse than the Expedition when towing. That solidified our decision to trade Fran's 2016 RAV4 hybrid (32 mpg rating) for a 2021 RAV4 hybrid (40 mpg rating). We put a deposit on the new RAV4 on March 9 (by phone) and hoped to pick it up a few days later.

We also planned to continue looking for more efficient replacements for the Expedition, that could still tow the trailer. There were plug-in electric options on the horizon with the potential to tow. But their range when towing was likely to be impractically short. In the mean time, I planned to do as many outings as I could with the new RAV4.

+++

Spring was in the air – March 9 at 50°F. I opted to head for Canoe Creek State Park in Blair County. Species I needed had been reported and it was less than an hour from home. When I arrived, there was a lot of bird activity but many people as well. I had a good start with Hooded Merganser (03.11), Canada Goose (many), a Belted Kingfisher, a group of Tundra Swan, Bufflehead, and many other species.

I took a trail across a spillway (03.12). The trail was nearly devoid of birds, but I got Pileated Woodpecker and Carolina Wren.

From Canoe Creek State Park, I headed to the "Lower Trail--Mt. Etna Trailhead" hotspot. I was directed by the GPS down Polecat Road. Having done research on automated identification and mapping of geographic place names, I enjoy encountering interesting place names out in the world —and Polecat Road was certainly one.

03.12

Given the backwoods "Polecat Road" name, I was surprised to encounter a quite impressive stone house right near the trailhead (03.13). Unlike the ruin I had encountered earlier, this one was maintained and lived in.

03.13

+++

A couple days later it was again quite warm (53°F) when I walked our dog Skoti. It was a good day to start a new county. I picked Perry. It was not quite new since I had reported 3 species when driving through on my way to the Snowy Owl in January.

My primary site for this trip was Little Buffalo State Park, the location in eBird with the most species seen over the prior week. I had to take the *monster car* that day, our Ford Expedition. Fran's RAV4 hybrid was getting traded in on the new RAV4 hybrid in a few days, so I did not want to take any chances with it.

Little Buffalo State Park was quite interesting; I had not been there before. From a birding perspective, it was one of my better days, reaching 39 species in Perry County. I did not get many bird photos, but some images from Little Buffalo State Park show off the site that I had almost to myself. The site included a covered bridge, several trails, and a historic mill (03.14).

On this outing, I also added 20 species in Juniata County as well as a Fish Crow and a Mute Swan in Mifflin County. The best two bird photos of the day were a Brown Creeper in Perry County pretending to be part of a tree as typical (03.15-L) and the Mute Swan, quite enamored with itself, in Mifflin County (03.15-M). Also in Perry, I found an interesting creature "perched" in a bush (03.15-R).

While Juniata County yielded few bird photos, I got a nice image of the Mifflintown courthouse from across the river (03.16).

+++

A couple days later, on March 13, I headed west to Curwensville Dam in Clearfield County. It was a cold morning compared to what we had been having, with a temperature in the upper 20°F range. After the 70-minute drive, I turned toward the dam entrance and encountered a disappointing sign (03.17). The sign seemed explicit. Driving down the road to the lake was prohibited. So, I tried to figure out where birders had been going to see the water birds that were reported at the site over the past several days. I walked down the road a short way, but the sign was unclear whether that was allowed so I did not walk far. I was able to see glimpses of the lake and did find Wood Duck, Tundra Swan, Common Merganser, Canada Goose, and Mallard. But that was a small sample of the waterfowl I expected. I ended up going to the DuBois Reservoir. I sat there for 20 min. or so eating my lunch, but there were no birds to see.

While I did add 26 species for the county during the morning, it was mostly birding from the side of the road, in town, and similar places that were not very appealing. After that outing, I took a short break from birding to focus on work.

+++

I was teaching Geog 583: Geospatial System Analysis and Design in the online Professional Program. As mentioned above, that program has compressed 10-week intensive terms that start and end earlier than the regular academic classes at Penn State. "Spring term" would end on March 17 and final projects were being turned in. So, I put birding on hold for most of a week, other than from my desk overlooking our feeders and one 11-minute foray into the Scotia Barrens while Fran had an appointment nearby. Except for a Woodcock heard in the field behind our house (#68 for Centre County) and a Fox Sparrow under our Feeders (#69), I had no year birds in any county for a 9-day stretch. This was the longest run without progress toward the quest since we returned to Pennsylvania from North Carolina in January.

The time off from active birding allowed me to finish most of my grading. Thus, my time was becoming more flexible. The remaining job responsibilities were faculty/committee meetings, individual meetings with continuing graduate students, collaboration on papers for publication, and moving out of the office I had been in for 36 years.

+++

Saturday, March 20, was predicted to be a nice day, sunny and temperatures close to 50°F. I decided to go back to Cambria County, specifically to Prince Gallitzin State Park, the location with the most target species. I was hoping for missing waterfowl and woodland species.

The drive along the ridge on I-99 was getting very familiar given the number of trips west already. On that clear windy day, the many wind turbines spinning on the far ridge really stood out. While not the most attractive part of the landscape, they are a lot better than strip mines.

I arrived a little after 8:00am. It was colder than I expected, about 21°F. Still, I saw some birds right off the bat. These included a Belted Kingfisher, Wood Duck, and Lesser Scaup (03.18-L). Then at the main lake I picked up Red-breasted Merganser (03.18-R) as well as Eastern Phoebe. It remained cold at 24°F.

03.18

I ultimately added 23 species to my Cambria County list before heading home. One highlight was a Barred Owl that flew out of the woods, turned toward me briefly, and then continued across into woods on the other side of the road. The other was a Red-shouldered Hawk that flew nicely in the sun so that I could see the red shoulders clearly. When I got home and checked eBird, I saw reports from Prince Gallitzin by another birder of several species that I missed. But I saw a couple that he did not; that's the way birding goes.

+++

The next day (Sunday, March 21) I headed back to Canoe Creek State Park because of reports from the day before. As I left home, it was a very clear morning, without a cloud in the sky, but also not a bird visible. But that was unsurprising as it was 6:59am. I did hear several species calling for their feeders, which I put out before I left. When I arrived at Canoe Creek State Park, it was cold, 21°F again. It was a bit hazy, but also quite picturesque, even in monochrome (03.19).

03.19

I added only 2 species at Canoe Creek SP (Rusty Blackbird and Horned Grebe), without good photos. But, I was happy to capture a Common Merganser running across the water just before liftoff (**03.20**).

03.20

+++

My next outing, on the 23ʳᵈ, was to Faylor Lake in Snyder County. I thought I might also stop in either Juniata or Union County. As I headed out, my app said 42°F, thus it promised to be a nice day.

I drove Fran's new RAV4 hybrid, which was a step up from the previous one. The milage rating was quite a bit better than her old RAV4 and I really appreciated the heated steering wheel! On that first outing, the mileage was not quite as good as expected. I got about 36 mpg. But that was still about 5 mpg better than the prior RAV4. As I drove past Lerch RV, the local dealer that found the problem with the lights on our trailer, it made me really wish that our camper was fixed so that we could start exploring more of the state. I was hopeful that we would get it back by mid-April when we returned from our house on the OBX (where we planned to go for about 10 days early in the month).

I got to Faylor Lake and was the only person there. So, after checking a map and seeing a route around the lake (purportedly marked in pink) I decided to do the whole loop. Birding was slow, but I ended up with quite a few good bird photos. These included some Mallard showing off, a male Northern Cardinal, a Northern Mockingbird, and both Red-breasted Merganser and Common Merganser together (03.21).

Beyond the birds, the view (03.22) from near the start of the walk was quite good. The trail took me along the lake and through some woodlands. About 2/3 of the way around, I heard what sounded like an Osprey. I saw a raptor flying away but could not get a photo or see it clearly due to trees. I was pretty sure it was an Osprey from the call, but the visual impression did not seem right — too brownish on top (which was all I could really see). So, that one was left as a miss.

Starting with 34 county species, I reached 41 at the lake. I might have had a better day if not for what happened next. I got to about the 2.5 mile mark and was near a small bridge I'd seen from a distance. But, just like a couple weeks back (with a longer distance walked this time), the path was submerged (**03.23**).

I initially followed some more pink trail ribbons, hoping the trail would cross over the stream somewhere else. But the path went uphill steeply and looped back on itself. I decided that the practical option was to head back the way I came — retracing the 2.5 mile treck. That seemed better than continuing 3.5 miles along a road, with probably much less chance to see many birds. On the way back I saw a juvenile Bald Eagle and realized that must have been the bird I saw — not an early Osprey — a bit disappointing, but good to get a definite ID.

+++

I had temporarily settled into an every-other-day pattern of birding and work. On March 25 my destination was Clinton County. It was predicted to be our warmest day of the year, hitting 70°F. I had a bad start to the morning, leaving my lunch behind and having to come back for it. That was particularly frustrating since I was driving the Expedition, which I hated taking out unless towing the trailer. But Fran needed her car.

The day improved slightly. The first stop, at a game lands, netted 6 new species. I also picked up an American Coot at the Central Mountain High School wetland, a site with a couple ponds surrounded by reeds. A black and white photo (**03.24**) works well for a Coot, except for the bright red eye. From there, I set off in search of the Ring-necked Duck reported at a nearby wetlands.

When I reached the hotspot that had Ring-ncked Duck reported, it appeared to be on private land. I called the Bald Eagle Township office, right in front of the wetland. But they said they had nothing to do with the wetland and it was private. I emailed one of the local birders who had reported from the site but did not hear back right away. I finally took a chance to walk in because I could see a sign about the wetland, which implied that the public was allowed. I quickly found Ring-necked Duck (two of them) but couldn't find anything else. I was hoping for at least Swamp Sparrow. I thought I heard one at a distance, but I was not certain enough to list it.

+++

I remained on the every-other-day pattern, heading back to Prince Gallitzin State Park in Cambria County on the 27th. Since I was at 46 species, the target seemed to be getting within striking distance — 21 to go. As I started out, it was 44°F and heading towards 70°F. Shortly after I arrived so did the people and the boats; the lake and shores quickly got crowded with fisher folks. The best photo, before the boats arrived was of a male Bufflehead (03.25), another bird well suited to a black and white photo.

The outing was good, but not nearly good enough to hit the target. I ended the day at 59 species. Highlights were Horned Grebe,

Red-breasted Merganser, and at the marsh across from the Park itself, three Wild Turkey. I didn't get as many ducks as I hoped for.

+++

As the month (and the year's first quarter) ran out, I tried to pick up the pace. This also anticipated our planned trip to the OBX where I would not be able to make progress on the Pennsylvania quest. On the 28th, even though it was rainy, I headed back over to Canoe Creek State Park in Blair County. I was at 47 species, so just like Cambria County, I was getting within striking distance. Many water birds had been seen in the prior couple of days and I figured rain would not bother them. It was not actually raining when I pulled out of the garage, but by the time I reached the end of the driveway it was coming down hard.

I spent the better part of the morning at the park without much success. The only water birds seen were three Double-crested Cormorant and a Common Loon. The weather was not suited to any photos. Discouraged by the rain, I headed home at just 53 species for the county.

+++

March 29 was my second COVID-19 vaccine shot appointment. I was looking forward to it. Once the shot took effect, I expected to start feeling a bit safer if/when I encountered others out birding. It would also decrease the Covid-anxiety of doing overnight trips.

Since I had to drive down to the Lewistown Hospital again for my shot in the early afternoon, I decided to take the morning to try to pick up a few more species in Mifflin County. I chose a back route through a bit of Huntingdon County so I could stop at Lake Perez endeavoring to finish that County. I had a great start at the lake, picking up six species, reaching 65; but could then not find anything else.

Since I still had 4+ hours before my vaccine appointment, I decided to head toward Belleville in Big Valley, the hub of the Amish community in Mifflin County, and check out some of the country roads, small streams, and farm fields. I captured a photo of a horse team pulling a manure spreader, a typical scene for Big Valley (03.26). Our local State College Bird Club has an annual "manure chase" field trip (usually in February) to look for fields with freshly spread manure. They attract Horned Lark, Snow Bunting, and Lapland Longspur. So, I was on the lookout for all of these.

03.26

I ended up adding 11 species to reach 45 for Mifflin County. Among the best were Horned Lark (no Snow Bunting or Lapland Longspur), Winter Wren, Swamp Sparrow, Cooper's Hawk, Wood Duck, and four Greater Scaup (at Victory Park on the river). Most were not very photogenic; the best bird photos of the day were a Horned Lark (03.27-L), showing off its horns, and a Carolina Wren (03.27-R), singing loudly.

03.27

After the drive through Big Valley and the stop at Victory Park along the River, I then went over to the hospital (about 3 minutes away). I got in and out quickly for vaccine shot two. But it was nearly 3:00pm at that point, so I headed home.

+++

On March 30, with only two days left in the month (and in the year's 1st Quarter), I decided to see how far I could get in Juniata County where I had 23 species. I had slept poorly after my COVID-19 vaccine shot; this second shot had a bigger kick than the first. But I decided to go out as planned anyway.

Juniata County seemed to have fewer attractive birding spots than any county I had worked on thus far. There were quite a few boat launch areas along the rivers. But those tended to be busy, and birds were scarce at the ones I stopped at. I also tried some farmland roads and a small reservoir. The latter had an interesting castle-like building (03.28) that I assume contained equipment to manage the lake level. But that was the only interesting thing there; no birds were seen at all.

I posted eight lists that day, but only added 18 species. The strangest event was at one of the eBird hotspots along the river, Castings Crossing. The site is along a dirt road that parallels the river and at which local birders post lists frequently. But there is no public access to the river. No trespassing signs dot the land strip between road and river. I had been there once before and parked in a space across the road from the river and the no trespassing signs. The parking spot looked like it was used often by others. I then walked along the road, as before (for about an hour). I added 6 species, but most were too far away for a good photo. One Tree Swallow (03.29), however, was quite cooperative.

After walking up and down the road, I got in my car to eat the lunch I'd brought along. A fellow drove by in a big black car, slowed down and stared at me for a bit, then pulled in next to me. He got out of the car. He headed my way. While younger than me by quite a bit, he was walking with a cane; and he was dressed in a dark suit, which seemed out of place on that dirt road. The fellow flashed a badge of some sort, not giving me a chance to look at it properly. He said he was in "law-enforcement", not saying what kind. Then my black-suited, cane carrying questioner started asking about why I was there, saying he'd seen me multiple times in different cars. He was correct about different cars, but "multiple" was a stretch. I was there once before in our RAV4 (today I had to drive the Expedition since Fran needed her car).

I told my inquisitor that I was birdwatching. He clearly did not believe me. He then said I was parked on private property. Perhaps he was right, although it was a gravel pull-off (big enough for 4-5 cars) along the dirt road with the river on one side and train tracks not far on the other. I had seen someone else park there to eat lunch on my one other time at the hotspot. That said, I was in no position to argue the point. And the somewhat vague information I got about the guy's credentials made me a bit nervous in this rural and out of the way spot. Thus, I did not think about how to convince him that I was a birder — I should have shown him my eBird app and photos, of course.

At that point, the man said he lived nearby, had kids, and worried about strangers in the neighborhood. That made sense. I told him I was happy to move on and that I wouldn't come back. That seemed to satisfy him (somewhat); although I think he doubted that anybody would come there (or perhaps anywhere) to birdwatch.

+++

It was the last day of the 1st Quarter of my Geo-Big Year and I had reached 67 species only in my home Centre County. I did not plan to go out that morning, given our upcoming trip to the OBX. But I was only 2 species short in Huntingdon County and eBird alerts listed 17 species I had not yet seen. So, I headed for Lake Perez at Shaver's Creek. I thought several species would be easy, including Golden-crowned Kinglet, Tree Swallow, and Song Sparrow. All were on 5 or more reports the previous day. Osprey was also likely with 4 reports. And, I was on the lookout for Green-winged Teal, reported once.

Things started great with a Pine Warbler (#66) in the parking lot (03.30-L), another species on a single prior day report. I tried the boardwalk, looking for Green-winged Teal or Osprey. As typical for birding, what I most expected was nowhere to be found. I continued across the boardwalk hoping for Golden-crowned Kinglet. No luck on that, but then I heard an Osprey call from where I'd been. I walked back along the boardwalk and saw it perched in a tree (#67). I managed to snap several photos. None were perfect but one flying away to join its mate (seen later) was identifiable (03.30-R). Another 10 minutes had me back at the parking lot, still with nothing else new. I headed for home.

+++

With the end of Quarter 1, and a planned trip to the OBX in April, it was time to assess my Geo-Big Year progress. My first step was another map, which I had been updating periodically along the way so knew what to expect (03.31). As is clear, I was making progress in the center of the state, but not at a pace that would achieve the end goal. Based on the map, I was beginning to wonder whether this Geo-Big Year quest was a good idea or not. It might be an achievable goal, but it would not be as easy as I initially expected.

Pennsylvania Geo-Big Year - March

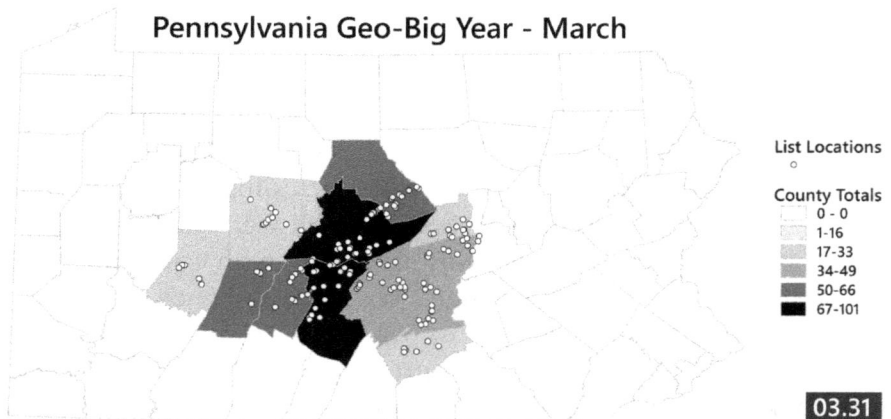

List Locations
○

County Totals
- 0 - 0
- 1-16
- 17-33
- 34-49
- 50-66
- 67-101

03.31

To complement the map above, I also generated a bar chart (**03.32**) depicting progress toward the 67 species target by county for all counties in Pennsylvania. The counties are listed alphabetically and vertical black lines on the bar graph highlight the category break points from the map above. The bar chart presents a much more discouraging picture than the map.

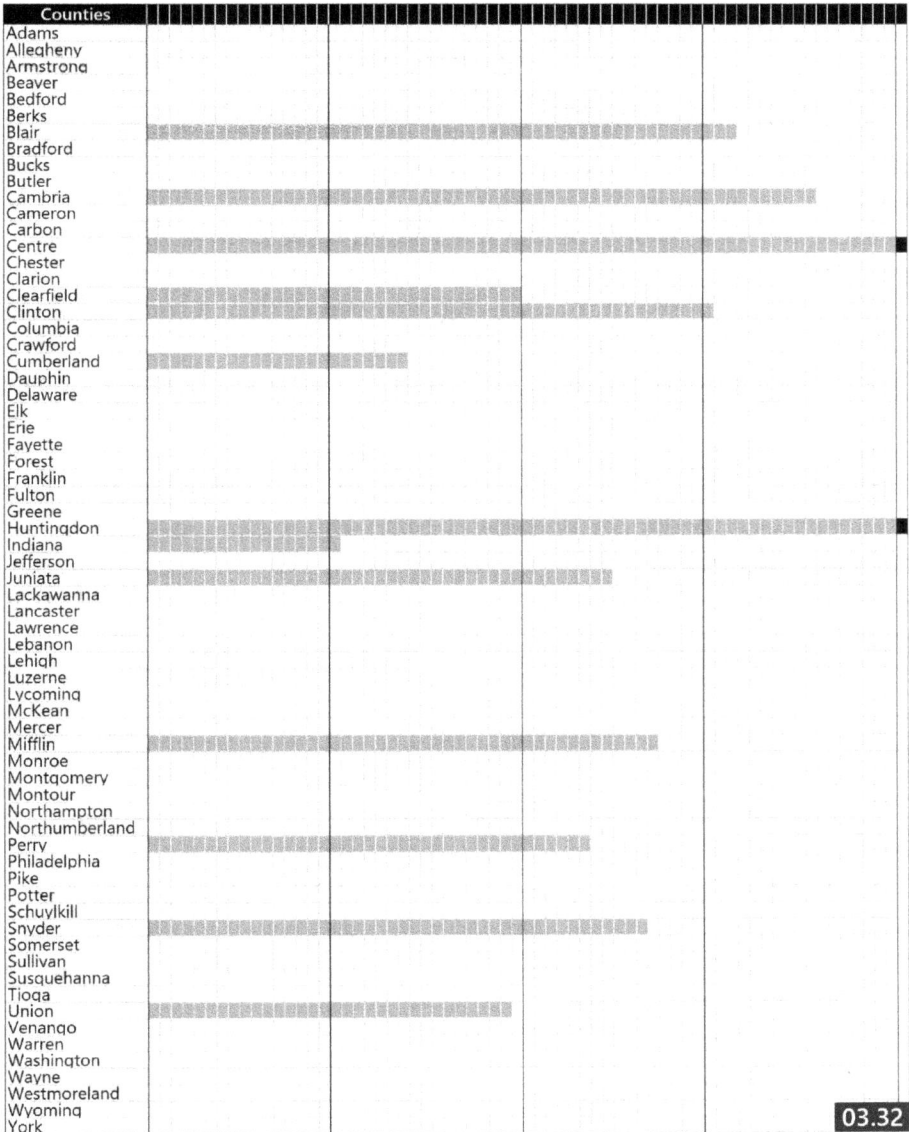

As clear from the map above, I had stuck close to home in Quarter 1, due to the combination of COVID-19 risk, continued work at Penn State, and the fact that we still did not have our camping trailer back. Now that I had my vaccine shots and the teaching part of my job was done, camping trailer repairs were the main impediment to extending the quest to more distant counties.

I had generated maps as the year progressed, but not the bar chart. I suspect that if I had seen the mostly bare chart earlier, I might have given up. At the time, I was already looking ahead toward spring migration — and continued to do so.

But ... the "Geo" part of the year means that seasonality of birds is as much of a challenge as it is an opportunity, since one cannot be everywhere at once. A traditional Big Year does not have this issue, because the focus is only on the species and there is no need to be comprehensive in where one birds.

One reason I opted for a Geo-Big Year rather than a traditional big year is my expectation that it would be (at least somewhat) less environmentally unfriendly. A traditional big year prompts long distance chases, often to pick up just one unusual species in a particular location. You might gain few other species on the trip. With a Geo-Big Year, each place (county here) will be visited, but the more distant ones only once or twice for longer periods of time. This means less chance for rare species, but fewer miles driven across the year. In addition, as discussed further in Reflections at the end, it generates data for places that might otherwise be ignored.

In early 2022 after the Geo-Big Year that I am recounting here ended, I did one "traditional" chase — for the Steller's Sea-Eagle in Maine; I put about 1,300 miles on our hybrid car with a stop in Connecticut for a lifer Pink-footed Goose and then on to Maine where I managed to see the Sea-Eagle the afternoon before it disappeared the very next day. I felt guilty about the miles driven, but it was a spectacular, once-in-a-lifetime chance. My view was brief, distant, and yielded only poor photos, but worth the trip. To (somewhat) offset that trip, I used a carbon calculator (http://www.carbonify.com/carbon-calculator.htm), which estimated 2 trees. In 2022, we added a Mulberry tree and a Pin Oak to our yard.

Second Quarter
Spring Toward Summer

Green is in the air
Songs to attract and repel
Fledglings on the way

We left for our house on the OBX in North Carolina on April 1 and returned on April 11. I had some nice birding there, adding 24 species to my Dare County, NC year list, but obviously made no progress toward the Pennsylvania Geo-Big Year quest. Thus, my initial Second Quarter outing did not happen until April 14.

APRIL

There was still no progress with our camping trailer's stove, so day trips remained the main option as I started Quarter 2. I checked eBird for opportunities in several nearby counties. The best choice looked like Union County, particularly on the Bucknell University campus and nearby.

I started the day there just under the halfway point to the target of 67. It proved to be a good outing with 17 new species including Wood Duck and Red-breasted Merganser plus many wood and field species including a Northern Flicker and Chipping Sparrow (04.01-L&R). An Eastern Bluebird I also saw was not new, but it was the best photo of the day (04.01-M); the color version is particularly nice.

04.01

From the Lewisburg area, I moved over to the corner of Northumberland County since I was close and it was a blank county at that point. I got a decent start of 22 species. All were at Milton State Park, which consists of a small island in the river. There was a 2.5-mile loop trail around the island, which I took.

+++

Despite the decent day, I continued to worry about achieving the end-goal of 67 species in all counties by year's end. Our two-week "vacation" from the Geo-Big Year quest was early enough that most warblers were not back in PA. But the numbers for some waterfowl, sparrows, and others were already waning. The added worry was the task of moving out of my Penn State office of 36 years. I spent about 2.5-hours emptying one set of drawers; and I still had not figured out what to do with everything removed. The dust also made me feel like I was coming down with something, so I took a day off from that.

During 2020, I had done a first round of "thinning" in my office. But that hardly made a dent. It would be an arduous task to get through the large amount of "stuff" I had there by my last day of work on June 30. I was particularly stressed about all the sheet maps I had collected over the years. As a cartographer/geographer, I was loath to discard maps, but had no place for them at home.

I was also uncertain about all the books I had. I estimated that I might have room at home for about 15-20% of them if I first thinned out the home bookshelves. That would mean recycling our collection of National Geographic Magazines, which went back to the 1960s due to inheriting a bunch from before we subscribed. In pre-COVID-19 times, passing on books was easier due to the annual AAUW book sale on campus, which featured about half a million donated books when it ran for the 58th time in 2019. But the long-running book sale was canceled in 2020 due to COVID-19 and the 2021 sale was postponed for the same reason, to an uncertain date, but clearly to be well beyond when I needed to dispose of books. *As I write this in February 2022, the AAUW just announced that they will have their next sale in October 2022.* At the time I was cleaning out my office, the local AAUW had also just lost the lease to the building where they sorted and stored donated books. Since they were coping with nearly 2 years of donations they already had, they stopped collecting all books.

+++

I set my quest completion and office worries aside and got back to birding. The next morning, I focused on Blair County, where I needed 14 species. That seemed within reach. I opted to begin back at Canoe Creek State Park. The morning was windy, but birds were about. After a couple hours I was at 62 and switched sites; I added a Wild Turkey on the way out. I drove down Polecat Road again to get to Lower Trail. I managed to add Northern Rough-winged Swallow, Barn Swallow, Louisiana Waterthrush, and Ruby-crowned Kinglet (the latter for #67). The Kinglet was doing its typical flitting around in bushes and I could never get focused on it with the camera. But the Waterthrush was singing in a tree (04.02); I was happy to get a photo of a bird that's often in hiding.

04.02

+++

Having completed 3 Counties (Centre, Huntingdon, and Blair) I started focusing on others close to home. On April 17th, I headed back to Victory Park in Lewistown, Mifflin County. It was a short outing because I wanted to spend another couple of hours back at the office sorting and tossing stuff. In about 2.5 hours at the park, I added 13 species to get to 58 in the county. These included: a Wood Duck, a Double-crested Cormorant (across the river in a tree), and a Northern Rough-winged Swallow (04.03).

+++

The task of vacating my office remained daunting, thus the need to restrict the day's birding. Between this point and my last day (June 30), I needed to balance three activities: the Geo-Big Year quest, continuing job responsibilities (paper and proposal reviews, writing, evaluating dissertations, faculty and committee meetings), and the task of sifting through the detritus of 36 years as a Penn State Professor to extract a few still-meaningful bits. I would come to regret being a saver.

I knew that choices on which physical artifacts to keep, which to toss, and which to try giving away would be difficult (*but in April I was only beginning to guess how difficult*). At least the decades of digital documents and email I saved required no physical space — they could simply be copied to small storage devices.

I did have a productive afternoon sorting at the office. The Department arranged for huge recycle bins on wheels (about 7ft long x 4ft wide x 5ft deep). The first bin was there when I got to the office that Saturday afternoon. I started with multiple sets of free GIS-related magazine issues that I had been sent over the years (when they still came in print form). I checked to see if the library had copies. They did. So, issues occupying about 8 feet of counter space went into the recycle bin.

While I never disposed of maps in the past, I did not have that luxury now. I recycled a bunch of old maps that were common titles of no value to anyone. I also got rid of seven file drawers of photocopied journal articles. I still remember the days when I would spend hours in the library photocopying papers that were important to me. That's partly how my Endnote digital library grew to more than 23,000 citations! The photocopies topped up the recycle bin (04.04) but I retained the digital library of citations since I planned to continue some research and writing projects once I became Emeritus.

This day of sorting was easy. It was all stuff I had no trouble parting with (except perhaps the maps). I could tell that the sorting would get harder as I got to more personal items. Beyond paper, I went through old memorabilia from the GeoVISTA Center and my earlier days in the Department, setting aside items of possible interest to continuing colleagues. One find was an Association of American Geographers Cartography Specialty Group *Student Paper Award Publication*. It contained a paper by Cindy Brewer (current Department Head) when she was a graduate student. It won first prize in the competition back in 1990.

On the birding front I encountered decisions as well. An American White Pelican was seen at Bald Eagle State Park, in Centre, County. Since I had "finished" the county, my choice was to chase a Pennsylvania life bird (one I see routinely in North Carolina) or focus on completing the next county. I (temporarily) opted for county completion.

+++

The next day the American White Pelican was seen again at Bald Eagle State Park. I decided to head to Clinton County, in part because one logical route could take me near Bald Eagle State Park and the White Pelican. I was up early and off at 7:01am. The White Pelican was still at the reservoir, a bit distant but no doubt about the ID (04.05).

Starting with the White Pelican, number 255 on my Pennsylvania life list, it was a great day. I finished Clinton County about 1:00pm, with one species extra (Ruby-crowned Kinglet). My 67th was Brown-headed Cowbird, not the most popular of birds (being an obligate brood parasite). I had been thinking about dropping Rock Pigeon from my lists due to the recent switch in eBird to report them as "Feral Pigeon." That would have made the Kinglet number 67, a much nicer "last bird". However, after a bit of investigation into recent Big Years by others, results from the World Series of Birding, and other listing efforts, I saw that Rock Pigeons had not dropped off any lists. So, I decided I would continue to count Rock Pigeons — which meant that I had to settle for the Brown-headed Cowbird as number 67.

Because I reached the Clinton County target early, I decided to drive on to Williamsport in Lycoming County for a quick first pass. I picked up 18 species there (including Rock Pigeon).

+++

To add to an already good day, I was able to listen to Cleveland baseball on the way home. Shane Bieber was pitching for Cleveland against Cincinnati. Cleveland was ahead 4-2 and won 6-3. I am a life-long (and long-suffering) Cleveland baseball fan, having grown up in a Cleveland suburb. As a kid, I usually listened to games on radio, even if on TV. Later, I remember working hard at night to get a weak radio signal to hear games, first as an undergrad in Athens Ohio, then as a grad student in Lawrence Kansas (where the signal was hit-or-miss and only at night), next in Blacksburg, VA (my first faculty job, with a similar hit-or-miss signal), followed by Boulder, Colorado (my second faculty job, and a location where I was surprised I could pick up the Cleveland radio broadcast … on clear nights). When we moved to State College, PA in 1985, I was still listening to ballgames on traditional radio with weak signals, accessible mostly at night. That prompted Fran and me to also become Pittsburgh baseball fans, since they were on local radio. Since 2001, I had subscribed to Gameday Audio, which was how I heard the game when driving home from Williamsport.

+++

A couple days later (April 20) the weather was good. I decided to try completing Cambria County, and perhaps make a bit of a dent in

Clearfield County. My first stop was Prince Gallitzin State Park (again). As I arrived, a hawk flew by. My impression was Cooper's Hawk, but it went by too quickly for certain ID, so it got left as a miss. I then caught a glimpse of a swan, expecting a Tundra Swan. But I needed a closer look to be sure. As I shifted position, 3 Double-crested Cormorant flew into the lake; they were the first new species of the day. As I got within better scope and camera range of the Swan, I was surprised to see that it looked like the Trumpeter Swan that I had missed in prior visits. The views were rather distant, so I did not post my list immediately. I decided to wait until I could see my photos on a larger screen before submitting that report. When I returned home and reviewed the photos (I had taken about 20), I was happy to find that all the field marks said Trumpeter (04.06-L); I reported it and that report was accepted by the eBird reviewer.

I made steady progress over 3 hours at sites around the reservoir. As a follow-on to the Brown-headed Cowbird as number 67 in Clinton County, number 67 for Cambria County was a Turkey Vulture (04.06-M). I came close to having a much better number 67; I found an early Northern Parula for number 68 (04.06-R). Then, I added Blue-headed Vireo and Osprey to reach 70.

+++

A day off from birding (April 21) resulted in progress at the office on sorting through and deciding what to do with some "stuff". I generated piles of folded and flat maps plus some atlases that I planned to put up for grabs in the department. I also got my desk completely empty and scanned the original unbound copy of my own dissertation from 1979. I decided to scan many old records from the desk before having them shredded. I'll probably never need them, but digital copies do not take space. I went home for dinner, then came back. Recycle bin 2 was full by the end of that evening shift (04.07-L). The bulk was Geography journal issues, some going back to when I joined the Association of American Geographers at the start of grad school back in 1974, plus others from the National Council for Geographic Education that I belonged to for many years. There were also surveying journals from the now defunct American Congress on Surveying and Mapping. The room was emptying only slowly (04.07-R).

+++

April 22 was a cold morning ... with every birder in the area (it seemed) talking about "fall-out". I did not plan to bird. We had scheduled an appointment to get a geothermal heating retrofit estimate for our house — along with an estimate for other options to replace our ancient furnace. But given the fall-out reports, I decided I better get out and take advantage of it. The only below-target county that I could manage with time available was Mifflin. I had spent bits of 7 previous days there but had only 58 species to show for it. I decided to stop at a site I had not tried before, Laurel Run Reservoir, just over the mountain coming in from Centre County. The plan was to head on to Victory Park in Lewistown (again) if I did not have luck around the reservoir.

Most of the reservoir is east of U.S. 322, but there is no easy access to that side. I parked on Stone Creek Road and walked to the small bit of reservoir on the west side of the highway. I picked up five species, including Belted Kingfisher, Red-breasted Nuthatch, and Blue-headed Vireo. Continuing from there down Spruce Mountain and then Lingle Valley Road I added Hermit Thrush as well as Louisiana Waterthrush to reach 65 species for the county. I was only two shy of the target but needed to head home for the heating estimate appointment.

+++

With another evening session back at the office I managed to clean out every drawer except in my map cabinet and one with a bunch of CDs and DVDs from Conferences. Because the office had a lot of built-in file cabinets and drawer sets, that was a lot of drawers. One set ran floor to ceiling with more than 25 drawers, each about 2in high (04.08-L). I was never sure what they were designed for (perhaps topo maps) but over the years they collected some of my sheet maps, some folded maps, newspaper and magazine clippings, and anything else that was relatively flat and could fit in the shallow open drawers. One *find* in a drawer was my first computer-generated map, an isopleth, produced on a line printer at the Ohio University's Computing Center in 1974 (04.08-R). It was one of a pair; the choropleth version is long since lost.

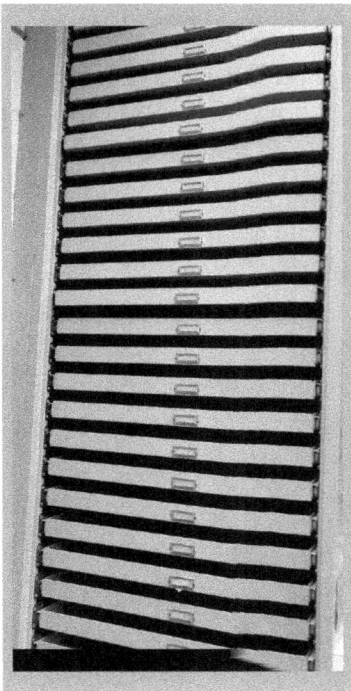

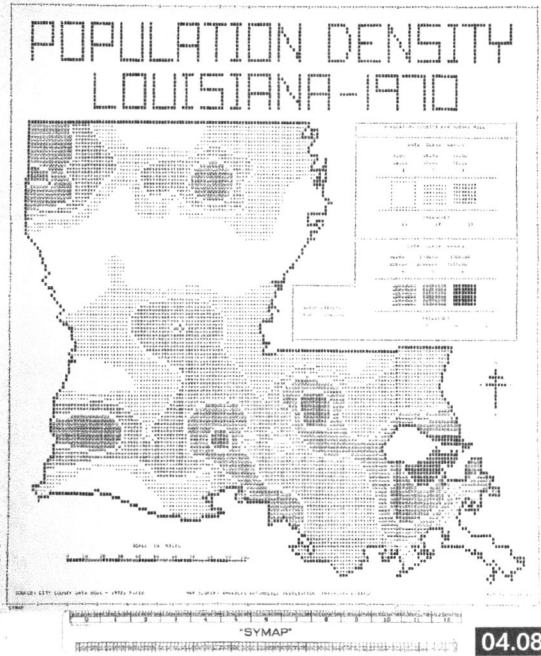

At that point, my office remained a mess with a huge amount of material to recycle. Among the hardest items for me to toss were my cartographic journals. These included all issues of *The British Carto-graphic Journal* (early in my career, I bought back issues starting with Volume 1 in 1964), *The American Cartographer* (which started the year I started graduate school - and its successors, *Cartography and Geographic Information Systems* and *Cartography and Geographic Information Science*), *Cartographica* (and its monographs, another journal for which I bought back issues to its start in 1964), and *Cartographic Perspectives*, along with a partial set of the *Bulletin of the Society of University Cartographers*.

In addition to cartography journals, I had issues of *Information Visualization* (from several years as an Associate Editor), the *Journal of Information Technology and Politics* (that I had due to a position on the Editorial Board), and *The Map Collector* magazine. I set the *Map Collector Magazine* issues aside and recycled the two other journals. I had filled 3 big recycle bins and estimated that I needed 3 more. It was strange to throw away so much of one's life.

Beyond journals, I had print *Proceedings* from cartography, GIS, and other conferences (**04.09**). I shared the image below with current colleagues to see if anyone wanted issues before they were recycled. As I sorted, I also checked all publications against Penn State Library holdings to make sure that I did not recycle something the library was missing. I found several items they said they could use. I also expected to have some bound dissertations from Ph.D. graduates at other universities that would be of use to the library. So, I set aside a bookcase where I moved the items the library already claimed and would put other items as I went.

+++

The next day (April 23), I checked eBird reports to pick a county for a day trip. Juniata County looked promising, but most reports were from the site I got chased away from. Since I did not intend to go back there, I settled on Snyder County. I added 11 species for the county in the morning; the best photos were of a diving Osprey, an annoyed Northern Rough-winged Swallow, and a curious Wood Duck floating on a pond (04.10).

04.10

In the afternoon, since I was close, I moved over to a game lands site in Northumberland County. I added 7 species, including a Ring-necked Pheasant, a Common Raven, and a Cooper's Hawk (04.11). But I remained below half-way for that county.

04.11

+++

Finally, on April 27, the RV dealer replied to my latest email prompt for an update — the stove kit for our camping trailer was in and it would be fixed in a couple days. It was a good thing I checked; otherwise, our trailer may have slipped down the priority list. Given that I took the trailer to the dealer for a "minor" repair in October, getting it back at the end of April had us questioning the original decision to buy the trailer and the Ford Expedition.

While I waited for the trailer repair, I returned to the office for more sorting and discarding. I focused on recycling Proceedings that the library did not need plus a mix of stuff gathering dust on a top shelf for years (e.g., Association of American Geographers Meeting programs, field trip guides, etc.). I filled two more recycle bins with journals and occasional papers that I could not find a home for (04.12).

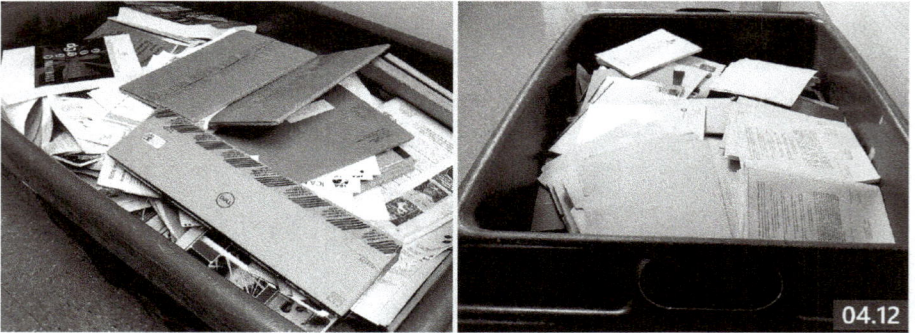

04.12

I began sorting books as well, making me painfully aware of how much more shelf space I had at the office than at home. I would be able to retain only a small subset of books and no journals (my cartography journals would have to go — but that would wait for another day).

Over the years my personal library had grown both large and diverse with titles covering cartography, many other aspects of geography, history and philosophy of science, environmental science, art, design, usability engineering, statistics, psychology, and more. As I started picking what to keep, I found that I kept focusing on the cartography books. All the psychology, statistics, scientific and information visualization, user-centered design, usability engineering, and others seemed to hold less excitement for me at this point, and much of that material was available digitally. That said, most of my philosophy of science titles, some of the more important books on visualization, and most of the art and design books were already in my home library.

Advice for academics: if you stay at the same university for most of your career, it's a good idea to move offices multiple times. STAYING IN THE SAME OFFICE FOR 36 YEARS IS A BAD IDEA. Changing offices encourages thinning things out, which you will appreciate in the long run. If you have stayed in one office for decades, moving out after a year of pandemic turns out to be a plus. I am pretty sure that it was easier to let go of books, maps, paperwork, notes from classes, and other artifacts of life when I had not seen them for the past year anyway!

+++

Since our trailer was not quite ready, and I had made good progress toward emptying my office, I decided to head to Juniata County before the month was over. Juniata had been tricky to bird because the best eBird hotspot was the one I got chased away from and now avoided. In-stead, I focused on river access locations that had parking, quick access to the river, and a chance for woodland birds in the vicinity. Warblers had started to appear, so I was on the lookout. I found Yellow-rumped Warbler (several) plus one Palm Warbler (04.13-L). But I was also happy to find an American Pipit, a Northern Waterthrush (04.13-R), as well as a Baltimore Oriole. Overall, I added 11 species for the county.

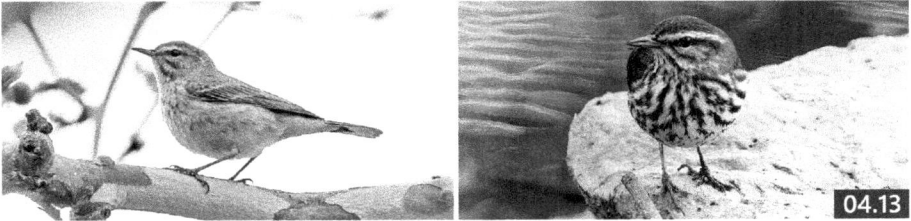

+++

On April 29, after six months at the dealership, our camping trailer was fixed. It was a long saga (detailed above), with the manufacturer's running light glitch, a bungled repair, a long wait for the wrong part, another wait for the right part, then the stove recall and wait for that repair kit. We were looking forward to finally doing some camping.

My route to West Virginia went through Fulton County, PA. I stopped briefly at a turnpike rest area and walked around the perime-ter near fields and a woodlot. I added Northern Mockingbird, Eastern Meadowlark, and the prize of the trip, a Wild Turkey, which I heard first, then saw out in the field. With my camera in the car, I tried to take an iPhone photo; but it turned out to be a little blob in the middle of a landscape. The short stop netted 10 species for Fulton County.

+++

Those few Fulton County species were the final new species in any county for April. Thus, it was time to assess progress again by gener-ating a monthly map. As shown (04.14), I had completed several coun-ties and the core territory birded was expanding. The ridge and valley topography of Pennsylvania is apparent in the map, which shows that it is easier to go northeast and southwest from Centre County than to cross the ridges. Day trips had focused on places I could reach within about an hour. While I had made progress, the map emphasized how far I had to go. Each month's map had me questioning the quest. But getting the camping trailer back provided a boost; it now seemed practical to start on counties at the extremes of the state.

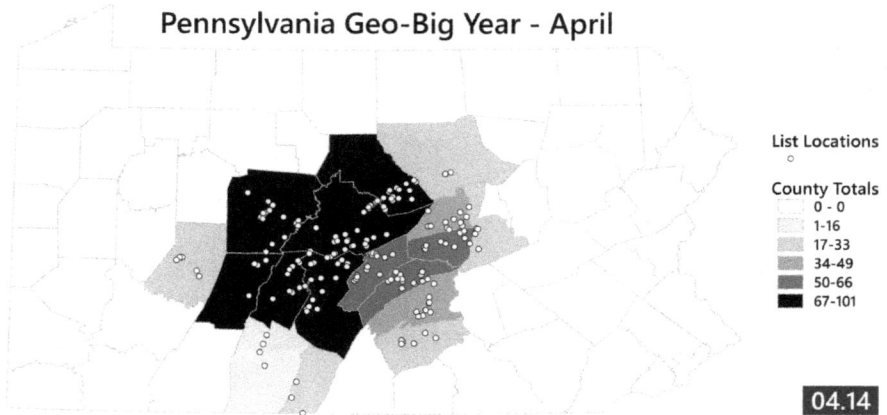

Pennsylvania Geo-Big Year - April

List Locations
○

County Totals
0 - 0
1-16
17-33
34-49
50-66
67-101

04.14

The last evening of the month found me back at the office sorting. The end of that task was not yet in sight, but I had made a clear dent (04.15) — compare this to the April 21 photo.

04.15

+++++

MAY

With the camping trailer back, we quickly booked a 2-night (May 2 -3) camping spot at Shawnee State Park in Bedford, PA. It was a county in which I had only 5 species, picked up on the way to the NC OBX in early April. Given the time of year and the increasing bird activity, I set out to reach the target of 67 on this short trip.

It took longer than expected to get ready to leave — too long between camping trips. My target departure time was 1:00pm for a 3:00pm check-in time; Fran, I and dog Skoti left home at 1:45pm. It was very windy, and the trailer was hard to handle. The car and trailer behaved like someone was pumping the brakes repeatedly, which was nerve racking. I ended up stopping three or four times to check things, but found nothing wrong, just the wind (and my lack of experience pulling a trailer in conditions like that).

After a very jerky ride, culminating with a rollercoaster-like trip on the back roads to the park, we pulled into the campsite an hour later than expected. To make things a bit worse, I had trouble figuring out how to use their water hook up, since it was the first camping trip without filling the water tanks before leaving home. It turned out being simpler than I was trying to make it.

At the campsite, I saw a few good birds including Baltimore Oriole. But by the time we finished setting up it was time to start organizing dinner. When we finished dinner, it was getting a little dark, thus there was not much chance to see more that day.

Fran had a very bad night sleeping, due to the combination of the jerky trip to the campsite, the mediocre camper mattress, and extreme lower back pain (due probably to both). We also both got quite hot at first, and then cold toward morning. The trailer was 65°F in the morning which was not bad once we got up and dressed.

+++

May 3 turned out to be an amazing birding day. After a very early walk with Skoti, then breakfast, I started the day with a quick outing near the campsite in the State Park (picking up 11 new species). I was ready for my first real outing of the trip and using eBird picked the Whitetail Wetlands hotspot as the best place to spend some time. I got an early start, considering that I walked Skoti first.

As I arrived at the wetlands, I saw a hand-painted sign that said "birders" with an arrow that I followed. But I found myself on what seemed like a loop drive on a farm, heading toward the barn with someone following me. An older fellow, older than me, got out. He was a big, bearded man. He started asking questions about what I was doing there, how I learned about the site, and so on. I started to get a little worried. It was reminding me of the situation in Juniata County where I was chased off.

But, as we talked, it became clear that this fellow was owner of the Whitetail Wetland. Several years earlier, he and his wife had turned their farm into a nature-retreat and B&B that attracted a lot of birders. Most who birded there had been B&B guests. He had experienced a sudden big influx of other birders recently and didn't know why.

We introduced ourselves and I learned that the owners name was Mr. Fetter (he said his first name, but that did not stick). He and his wife had shut down the B&B, but he was still running the farm. Mr. Fetter said he was still happy for birders to come out there, but he wanted to know why he was getting so many and wanted advice on controlling their activity. Apparently some of them had been rude and even tried to tell him that the conservation easement he and his wife established meant that the land was public and that they could walk anywhere they wanted. It is a shame that a few birders are both ill-informed and inconsiderate. That impacts the rest of us and does nothing to encourage non-birders to maintain habitat or allow access to their land.

It seemed clear to me that the listing of the Whitetail Wetlands as an eBird hotspot was behind the sudden influx of birders. Mr. Fetter did not generate the hotspot request to eBird and since I had not spent time in the county I could not tell him how long it had been in eBird. I promised to contact one of my former grad students who works at the Cornell Lab of Ornithology with the eBird project and ask what can be done about the hotspot listing.

Mr. Fetter turned out to be very helpful and open to letting me bird the wetland. He gave me a map of the site, detailing its 100+ acres and 10+ miles of trails winding through wood lots and marsh. I walked in the rain for about 2.5 or 3 hours and saw about 40 species (29 new for the county). It was wonderful.

When I got back to my car, Mr. Fetter was waiting to talk more about the issues he had been having with birders. He also wanted some help from me (in my position as a Penn State faculty member who knew other faculty whose work related to wetlands and conservation) to make contacts at Penn State. I was not sure exactly what he wanted to discuss with people at Penn State, and I did not ask for details. But I told him I would try to arrange a contact. He gave me an email address and phone number and I passed them on to a colleague on my return home.

Mr. Fetter encouraged me to come back with Fran so that she could enjoy the site too. I mentioned that she was having some trouble walking (particularly on uneven ground) due to the back pain. He offered to let us use one of several electric golf carts that were part of the B&B experience they had offered. I brought Fran back that afternoon and we did a nice loop around the Whitetail Wetlands in a cart; I added 6 more species, including an Ovenbird. The best photos of the day were of a Green Heron, a Killdeer with 2 chicks, and a Great Egret (05.01).

Fran had a terrible night, her second in a row, due to extreme back and leg pain. At that point, it was starting to look like the camping trailer was a bad idea. It seemed possible that we might need to give up on our traveling/camping plans. Despite the night, once Fran was up for the day on May 4, she encouraged me to spend the morning birding before breaking camp after lunch to head home as planned. So, I did.

I had reached 60 species by the end of the prior day, so was within striking distance of 67 before we left for home. This time, I stuck to the State Park. I started with a Barred Owl (poor light, thus no usable photo). I then made steady progress through the morning, including adding a Pied-billed Grebe, a Yellow-rumped Warbler, and a Ring-billed Gull (05.02-LB). Number 67 was an immature Bald Eagle (05.02-R); shown 20 min. later when I got closer). After the Bald Eagle, I added a White-crowned Sparrow (05.02-LT), a Brown-headed Cowbird, and an Orchard Oriole. I had reached the target of 67 species more quickly than in any county so far.

05.02

At that point, it was not quite 9:00am. I checked with Fran. She said I should stick to the plan to stay at the campground through lunch, then pack up and head home. I decided to see how far I could get on adjacent Somerset County in an hour. On the way, I added Indigo Bunting for Bedford County.

Given the short time I had, I did not try for any of the active hotspots in Somerset County, but instead drove to the nearest game lands that was just over the county border into Somerset. I clearly picked the right spot. I recorded 23 species in the county in just over one hour. Nice ones included Ovenbird, Black-throated Green Warbler, and Broad-winged Hawk. Most were not very photogenic, but a Common Yellowthroat and an Eastern Towhee (05.03) struck nice poses.

05.03

The trip was amazing for birding. Reaching the 67 species target for Bedford County quickly, then adding over 20 for Somerset County was great. But the rotten time Fran had on the trip due to extreme back pain turned our plans for the rest of the year on their head.

+++

We packed up at the campground on May 4 and headed for home. We got in late afternoon, and I unpacked things while Fran coped with more pain from the 3 days of bouncing around in the Expedition and sleeping on the stiff mattress.

I contacted my former student at Cornell about Mr. Fetter's hotspot problems. I passed along Mr. Fetter's preference that the hotspot listing say "by permission" and list his phone number. I heard back that the only option was to list the site as "restricted access." Then, the property owner should post access information at the site or through other means (e.g., local bird clubs).

Over the next days, Fran and I continued being uncertain about her health. She could barely walk the day after our return. A tele-meeting with her doctor resulted in pain medication as well as some new medication for neuropathy. The meds seemed to help a bit during the day, but she still could not sleep that night.

It was clear that we would do no trailer camping together any time soon … if ever again. The key thing was for Fran to rest, take the medication, and see how much it helped. With Fran resting and my official responsibilities at Penn State due to end on May 9 with spring commencement, I planned to get out locally over the next week or so. I could fill in remaining species for nearby counties while we waited to see whether Fran's medication helped. If it did, I would buy a mattress topper to try making the trailer's mattress more comfortable. Then we might try another overnight outing to see how that went. The fallback plan was for me to travel with the trailer on my own to the distant counties. That option was far from ideal and not what we had in mind when planning a Geo-Big Year and buying the trailer.

The planning went back more than a year and did not start with a trailer. It began with the idea to bird all 50 states of the U.S. For that, we initially considered small motor homes and a towable car. I spent my spare time over the better part of a year investigating options for both small motor homes and the car to tow. The best motorhome option looked like a 26' Coach House. The big attraction was its one-piece molded body (no chance for seam leaks).

I was certain enough that we bought a Jeep Cherokee (05.04) with disengage-able transmission enabling flat towing. That was a saga of its own. To find the model with a 4-cylinder turbo engine (for better milage) and the transmission that could be disengaged for towing, I ended up buying remotely from a dealer in Maryland. I rented a car to drive there to pick it up and arrived to find that the *brand-new* car had about 5000 "dealer miles" on it. I later wished I had canceled the deal … but the dealer dropped the price and provided documentation that I would still have the full warranty. I went through with the purchase. It proved to be a very nice car. But after I got it, we could not find a new-ish used Coach House motorhome; the new ones were both beyond our budget and would have required a very long wait.

05.04

We then traveled to the big RV show in Harrisburg to explore options. With that input, I switched focus to a Leisure Travel Vans model. It had the advantage of a Mercedes diesel platform (meaning better gas milage) but the disadvantage of being just barely sufficient to tow the Jeep we already had.

After a series of near misses. where we almost made offers on both Coach House and Leisure Travel Vans models. we gave up on the motorhome option. I was uncertain whether we could keep the weight sufficiently low in the motorhome and car to allow the Jeep to be towed by the diesel-powered option. The Coach House or other options that could easily tow the Jeep were based on a Ford 350 or 450 chassis, which would get horrendous mileage.

That led us to investigate camping trailers and to plan on trading the Jeep for something that could tow one. As detailed earlier, we ultimately ordered a custom Lance model 1985, fitted out for the travel we planned. After exploring a range of pickup truck and SUV options, we nearly bought a 1-year-old Audi Q7 configured for towing. But the specs were just barely sufficient to tow the Lance trailer. Instead, we ended up with the Ford Expedition. If we had bought the Audi with its air suspension, the better ride might have avoided Fran's back pain — we will never know.

When Fran had the bad experience on our first camping trip of the Geo-Big Year, I briefly thought about trading the Expedition for an Audi

Q7. But I was still not comfortable pushing weight limits for towing, and we did not want to make yet another vehicle purchase mistake. Thus, we decided that we either would make the current combination of Expedition and Lance work or give up on the camping option for traveling together.

In the short run, Fran preferred taking time to recover, meditate, quilt, and write rather than trying to travel again soon. So, I switched back to day trips. That beat sitting home trying to find other things to replace work (and I wanted to take a bit of a break from academic activities as I eased into Emeritus status following commencement in a couple days' time).

+++

On May 7, despite the 44°F morning temperature (cool for May), it seemed like it was going to be a nice day … until mid-afternoon rain. I decided to start by going after the Least Bittern that had been seen at Bald Eagle State Park locally in Centre County. While I was well past my Centre County target, it would be a Centre County and Pennsylvania lifer. I had only seen two others anywhere, on the Outer Banks in NC. I was lucky enough to find the Least Bittern, hiding in the reeds (05.05). It did not appreciate my presence as much as I appreciated it.

05.05

I had a lunch along, so after the Least Bittern I moved on to Union County where I was sitting at 49 species. I spent the rest of the morning at Dales Ridge Trail, my 2nd time at the site. I added 18 species to reach 67 with a Yellow-rumped Warbler. I did not manage a good photo, but I did have nice photos of others, including Red-headed Woodpecker, Wood Thrush, Spotted Sandpiper, and House Wren (05.06) — clockwise from the top left.

05.06

From Union County, I moved on to a game lands in Lycoming County. With an 18 min. stop, I added 8 species, but was still below halfway. Lycoming would take two more trips to finish off.

+++

That night, after what had been a productive birding day with a Pennsylvania lifer along with completion of another county, I spent a couple more hours up at the office continuing to sort and toss. I found that on previous trips to the office I missed one whole shelf in a glass-door bookcase containing my history of cartography books. I decided to retain most of those, giving away only a few. I was not sure where they would fit at home, but I packed them up, gathered my drawer of antique sheet maps, and selected a few other books to cart home.

When I realized that I would not be able to donate any books to the AAUW book sale, I decided to make all books I could not keep available to anyone in the department, with the rest to be recycled. I had been given an OK to use the Department's small conference room as a space to lay out books (and maps) for faculty, grads, or staff to check out and take any they wanted. I began shifting things to that space. In the process of sorting maps, I came across a huge tactile, multi-sheet map of Washington, D.C. (**05.07**). One of our Ph.D. students (Harrison Cole) was doing a dissertation (with Anthony Robinson) on tactile maps, so I contacted him to see if he wanted the map; it is now his.

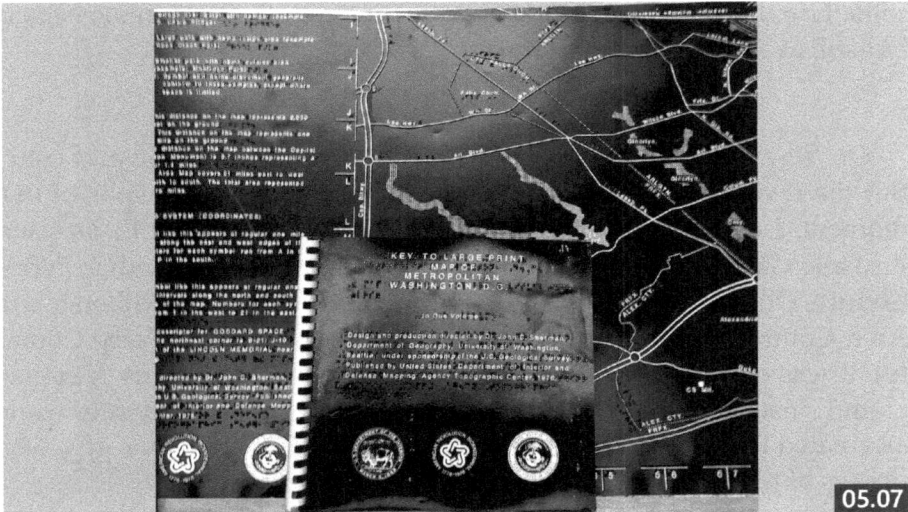

+++.

On Saturday, May 8, I opted for a short daytrip back to Snyder County where I had 58 species. I wanted to get back in time to pick up quiche (and, more importantly, espresso brownies!) at Café Lemont before they closed at 2:00pm. I stopped at a road in Bald Eagle State Forest, just across the Snyder County line. I had good luck that included three warbler species, Black-throated Green Warbler, Hooded Warbler, Black-and-white Warbler. I managed passable photos of the latter two (05.08-L&ML). I went on to Walker Lake. There I added Baltimore Oriole, Gray Catbird (05.08-MR), Cliff Swallow (#67, but photos were marginal), Lincoln's Sparrow (05.08-R), and Great Blue Heron.

Having completed Snyder County (and then some), I moved to Juniata County, which was on the way back to Lemont. I added 9 species, reaching 61 for the county. From there, I went to Café Lemont to pick up our quiche; they were (disappointingly) out of espresso brownies. I settled for the gluten-free brownies (too much sugar, no espresso beans, but still at least some chocolate).

+++

On May 9, I intended to stay home due to predicted rain and cold. But the revised prediction was for afternoon rain. On the spur of the moment, I decided to bird. I picked the Brig. Gen. Frank E. Tressler Bird and Game Sanctuary and the little Buffalo State Park, both in Perry County. On the way I decided to make a quick stop at the Millerstown Area Community Park, a place I visited in March (also Perry County). It was quite productive for both birds and the arts/crafts "Gnome Home" installation (05.09). I learned later that the Gnome Homes were all created by Steve Hoke, known locally as the Gnome Home guy. My photos of his work are included here with his permission.

I added 11 species at the park; the best was Baltimore Oriole (05.10). I then moved on to the Brig. Gen. Frank E. Tressler Bird and Game Sanctuary, where I added 8 additional species.

Next, I continued on to Little Buffalo State Park where I added 7 more. Rain that began at the Sanctuary gradually got heavier at Little

Buffalo. Birds took shelter. I had progressed from 39 to 65 species in Perry County. I gave up for the day 2 species short and headed home.

+++

The night prior to my trip back to Perry County, Fran had another unpleasant bout with back pain. Recovery from our camping trip was slower than we hoped. We were still optimistic that the medication would start having an effect, but it was looking less likely that Fran would be able to travel again with the Expedition and camping trailer.

The situation was making my quest plans challenging and brought into question whether it was an important thing to try at this point. Having heard just the week prior that a recently retired colleague had contracted a fatal illness, however, was a reminder that (at our time of life, both 69), postponing anything can mean never doing it.

+++

On May 10, I woke up discouraged about the chance to achieve my Pennsylvania Geo-Big Year. More than a third of the year was gone. I had visited only 18 of 67 counties, completing about half. Coming close to finishing Perry County the day before without doing so did not help. And, facing long drives to "nearby" counties to avoid overnight stays was draining. Still, I was not ready to give up (yet). I decided on Lycoming County for a day trip, where I had 26 species. Several species I needed had been reported there in the prior three days.

No rain was predicted, but it looked like the prediction was wrong. I had to wear old hiking shoes that I had intended to throw away. My new ones were still soaking wet from the day before. I started at State Game Lands 252 and did two walks there, each a productive hour and a half. I reached 55 species by the time I moved on. Highlights were Black-billed Cuckoo, Chestnut-sided Warbler, and Indigo Bunting (05.11). I also had Hooded Warbler and Northern Waterthrush.

05.11

After the game lands I went to Mill Street near the municipal airport in Williamsport. I picked up a Warbling Vireo, then saw some birders who mentioned they were looking for a Clay-colored Sparrow seen earlier in the day. I started looking for the sparrow, of course, since it was a potential lifer I'd missed earlier in the year. It had been seen near the airport gate. I walked the road slowly, scanning on both sides, then retraced my steps. But I had no luck finding the sparrow. It was time to head home for dinner.

Just as I was getting in the car, a Belted Kingfisher flew past for number 63 in the county. Spotted Sandpiper had become my go-to bird at the end of the day when I'm trying to add to the count and have any water nearby. I was next to the river, so I started scanning the opposite shore. Not too surprisingly a Spotted Sandpiper flew by, turned around, and landed right across from me. Then as I was driving out, I added an Eastern Bluebird to get the count to 65 for the county.

It was a good day, but one where I came up short for the target (by 2 again), meaning I would need another trip back. At least I had many good photos; which included: Red-winged Blackbird, Killdeer, Veery, and Warbling Vireo (05.12).

+++

At this point, it was about 10 days since we returned from our first camping trip of the Geo-Big Year. Fran was still having regular pain, difficulty walking, and difficulty sleeping. She felt that the chances of traveling in the trailer again were near zero. I was not certain what we would do. Fran encouraged me to keep at the quest, traveling by myself to those places I could not do as day trips. I was unsure whether I wanted to do that, particularly since it would mean leaving Fran at home with Skoti, who likes lots of walks. Since we were in spring and heading to summer, however, it was increasingly possible that Skoti's buddy Diggity would be brought over by his owner to play.

As I was considering what to do, I took a couple days off from birding to catch up on moving out of my office. I spent more time shifting things I would not keep, but that someone else in the Department might want, over to the small conference room. This included several hundred sheet maps and about 3/4 of the books that I had no room for at home (05.13).

I was happy to hear that my colleague Cindy Brewer was interested in issues of cartographic journals she did not have in her collection. I set aside issues from The *American Cartographer, Cartographica,* and *The British Cartographic Journal* for her (05.14). The rest of the issues I had were relegated to the recycle bin.

In the process of sorting, I separated out more than 35 bound dissertations sent to me over the years by Ph.D. grads or advisers from around the world. They were mostly from ITC in the Netherlands, ETH and University of Zurich in Switzerland, and multiple universities in Germany, Australia, and the U.K. None were in our Penn State Library, so I checked about library interest. I received a "yes" response to all; so these dissertations went on my "save" shelves along with the Proceedings volumes previously set aside for the library (05.15).

05.15

By the time I left in the evening of May 11, my office was starting to look rather empty — the end was in sight (05.16).

05.16

After thinking about things for a couple days and discussions with Fran, I decided tentatively to continue the quest and do some traveling on my own. While traveling with the trailer solo seemed like overkill, it was safer in relation to COVID-19 than hotels. Plus, we owned the trailer. So, while I was still hoping Fran would feel sufficiently better to give camping another try, I was not optimistic. If it happened, it would be well into the future. For now, I started to plan a solo camping trip, focusing on the northwest corner of the state (Erie County and nearby).

+++

While considering when and where to take the trailer, I decided to continue local day trips to counties within reach that I had not completed. On the cold morning of May 13 (36°F), I headed to Northumberland County where I had 29 species. I knew it would be a challenge to hit the 67 target, but I decided to spend a full day and give it a try. I also wanted to have a stop in Lycoming County where I had just 2 more to go.

Birds in Northumberland County were scarce that morning. I started at Milton State Park (the one on an island in the West Branch of the Susquehanna River). In an hour and a half, I netted only 7 new species. The only warbler I added was Yellow Warbler.

I shifted to Lycoming County, hoping to at least finish it off. After more than an hour (at a site in Tiadaghton State Forest), I got number 67, Worm-eating Warbler (05.17-L) and three extras (Black-and-white Warbler, Blue-gray Gnatcatcher, and Black-throated Green Warbler). I was particularly happy to get a photo of the Worm-eating Warbler (I had not been having good photo luck for the 67th in many counties). I also got a nice photo of an Ovenbird (05.17-R).

I planned to move back to Northumberland County, but on the way went through a part of Montour County, a county I had not started. I made several stops, cutting back and forth across the Montour-Northumberland border. In Montour, I picked up 10 species, including an Ovenbird and a male Scarlet Tanager. In Northumberland, I added Hairy Woodpecker and Red-headed Woodpecker at one stop (05.18) and Scarlet Tanager in another.

Near the woodpeckers, I also captured a photo that illustrates some of the culture of rural Central Pennsylvania (05.19).

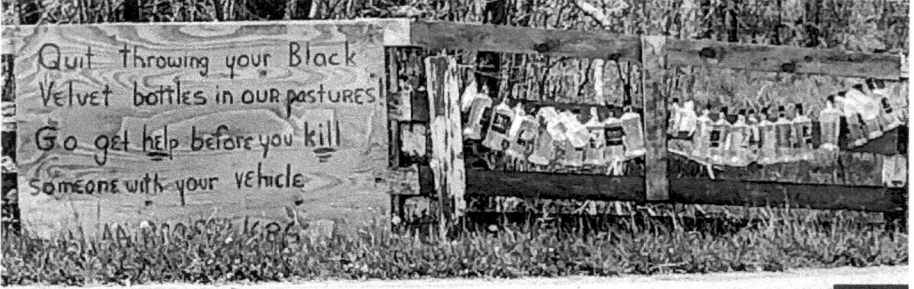
05.19

I needed to head for home. I had managed only 42 species for Northumberland County. Google indicated a 52-mile drive home — time for WCPE (the Classical station through Apple CarPlay). While I did not make the hoped-for progress in Northumberland, the trip was successful in completing Lycoming County and starting Montour County.

That evening, I began exploring campgrounds for the trailer in or near Erie County. I planned to start on Wednesday, May 19 since midweek typically had more openings. But, even mid-week, I found no State Parks with spots convenient to Presque Isle, my key destination. I opted to wait to book while I explored recent eBird sightings in Erie County and nearby counties and watched the weather reports.

In the meantime, I decided to try for a *trifecta*, finishing Mifflin, Juniata, and Perry Counties. I needed 2 each in Mifflin and Perry plus 5 in Juniata. Dickcissel had been seen in both Mifflin and Juniata Counties. So, I made that a priority since it would be a PA lifer.

I started with Mifflin. One 30-minute walk/drive on a country road near Belleville netted Savanah Sparrow, Eastern Meadowlark (#67), and Northern Mockingbird — but no Dickcissel. Since I was working on my *trifecta* and Dickcissel was seen in Juniata County, I moved on — but stopped to capture a view of Big Valley before heading off (05.20).

05.20

I tried back roads east of Lewistown and north of U.S. 322 where reports had been posted of species I had not seen. I ended up adding 9 species to reach 70. A Red-Shouldered Hawk was number 67. The best photo was of a Grasshopper Sparrow (05.21). Again, no Dickcissel.

I moved on to Perry County and added an American Pipit (#66) and a Horned Lark (#67). While my photos of number 67 for each county were not the best, it was great to finish three counties and have at least an identifiable image of number 67 in each (the Eastern Meadowlark taking off, the Red-shouldered Hawk circling, and the Horned Lark posing (05.22).

+++

I spent the next day at home catching up and heading back to the office to continue the push to empty things out. Not surprisingly, I had conflicting feelings as the last remnants of the 36 years I had spent at Penn State disappeared from my soon-to-be former office. I was looking forward to the freedom from course preparation and grading (particularly grading) and from faculty and committee meetings. But I knew I would miss interacting with students, particularly graduate students. It was the opportunity to mentor students one-on-one and in small groups over the years that kept me in academics. I would also miss the interdisciplinary research project collaborations that had been central to my time at Penn State. While I would explore opportunities to collaborate with others in my soon-to-be Emeritus status, I was tired of chasing funding, thus a big positive would be no more grant proposal writing. Despite mixed feelings, by the end of that day on May 15, I had made real progress on vacating the office (05.23).

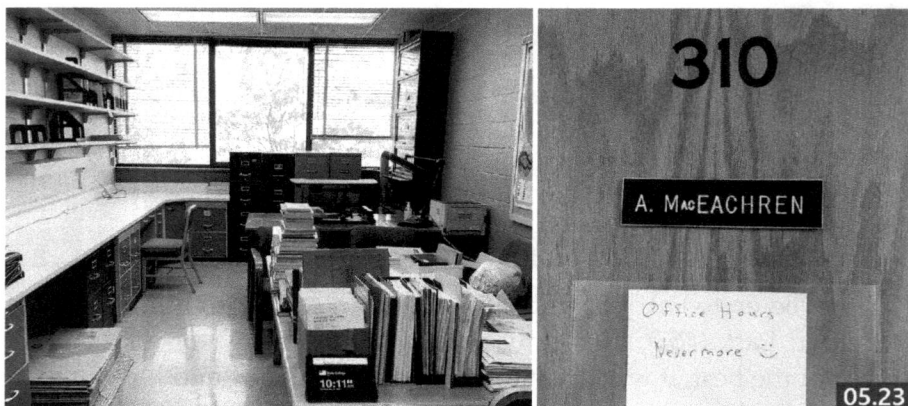

Before returning to my quest, I had a dissertation defense to attend on Monday (May 17) — my last. After that defense, my only remaining Penn State responsibilities were to finish moving out of my office and return my ID and keys. At that point (while official retirement would begin July 1), my standard 36-week academic appointment would be completed, leaving me free for multi-day birding trips to the more distant counties.

For my first such trip, I stuck with the plan to head to Erie while migration was still at its peak. I ended up booking at a KOA (checking in on the 19th and out on the 22nd). It was the closest spot to Presque Isle I could find with spaces available.

+++

I needed to stay at home through the defense on Monday; even though it would be held on Zoom, reliable internet was essential. So, I opted for a Sunday day-trip to Cameron County. Of counties I had not yet started, it had the closest hotspot, part of the Quehanna Wild Area, about 1-hour from home.

Heading to the Quehanna area took me (mentally) back to the beginning of my time at Penn State. My first Ph.D. student, John Krygier, now a Professor at Ohio Wesleyan University, did a dissertation entitled *Visualization, Geography, and Landscape: Visual Methods and the Study of Landscape Dereliction.* The multimedia artifact that John built as part of his dissertation was (in my view) an early precursor of what Esri (the GIS company) now calls a "Story Map". The landscape "dereliction" of John's title was the antecedent to the Quehanna Civilian Conservation Corps (CCC) project in the 1930s. The Quehanna CCC sites were repurposed and abandoned multiple times, with some activities generating toxic waste and others simply leaving environmental scars.

A tangible reminder of the Quehanna Wild Area's non-natural history is the Pennsylvania Department of Corrections *Quehanna Motivational Boot Camp* that straddles the main road just before the Cameron County section of Quehanna. Passing that, I stopped at the Hoover Farm site to bird. I got my bearings with the signage (focusing on Elk rather than birds) and map posted there. Here, I include a terrain map from OpenStreetMap showing the Wild Area boundary (05.24).

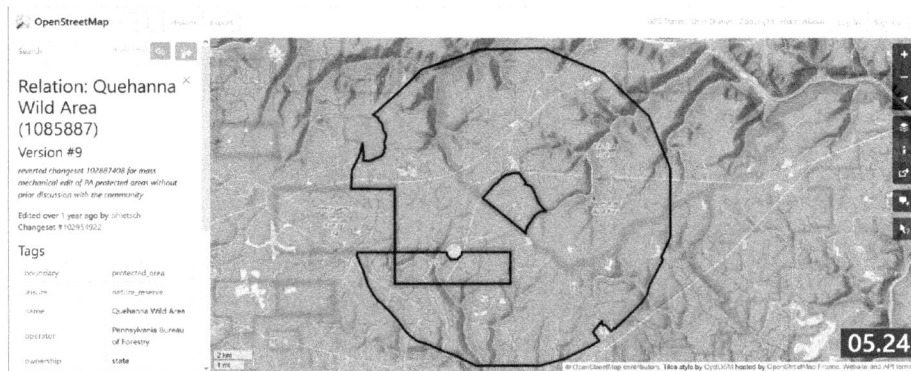

I spent an hour walking trails and fields. It was odd birding this "natural environment" knowing its past. Reminders popped up unexpectedly, including old oil wells and building ruins. Despite these scars on the landscape, a PA DCNR sign said: "Snowmobiling, vehicular camping, and off-road vehicle use are prohibited to protect the wild character of the area." On my walk, I recorded 24 species that included a female Rose-breasted Grosbeak, Blackburnian Warbler, Ovenbird, Magnolia Warbler (05.25-L), American Redstart (05.25-R), plus a Black-and-white Warbler and Ruby-throated Hummingbird.

After the Quehanna Wild Area, I drove to Sinnemahoning State Park. I stopped at the Dam and the main park area. Overall, I had a good day, reaching 53 species before heading home. These included Eastern Bluebird and Veery (**05.26**) plus five warbler species.

+++

That evening back home, I had photos to process and a dissertation to finish reviewing for the Monday defense. Skoti (**05.27**) was unhappy with this; he wanted a walk.

I attended the Ph.D. defense as planned; it went well for Jiawei Huang (advisor: Alex Klippel, dissertation: *The Effects of Visual Realism on Cognitive Constructs, Spatial Memory and Learning in Virtual Reality*). It was great for Jiawei and a nice bookend to the Penn State years for me.

The rest of that day and the next I got organized for my first solo trip with our trailer — to Erie County and nearby Counties. Fran and I were contemplating some non-camping travel to at least a few of the counties. But it had become clear that if I planned to continue the quest, much of the travel would be solo.

+++

On the morning of the 19th, I pulled out with the trailer about 9:30am. My goal was to arrive right at 1:00pm, leaving 5-6 hours of daylight to bird. I thought that might give me an outside chance to do a full 67 species for Erie County on the first partial day. At this point in my Geo-Big Year, I had not yet managed 67 species in one day. But it was the middle of migration (based on BirdCast), so I expected Presque Isle and nearby places to be awesome. In the past 3 days of eBird reports, more than 100 species were listed.

My first stop on the trip was a rest area in Jefferson County. It yielded 10 species. The best were Wood Thrush and Ovenbird. An even quicker stop in Venango County netted 7 species. The best there was an Alder Flycatcher that I heard, my first of the year. I then got on I-79 heading north toward Erie, with the KOA exit a bit short of that.

I got to the KOA and set up quickly. Compared to State Parks we had camped in, the shade trees were rather pitiful (05.28). Other than that, the campground was fine, particularly for the minimal time I would spend there. As soon as I set up, I headed over to Presque Isle State Park, starting birding at 2:30pm.

I was too busy with birds to spend much time admiring or photographing the environment. But I like lighthouses, so when I drove past it, I could not pass up taking a photo of the Presque Isle Lighthouse

05.28

(05.29). A view from the water side would have been better … but I had no boat.

I birded 7 locations in the park. The experience was exhilarating due to the variety of species seen. Many species represented the first state-wide sightings for me during the year.

I started with some sites near the Park's entrance that proved to be productive. Gradually, I worked my way out to and part way down the peninsula. Since Presque Isle State Park is situated on a peninsula jutting into Lake Erie, water is abundant, and habitats are varied. There is the lake itself, Presque Isle Bay, Misery Bay, and many ponds (some marshy, others more open). As a result, there was no shortage of waterfowl and shorebirds. Plus, the weather was reasonably cooperative for photographs.

On that first day there, I saw 17 species of ducks and shorebirds. Many of these were toward the end of the day along the Sidewalk Trail and from the shore at Misery Bay. Sightings included: Spotted Sandpiper, Redhead, Green Heron, Common Goldeneye, Ring-necked Duck, and Lesser Scaup (05.30).

05.30

I ultimately quit at 7:30pm, heading to the trailer for a late dinner. I was within striking distance of 67, but ran out of light. I managed 62 species. The best additional photos were of: Blackburnian Warbler, Bay-breasted Warbler, Magnolia Warbler, Rose-breasted Grosbeak, Blue-headed Vireo, and Least Flycatcher (05.31).

05.31

+++

I sat down to dinner at 8:41pm and sent a text to Fran: *Just sat down to dinner. I guess I'll pretend I'm in Spain :-)*. The text was a reference to the International Cartographic Conference we attended in A Coruña, where it was hard to find a restaurant open for dinner before 8:00pm.

I listened to Cleveland baseball during dinner. Jose Ramirez is Fran's favorite player on the team. I was able to text her about him stealing

3rd base, then scoring on the next play. Cleveland won 3-2 (over the LA Angels) but I was asleep before the end, planning to be up at 4:30am.

The next morning, I was up early, 4:30am as planned. An email brought distressing news; the former colleague who had retired ahead of me had passed away. We had known him and his wife for 36 years. When colleagues pass away, particularly when they are your age, it makes you realize how every day really counts.

+++

After breakfast and the drive from the campground, my first list was for the Presque Isle SP -Thompson Bay hotspot starting at 6:17am. I got to see a great sunrise looking east across Presque Isle Bay (05.32).

I reached 67 species by 7:30am. Additions included Warbling Vireo (warbling) and Peregrine Falcon flying (number 67). I continued to the end of Gull Point in case this was my only chance to bird Presque Isle. I added 7 more species to get to 74 by about 8:15am. Photos (05.33) show three of the morning species: the Peregrine Falcon (moving a bit fast for a crisp photo), a Black-bellied Plover in breeding plumage, and a nicely posed Great Egret fishing.

After the long walk back from Gull Point, I headed to the campground to pack lunch and pull fish from the freezer to thaw for dinner. I then headed south to Crawford County where I posted lists from 9 different places. I started at a pair of ponds that were on State Game Lands 214. An Upland Sandpiper had been seen there, which would have been a lifer for me. I had no luck finding it, but added 14 species in 26 minutes, including Savannah Sparrow and Purple Martin (05.34).

I then stopped at Pymatuning State Park (2 sites), getting 26 species by the end of lunch. I tried Conneaut Marsh but had little luck. Then, I did a 3.5-mile loop at the Erie National Wildlife Refuge Deer Run Trail site. The highlight was a Barred Owl (05.35-L). I also had a cooperative Yellow-bellied Sapsucker (05.35-R). Two final stops got me to 55 species in Crawford County before I headed back to the campground for dinner, this time a bit after 7:00pm. I had to use the trailer air conditioning for the first time ever — it was over 80°F and humid.

+++

The next morning, May 21, my first objective was completing Crawford County. Checking eBird was discouraging since others saw several species the prior day that I tried for unsuccessfully, including Blue-winged Warbler and Yellow-throated Vireo. But — that is birding, I suspect I saw things that others did not as well. Despite the previous day's misses, the morning went well with a Bonaparte's Gull and Bald Eagle (05.36-L&M) at Pymatuning SP and steady additions at State Game Lands 214, including Great-crested Flycatcher (05.36-R).

I added Wood Duck (05.37-L) for number 67 before 9:00am, followed by White-crowned Sparrow and Eastern Meadowlark for 68 and 69. The best bird for the county, was a lifer Upland Sandpiper. I had missed it the day before, then missed again on my first try of the morning. I finally found the Upland Sandpiper on try three. If I had scanned only the fields, I would not have seen it. To my surprise, it was perched on a wire (05.37-R).

Next, I moved south again to Mercer County. I was not starting at zero; I had picked up 3 common species on my way into the area. I was able to start my first Mercer County list at 9:40am. Based on successes in Erie and Crawford, it seemed likely that I could get into the 50 species range and perhaps finish the county early the next morning before breaking camp and heading home. Since most sites in Mercer County were an hour or more from the KOA, and check-out time was 11:00am, that could prove to be a challenge. So, I focused on getting as far as I could toward 67 with what remained of the day. After walks of 2.2

miles, .9 miles, 1.1 miles, and .5 miles, I had 41 species. I stopped at a shady spot for lunch (**05.38**) and picked up a couple more.

The remainder of the day was a long hard slog with walks of .5 miles, .1 miles, .8 miles, 1.7 miles, 1.4 miles, and .2 miles. At about 6:15pm, I picked up number 64, a House Sparrow. I was within range to finish Mercer County, so I tried Maurice K. Goddard State Park for a last push. First, I saw American Goldfinch (#65). Moving to the other end of the reservoir, just before 7:00pm, I added Purple Martin (#66) and a single Cliff Swallow (#67). Before heading back to the campground, I also got Black-capped Chickadee (#68). Due to 3 common birds seen while driving through on May 19 (Common Grackle, Barn Swallow, and Turkey Vulture), I did not go from zero to 67 in one day. But I saw those 3 again, so all 68 on my Mercer list were seen in one day! I did not manage good photos of the last birds; but I did get nice shots of a Yellow-bellied Sapsucker (taking off), an Orchard Oriole, a Yellow-throated Vireo, and a Yellow Warbler (**05.39**).

+++

It was odd to see zero Chickadees until after 7:00pm. But, as reported by multiple authors, Black-capped Chickadee numbers have experienced steep decline. Nick Bolgiano (a Centre County birder, and a Seasonal Editor for *Pennsylvania Birds* who analyzes data and writes about his results) reported evidence that West Nile Virus may be a factor (*Pennsylvania Birds*, issue 33:1, 2019).

After a successful three county blitz, I had to plan my travel-home day (May 22). Checkout was 11:00am. Possible next counties were east of the KOA, which made it impractical to start another county before breaking camp. I opted to break camp early, then try birding in Warren County, the next county to the east. Since I would be towing the trailer, I needed to find a place with room to park and a chance for birds within walking distance from the parking. I would check options during dinner, which was again going to be late since my last stop in Mercer County was more than an hour from the campground.

During and after dinner, I used the Google Maps satellite layer to check out parking for several eBird hotspots. I eventually picked Buckaloons Recreation Area as the best bet. It appeared to have long pull-in sites for people with boats, and I took the chance that they would allow short-term camping trailer parking as well.

+++

Buckaloons turned out to be a small but decent birding site, just right to park, then walk the entire thing in the hour and twenty minutes I spent there. They had a campground, which seemed to have most spaces filled, but the pull-in parking for boats was mostly empty. I did need to pay a *day-use fee*, despite my *America the Beautiful — National Parks and Federal Recreational Lands Senior Pass*. I was told it did not apply, even though the web site detailing what the pass covers says, "The passes cover entrance and standard amenity (day-use) recreation fees and provide discounts on some expanded amenity recreation fees." I did not have much choice, so paid the $5 for my short stay there.

In that time, I managed 33 species, one short of halfway. Highlights were an adult Bald Eagle pair roosting in a tree, Blackburnian Warbler and Chestnut-sided Warbler seen near the parking area, and one Green Heron in a stream (05.40). On the way driving out, I added European

Starling and Red-winged Blackbird to push the county total over the halfway point.

+++

I stayed home for a few days, spending time with Fran and Skoti, processing photos, dealing with non-birding obligations, and simply resting up from the long days of the multi-county trip.

The trip to northwest counties gave me some real hope that the Geo-Big Year might be doable. Hitting the target for three previously unvisited counties and reaching half-way for another in four days was my best result to that point. Camping in the trailer by myself was a drag, but it did allow me to bring my own food and avoid restaurants and the associated COVID-19 risk.

While staying at a KOA was OK, I preferred State Parks. They are more likely to have birds on site (and owls at night). So, I booked 2 nights at Cowans Gap State Park, straddling Fulton and Franklin Counties (May 27-29), 3 nights at Ryerson Station State Park in Greene County (June 2-5), 3 nights at Kooser State Park in Somerset County (June 9-12), 3 nights at Racoon Creek State Park in Beaver County (June 22-25), and 2 nights at Pine Grove Furnace State Park in Cumberland County (June 16-18). Since summer was coming on, it seemed best to lock in dates — while hoping for the best on weather.

+++

I had the trailer hooked up and ready to go the night before my trip to Cowens Gap State Park on May 27. Check-in was 3:00pm. If I left early, I would be there well before that. So, I went online to see if they had any rules about early check-in. I didn't find anything, but discovered that I did not have the reservation I thought I had. I must have missed hitting that last *submit* button! After a bit of panic, I found that there were still several spots available for that night and the next (my intended nights). Open spaces probably existed because it was supposed to rain for two days. But I was ready to go so I booked anyway.

My route took me south down US 322 past Milroy, PA. I knew I would pass a trailer scale. Since I had never done a weight check I decided to take advantage of it. The weight scales are designed more for tractor-trailer rigs than camping trailers, so it was an interesting experience. I had to pull up on the scales in a particular spot to get three separate weights, then pull-off to unhook the trailer and drive back on to get a weight for the Ford Expedition on its own. Once I did that, with a run inside to pay, I was able to use results to calculate the key weights. The outcomes were tongue weight of 640lbs and GVWR of 5,420lbs. Both were well within specs for the Expedition with nearly an 800lb cushion on the GVWR. I was reassured to know that I was not pushing the limits.

I got to the campground and set up quickly. Starting with 11 species in Fulton County (from an I-70 rest stop on the trip to retrieve the trailer in April), I began my first list for this trip a bit after 4:00pm. Five stops and 3.5 miles walking later, I quit for the day (or thought I had) with 37 species. The best birds were Black Vulture (a pair), a Scarlet Tanager, and Northern Rough-winged Swallow, none of which were cooperative for photos. The best photos were of a Cedar Waxwing and Wood Duck (05.41).

+++

The most interesting aspects of the day were not the birds but the places I drove through on the way to the state park. One was *Burnt Cabins*, a place Fran and I used to pass on our way to North Carolina before I-99 was built. It is a historic place listed on the National Register. The other was *The Pulpit*, a spectacular hang-gliding launch site on US 30 at the top of the ridge, for details about the site see: https://www.round-barnpress.com/category/central-pennsylvania/the-pulpit/

I learned to hang glide years ago, mostly because my father-in-law was Francis Rogallo (known as the "father of hang gliding" due to his invention of the flexible wing that inspired the first hang gliders). I bought a wing but flew infrequently. *The Pulpit* was beyond my skill level, so I never flew there. My trip focus was birds, not people (even ones who fly); so, I did not stick around at *The Pulpit*.

+++

The campground turned out to be the first place during the year that had bats flying around at night. I saw a lot of bat boxes earlier in the day, so seeing bats was not surprising (but a welcome sight). The only new bird I got in the evening back at the campground was a Great Blue Heron fly by. I was hoping for owls but had no luck.

While there were no owls, I did hear an Eastern Whip-poor-will call early in the evening, then a Woodcock in the background. I got recordings of both. The Whip-poor-will started up again at 3:00am and called nonstop till about 4:30am when I finally got up.

+++

On the 28th, I expected to finish Fulton County, then move to Franklin, but that did not happen. I got a slow start, due to rock-solid frozen blueberries that I had to thaw for breakfast. Birding started slowly too, and lighting was poor. One of the few photos I got was Worm-eating Warbler (05.42).

Just after noon, I reached 61 species as I walked along an abandoned section of a former turnpike (05.43-L). Then, it started to rain steadily (05.43-M). I checked the forecast (05.43-R) and it was not promising. It rained heavily much of the afternoon. I managed only one new species the rest of the day, a Blue-headed Vireo on an out-and-back half mile hike where I got quite wet.

Given the rain, I drove around in McConnellsburg, looking for House Finches and Tufted Titmice because I had seen neither. No luck. I returned to the trailer to get an early dinner.

+++

The plan was to go back out if the rain let up. That plan was foiled ... due to yet another issue with the trailer. The "fantastic fan" was leaking. There was water on the bedspread and a very slow but steady drip from the fan. I was not sure whether the fan had a broken seal or just something stuck in the opening. I climbed on the roof to try to assess the problem. But since it was raining heavily, I could not check things thoroughly and could not identify the leak's source. So, I rigged up a towel on a piece of plastic and put that on the bed to keep things from getting wet. I ended up not going out because it kept raining — I went to bed very early, at 9:00pm, hoping for a dry day.

On May 29, I rose at 4:30am — again. I was (again) trying to finish off Fulton County. The previous day was a tough one with scarce birds and heavy rain that continued through the night. Plus, I was getting no help from other birders, since there had been zero lists posted in the past seven days for the county (other than mine).

+++

At least the rain had stopped by 5:30am when I headed out. Given my experience on the Erie trip, I expected to finish both Fulton and

Franklin Counties easily, so was discouraged at my slow progress. Since I needed to exit the campsite by 3:00pm, I was hoping to reach 67 for Fulton quickly and then start Franklin. Lacking help from any recent eBird posts, I headed for a promising site that I had spent time at my first evening, the Haines-Seville Wetlands. Starting before 6:00am, I expected more variety than in my previous afternoon stop there.

Things did not begin well. The first hour added just Green Heron. I moved to Buchanan SF--Kerper Tract/Redbud Valley. On the way, I picked up Indigo Bunting. Another hour and a half netted just 2 more species (Ruby-throated Hummingbird and Northern Waterthrush) to reach 66. I decided to try Meadow Grounds Lake, hoping for Spotted Sandpiper, my "go to" bird when I was trying to finish a county. I found one for number 67! I also had a Red-tailed Hawk fly over for number 68. As typical for this trip, the very gray skies, off-and-on rain, and usually quite distant birds conspired against clear photos.

I had finished Fulton County just after 11:00am. So, I quickly moved to a nearby site in Franklin County, the Fort Loudon State Historic Area. I spent about half an hour there and recorded 12 species. The best were Bald Eagle (2 of them) and Black Vulture (3 of them).

I returned to the campground and was packed up and on the way home by 2:00pm after a disappointing three days.

+++

I had three days at home prior to my next camping trip. I took May 30 to process photos and catch up on other things. One of those "things" was to go back to the office for what I thought would be the last time. I moved all remaining stuff that might be of interest to anyone over to the conference room across the hall — shown as a panorama (05.44).

I brought home one more small bag of stuff I decided not to give away. I took a final panoramic photo of the empty office (05.45).

Another "thing" to do while home was to determine what caused the trailer's *fantastic* fan to leak. I climbed up on the trailer roof to take a close look. With the lid of the fan fully open, I examined the interior seal, the caulking around the outside of the fan, and the lid itself. I could see nothing amiss. That made me suspect that the electronic fan closure might not have pulled the fan fully shut. I planned to test this theory on the next trip, for which rain was predicted half of the time.

After the last trip to the office, then examining the trailer's fan, I sat down at my desk overlooking our bird feeders to process some photos. To my surprise, a rather ratty-looking bear ambled into the yard to check out those feeders. I banged on the windows and managed to chase it off, with time to get only one quick iPhone photo (**05.46**). Bears are frequent in our yard, since we live next to a small preserve and near State Forest land. We have lost many bird feeders to them over the years, when I forget to put the feeders in the garage at night. In this case, the surprise was that the bear showed up in full daylight.

As I processed photos, I reflected on the limited progress of the past trip. I was again discouraged. But I had multiple camping trips booked, so the choice was to give up or to pick up the pace. I decided to try the latter and to fit in a day trip, for May 31, between camping trips.

+++

My day trip was to Northumberland County where I had 42 species from three prior forays. It was a longshot to reach the target with one more day trip. But I got out quickly after an early breakfast and was able to get to my first stop by 8:17am, Warrior Run Wetlands (05.47-L), part of the Susquehanna River Watershed, for which I later saw a nice map plaque in Shikellamy State Park (05.47-R).

I spent nearly 2 hours there, adding 11 species including a Baltimore Oriole (05.48-L&M), shown in two images going to a nest and feeding its young, and an Orchard Oriole (05.48-R), singing.

During mid-afternoon, while navigating among sites, I made several quick stops in adjacent Montour County, reaching 18 species. It was a long but productive day. I finally got to 67 in Northumberland County with a Double-crested Cormorant shown below, along with the lone House Sparrow I recorded in the county, plus a nicely posed Tree Swallow (05.49). I added a Great-crested Flycatcher for number 68.

+++

With the end of May, it was time to generate another map (05.50) to check on progress geographically. As the map shows, by Memorial Day, I had completed most of the counties that were reachable from Centre County in day trips and made my first major foray to the edge of the state in the northwest. As the growing number of dots on the map show, I had posted eBird lists from many sites in most of the counties I visited to that point. While I had visited alot of sites, five months into the Geo-Big Year quest, it was clear from the map that I was far from half-way to the goal. June needed to be a good month. On the positive side, now that I had finally moved out of my office completely, obligations at Penn State were few, mostly paper writing, plus some letters of recommendation — activities that would continue into my soon-to-be official status as an Emeritus Professor.

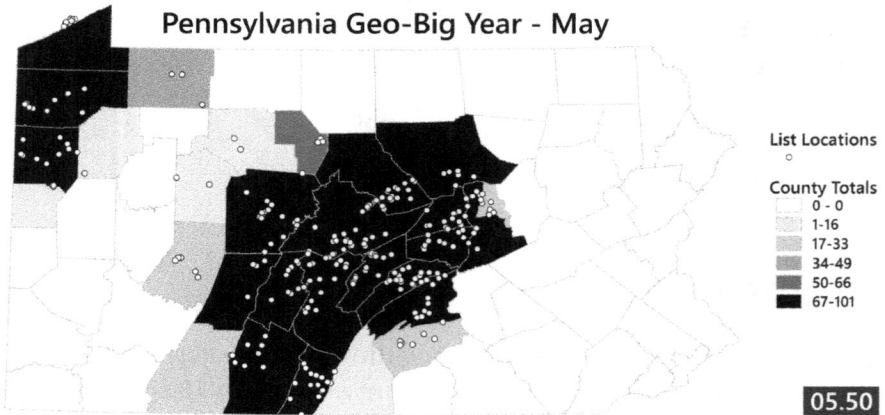

+++++

JUNE

It was a new month. On June 2nd I was off to the southwest corner of the state. It was another camping trip with Fran and Skoti staying home. I did not enjoy the solo travel, but it was better for Fran to stay home at that point. And, she encouraged me not to give up the quest.

As I passed Altoona, the skies looked dark and threatening and rain began. The weather report was less positive than it had been earlier; rain was expected for three days, with only Saturday (the day I was due to come home) being a nearly dry day. I tried to consider myself lucky that the prediction was for scattered showers much of the time rather than the torrential downpour I had on the last trip. That morning, I was just hoping to drive out from under the storm and I eventually did so.

Getting to Ryerson Station State Park proved to be a challenge due to Google directions. They took me down some rather narrow and winding roads (06.01), not great fun with the trailer.

06.01

I eventually got to the campground and found I had a tight camping space (06.02). I was unable to back the trailer straight in, needing to angle it quite a bit. That created a problem with my EZlift hitch. It popped off the rollers and I needed an Allen wrench to fix it. I thought I had one with me … I did not.

06.02

There was only one other campsite occupied, by a couple about my age. I walked over and asked if they had an Allen wrench. The guy was not sure, but he had a big toolbox in his pickup truck and agreed to look. Luckily for me he found an Allen wrench set (US rather than metric, which is what I needed). I got the hitch fixed with no problem and walked the wrench back, thanking the couple for their help.

It was after 3:00pm. I birded the campground a bit. Then I went to a location not too far away but remembered I needed to take shrimp out of the freezer to add to my dinner. After going back to do that, I went on to the dam area at the Park's small reservoir.

The dam site was a good one, with extensive wetlands. But ... I found a large part of the park closed off due to construction that I think was related to natural gas drilling activities. There also seemed to be a compressor station on the hill at the edge of the park. During my days there, I learned that Greene County had a lot of gas drilling activity, I encountered many big trucks and lots of noise on back roads — plus compressor noise nearby each night.

Despite these aspects of the setting, the afternoon was productive for birding. I got Cedar Waxwing, Northern Rough-winged Swallow, Scarlet Tanager, and Louisiana Waterthrush, (06.03) among many others. By 6:30pm, when I stopped for the day and headed back to the campground for dinner, I had reached 39 species for the county.

Greene county is mostly rural. Not surprisingly cell coverage was weak and in many locations I had zero signal. To check eBird (and text Fran), I drove out of the park onto a hill and got some cell coverage. I sat in the car for a while and searched eBird for places that I might go the next day. I marked the most promising ones on my downloaded Pocket Earth map. I then headed back to the campground for dinner.

+++

June 3rd started slowly, with 11 additions between my start at 6:22am and 11:00am. It had rained sporadically. I forgot my rain jacket, so had to go back to the trailer for it. That wasted an hour.

After a quick lunch, I picked a site at a game lands. It required a bit of bushwhacking and following deer trails to get to the best spot near a stream. I was looking for White-eyed Vireo and Rose-breasted Grosbeak but not having any luck. As I was getting to the point where

I planned to turn back, I saw movement in a bush. It turned out to be a White-eyed Vireo and I got a couple of photos (06.04).

06.04

Just before seeing the Vireo, I heard what I thought was a Rose-breasted Grosbeak. I played the call (quietly) to refresh my memory. It matched, so I scanned around. I saw a bird fly to the top of a tree at a distance. I couldn't tell what it was with binoculars. I took a few photos. In the first couple, the bird faced away. Probable, but I wasn't 100% sure. Then I found I had captured one photo with the bird facing forward. There was no doubt; it was a male Rose-breasted Grosbeak (the poor photo went in my eBird list). After nearly three hours and about a mile and a half hike, I had 59 species. Additions included a family of Common Merganser and an Eastern Kingbird (06.05).

06.05

With 8 to go for the county, the day was slipping away. I decided to go back to the state park. It was the only location where eBird showed recent species I had not seen. On the way I saw two Ravens hassling a Broad-winged Hawk. That 'ticked off' two species; then I saw one Common Grackle, also new for the county. I was up to 62. Close to the park I added Canada Goose (a family of them) to reach 63.

I parked at the ranger station, on the edge of a wetland. I put on my Muck Boots and went for a walk (about 1.2mi). That walk yielded a Killdeer, Spotted Sandpiper, Bald Eagle, and Cliff Swallow (#67).

It was almost 7:00pm. I returned to the nearby hill for the cell coverage needed to plan the next day's strategy for Washington County and to text Fran. Then, back to the trailer for dinner.

+++

On June 4, I had a good start, entering Washington County at 6:30am. I saw a Great Blue Heron at the roadside and added 5 species (including Chimney Swift) as I headed to Greencove Wetland. Enroute, I saw an intervening opportunity, a township park. I stopped and spent 30min. walking a trail. That *walk in the park* yielded 13 new species plus a deer fawn (06.06). The best bird was an Acadian Flycatcher. The hazy morning meant no good photos (of things smaller than a deer).

06.06

From the park I drove to my original objective, the Greencove Wetland. I spent about 2.5 hours there, walking 2 miles. It was a productive walk. I added 23 species, including Green Heron (06.07-L), Wood Duck, Warbling Vireo, Yellow-billed Cuckoo, and Wild Turkey. At one point, I got a glimpse of what I thought might be a Yellow-breasted Chat. I saw a bright yellow throat/breast, but too briefly to be sure. A short time later I saw a definite Yellow-throated Vireo (06.07-R). That could have been the first bird as well. Although a Chat was reasonably likely there in June it would remain a miss, at least for this site.

06.07

After the wetland, I headed to Canonsburg Lake. Again, Google Maps led me to a spot with no access … and it missed the fact that a bridge was out. Locating a lake access point was challenging. I finally found one where I could park and walk in about half a mile. But the walk added just 4 species. The highlight was Pileated Woodpecker. That put me at 50 for the county. While Canonsburg Lake did not add many birds, I did get to watch a Beaver swimming around and flapping its tail (06.08).

06.08

Next, I moved over to Peter's Lake Park and spent close to 2 hours circumnavigating the lake (walking a bit more than 2mi). I picked up 6 species, including a Ruby-throated Hummingbird and a Rose-breasted Grosbeak (in a tree with a Scarlet Tanager, which the Grosbeak ultimately chased off). The combination of trees and shy (or constantly moving) birds conspired to prevent decent photos.

At that point, it was about 3:00pm and my county total sat at 56. I picked Mingo Creek Park for one last push toward 67. By the time I got to the park, however, it was nearly 4:00pm and bird activity was slow — zero new species in the first 45 minutes. I generated two lists that spanned the time from 3:58pm to 6:30pm, walking 2.8 miles. I had nice views (06.09), but only 7 new species, reaching 63. The best additions were Broad-winged Hawk (flying along a ridge — I put a distant photo in my eBird list), Northern Parula, and Great-crested Flycatcher.

06.09

I quit for the day, since I was an hour from the campground (and dinner). I would try to reach the Washington County target the following day prior to campground checkout time at 3:00pm.

+++

The next morning (June 5) I headed to State Game Lands 302/Enlow Fork, the closest promising site in Washington County, arriving just after 7:00am. I walked down a trail and birds were scarce initially. There were many American Redstart (a new addition, that I did not realize was new), but nothing else.

I got to a place where the road crossed a stream. If I had crossed, I would've been back in Greene County, so I did not. I stayed on the bank to watch and listen. There were multiple bird calls and I had trouble sorting them out initially. The first new species I saw was a Baltimore Oriole going to a nest (06.10-L). Next, was Cedar Waxwing (06.10-M) then Blue-gray Gnatcatcher that I thought was number 66 because I had not realized that the American Redstart was new. So, I continued to look for one more. I got a glimpse of what I thought was a Blue-winged Warbler. I kept trying to find it again but was seeing only Yellow Warblers. While I may have had a Blue-winged, I could not be sure, so that was another one *that got away*. I was still hearing lots of birds, however, so I kept looking for number 67. Finally, I saw a Louisiana Waterthrush. I got a passable photo (06.10-R) of what turned out to be number 68 (with the Gnatcatcher as 67). Overall, it took me about 2.5 hours (and a mile and a quarter walking) to get the 4 species I needed (plus one).

06.10

On the way out I encountered three birders, the first I had seen on the entire trip. We compared sightings; they had seen nothing I had not. I debated where to go next. The nearest place in Fayette County was over 2 hours round trip. It didn't seem worth it for about 45 minutes of birding. So, I returned to the campground.

+++

I got back to the campground about 10:15am. It took a couple hours to break camp. My initial plan was to start another county on the way home; I had picked a site where I could park the trailer. But, given the time and the 4-hour trip home, I decided against that. Like the day before, it would have been more than an hour detour for less than an hour of birding. Instead, I went straight home for a welcome early dinner.

On the way out of Greene County, I had a Red-shouldered Hawk fly over. I had a great (quick) view of its translucent wing patches — it became a "spare" species on my already completed Greene County list.

I had a dicey trip over to I-79. Given the bad route in, I spent time picking a route I thought would avoid the narrow, winding country roads. My plan was to take State Route 21, which appeared to intersect I-79. But Google Maps navigation threw me a curve, which I foolishly "swung at". It told me to turn north on State Route 18. I assumed that Route 21 must not connect to I-79 as I expected and that this Route 18 was the one that would do so. I turned, but the route quickly got narrower, and Google Maps wanted me to turn onto an even narrower road. I skipped that turn, but things were not looking any better. So, I turned on the next road. That was a mistake.

The start of the new road was paved, and it looked better than the Google choice I had passed up. But as I continued, it turned into one of the "mini roads" that seemed common in this part of the state. The roads are about one and a half lanes wide. Two-way traffic requires someone to pull off or to rely on all-wheel drive if the ditches are not deep. Plus, this road was winding and bumpy.

At one point the road had a 9% grade (per my dashboard towing display). This was not a road I should have been on with the trailer. After coming over the peak and down the other side around a sharp turn, I encountered a farmer on a small tractor mowing his front yard. He smiled knowingly, assuming that I was lost (or crazy — or both). I smiled back, waved, and moved on.

After that point, the road was a bit straighter, but still narrow. I had about a mile to go to US 19. I managed to get through that distance without a car coming the other way — a deliverance! I got onto US 19, which then connected me with I-79, and I was finally *out of the woods* and on my way home.

After returning home, I tried looking up the road I had been on in Google Street View. Most of the road (particularly the very steep and sharply curved parts) was not in Street View ... apparently, it was too rural and/or unused to have been captured yet.

+++

On June 8, I posted my first-ever Twitter thread, detailing the process of vacating my office of 36 years. It summarizes the saga recounted in sections above and it remains available online:
https://twitter.com/alanGeoVISTA/status/1402397519624146946

That morning, after posting the Twitter thread, which I had prepared the night before, I planned a partial day trip that could get me home in time for the weekly farmers market that opened at 2:00pm. The choice was between Cameron County, where I had 53 species, and starting a new county. I decided to start Dauphin County, because the closest site was a little bit closer than any site in Cameron County. Starting Dauphin would also get me closer to an intermediate goal — birding (at least one list) in more than half of the counties before the year was half over. I was also trying to hit the 67 target in half of the counties in the first half of the year. But that second goal was looking very unlikely since I had only completed 20 counties with three weeks left in June.

+++

I got about halfway down to Dauphin County and realized that I left part of my lunch at home. So, "lunch" would be trail mix.

I got to the first site (State Game Lands 290 — Haldeman Island) and the small bridge to cross the river was closed to vehicles. I had seen many eBird lists from the site, so surmised that everyone parked and walked across, which is what I did. Then I encountered signs saying that the area straight ahead was closed ... and that the area to the left was closed. The area to the right was not restricted by signs, but there was a construction crew digging a trench. Given the noise they were making, the odds of finding birds did not seem good. Since I was already parked, I decided to bird the less remote of the two semi-island sites. That also turned out to be very noisy due to US 11 traffic. But I did see a Bald Eagle, a group of Wood Duck, and 10 other species.

From there I went to Detweiler Park and walked a 3.5-mile loop trail. There was nice grassland and woodland, but it was a very hot and humid day with few birds to be seen. I stopped for a chance to observe a field of thistles and get a bit of shade sitting in a conveniently-placed chair (06.11). The only interesting bird that appeared while I sat was a female Indigo Bunting. But she eluded my effort to get a photo.

Overall, I added 14 species there that day, leaving me at 28 for the county, well under halfway to the target. The list included Baltimore Oriole and Ovenbird. The only reasonable photos I managed were of Eastern Bluebird, Cedar Waxwing, and a Tree Swallow resident in one of several boxes around the site (06.12).

As I completed the loop, the skies started to look ominous. I reached the car just in time to avoid getting drenched. It was only about 11:30am, but with the next camping trip planned for the following day, I headed home while having my lunch of trail mix.

+++

On June 9, I got ready to leave for a 3-night campground stay at Kooser State Park, Somerset County. I planned to leave home after meeting with an HVAC guy scheduled to fix our new heating system's thermostat. That visit took longer than expected; they had installed a thermostat that lacked needed features. They agreed to replace it, but did not have the correct thermostat in stock. The HVAC system worked as is, but it required manual adjustment each morning.

I finally reached the campground at 4:30pm. My campsite was not flat. There solo, it was challenging to get the trailer leveled. It was 5:45pm by the time I was in place and hooked up. Given the hour, I decided to bird within Kooser State Park, even though it was quite small.

I started the day with 23 species (from the first camping trip of the year). I managed to add only 7 before stopping for dinner. One was a Spotted Sandpiper (06.13), so I would not be able to count on that as my go-to bird when I later approached the 67 target.

+++

That evening, I sent this text to Fran: *If I ignore the fact that there is a lot of road noise from the highway that's nearby, and that the trailer is out in the open with no shade, and that there are basically no trees in the campground itself, from my zero-gravity chair it looks nice ☺. I'm sitting out listening to Pittsburgh baseball and some birds -- hoping for a barred owl, 🦉 but none heard so far. I gave up on Cleveland when their starting pitcher gave up 4 runs in the second inning ☹.*

Later that evening, Fran and I had several texts back and forth as I adjusted the thermostat remotely to get air conditioning working for her. Hearing no owls, I went to sleep early.

+++

The morning of June 10 started slowly. I added 10 species between 6:30am and 9:00am. I got a Louisiana Waterthrush and a couple others with a quick 10-minute foray down a trail at the campsite. The rest were at a site in nearby Laurel Hill State Park. Those 7 took me nearly 2 hours and about 2.5 miles of walking.

From there I headed to Somerset "Lake". It was an eBird hotspot with promising bar charts for species I needed, although there had been no recent posts. I soon learned why. The road was closed to vehicles, so I parked and walked .5 miles in. Instead of the lake and birds I was anticipating, I found a dry lakebed, tall grass, and not much else (06.14). They seemed to be replacing the dam.

06.14

After Lake Somerset, I moved on to another eBird hotspot ... the most unusual one so far — the Flight 93 memorial. The roughly 2,200-acre site includes a huge expanse of grassland and some trees. The photo below (06.15) shows a view from one of the long paths with the Visitor Center on the hill at the top left.

06.15

Since my day's objective was birds, I used the site map, and walked the paths rather than going into the Visitor Center. While there for birds, I was somewhat overwhelmed by memories of the tragic events, both at this rural bucolic place as well as at the Twin Towers in New York and the Pentagon in D.C. Display panels posted around the landscape enhanced those thoughts, excerpts from two are below (06.16).

Overall, I found the memorial to be an incongruous place, as perhaps it is intended to be. It is in a rural setting and visitors pass through farmland to get there. The site combines a visitor center, artifacts from the disaster itself, a wall of names, a wind-chime tower, the resting places for individuals lost, and landscape elements that feature many trees, grassland, and wildflowers.

Trail of Remmbrance

This half-mile trail follows the route of Skyline Road, a quiet country thoroughfare for local residents prior to September 11, 2001.

Welcome to the Memorial Plaza

The Memorial Plaza is the culminating feature of the memorial. It marks the edge of the crash site, which is the final resting place of the passengers and crew of Flight 93.

06.16

The memorial explicitly embraces the natural environment. The image below reflects sentiment of another sign at the site (06.17). The site was by far the most unusual place that I ever spent time birding … while also reflecting on the past events and current state of the world.

Open to Change

Flight 93 National Memorial is a place of renewal. It embraces the natural environment, both stark and serene. Land scarred by decades of coal mining is being restored.

With time, this landscape will be transformed by nature, just as this place was changed by the events of September 11, 2001.

(excerpt from large display sign at the National Memorial)

open source image from the 'Flight 93 Memorial Website

06.17

Birding started slowly. I looked for grassland birds, since the habitat was ideal. As I walked the paths, things picked up. I had a Savannah Sparrow, then Indigo Bunting (06.18-L), then Grasshopper Sparrow, and finally Bobolink (06.18-M). I also got Eastern Meadowlark and a Killdeer (06.18-R) and saw American Kestrel and Northern Harrier over the fields. It started to rain … hard. I literally ran back to the car.

06.18

I moved on to a section of the Great Allegheny Passage trail that connects Pittsburgh to Washington, DC. I was at Meyersdale (06.19).

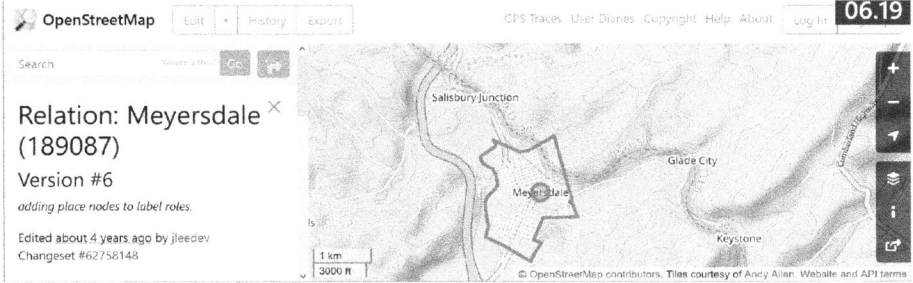

On the trail (wide gray line on map), I walked in both directions from that starting point. I picked up 8 more species, the best was Chimney Swift. I then drove to High Point Lake in the southern part of the county. It was pouring rain by the time I arrived. In the 8 minutes I stayed before giving up, I added only Eastern Bluebird. Given the rain, I returned to the campground. The rain let up by the time I got back, so I did a quick walk before dinner and added Red-breasted Nuthatch. I ended the day at 62 species for the county. During the evening I again listened for Barred Owl (or any other Owl), but I heard nothing.

A call (perhaps a bird) woke me about 3:30am — loud and argumentative. It did not match my memory of any Owl or Nightjar. Perhaps it was a mammal. If so, I could not guess what it was or what prompted calls at that time of night. That one would remain a mystery (for a time) — I went back to sleep.

+++

When morning came, on June 11, I got out about 6:20am. I still needed 5 species for Somerset County. I spent nearly 2 hours, walking 2.6 miles, not getting the first addition until about 8:30am when I heard a Red-bellied Woodpecker (#63). It was *like pulling teeth* to find the last few. Actually … although I had never pulled teeth, I suspect finding these new species was harder.

Although I was seeing few birds, I found an additional reminder of the impact that the Civilian Conservation Corps had in rural Pennsylvania. It was a monument, in Laurel Hills State Park, to remember those who undertook the hard work (06.20).

Due to slow progress, I checked eBird's *Target Species*. While it listed possibilities, few had been reported in the past week. There seemed to be too few eBird users in Somerset County. There also appeared to be less habitat variety than in some counties where I had better success.

06.20

About 10:00am I decided to go to Westmoreland County to get a start. As I drove through Forbes State Forest on my way, I heard calls and stopped. First, I saw Chestnut-sided Warbler (at least 4 for #65). Then I heard and saw a Rose-breasted Grosbeak (**06.21-L**). I walked down the road and encountered a female American Redstart (#66). After about 1 mile over an hour and a quarter, I again decided to head to a site in Westmoreland County. I started walking back to the car and I heard what I thought was a Scarlet Tanager song. My sound memory is not as good as my visual memory, so I thought I might be confusing it with the Rose-breasted Grosbeak. I wanted to see it to be sure. I kept hearing singing, and I was becoming more convinced I was right — but could not see the bird. I have always been amazed at how a bright red bird with dark black wings can be so invisible. I finally saw the singing bird near the top of a tall tree. No doubt then, it was a Scarlet Tanager. I got a marginal photo because the light was poor (**06.21-R**). But that was a quite nice number 67 for Somerset County.

06.21

I (finally) got to the Westmoreland County site I had been heading toward. The trail I walked was in Westmoreland County, but the parking lot was in Somerset County. Before I started down the trail, I heard and saw a Hairy Woodpecker in the trees of the parking lot, one more for Somerset.

I spent about an hour walking a trail at the Spruce Flats Bog Area, getting to 17 species in the county. These included a Dark-eyed Junco and a Yellow-billed Cuckoo, just visible through some haze (06.22-L&R). I then decided to try Fayette County for what was left of the day. On my way there, I picked up 4 more Westmoreland County species.

I made multiple stops once I reached Fayette County. The first was Mill Run Reservoir. In about one hour, I picked up 18 species including a surprise Green Heron as well as Cliff Swallow, a group were nesting under a bridge (06.23-L&R).

I headed south to Ohiopyle State Park. I added 6 species enroute (including Indigo Bunting and Eastern Meadowlark). On the way, I stopped at Fallingwater, but it was closed. A quick foray to a site across the road from it added Chipping Sparrow.

Once I got to Ohiopyle, mid-afternoon, I decided to focus on the Ferncliff Peninsula, the first section of park I got to. I parked and walked across the wide footbridge to the peninsula. From there, I had a great view back toward the small town (06.24-T). Overall, it was a picturesque site as also seen below in views from the trail, of the bridge I crossed and of the small waterfall a bit further along (06.24-BL&BR). While the site was picturesque, the river was very noisy with rapids, too noisy to hear birds. I managed only 6 additions (leaving me under halfway to 67). These included a couple female Common Merganser and several Chimney Swift flying overhead. I decided to quit for the day.

+++

June 12 was check out day. I had a great start, waking up to a Barred Owl calling — finally! I realized the call two nights prior was Barred Owl, I had not recognized the *caterwauling*. This time, I heard that plus familiar Barred Owl calls, with replies from a distance. The calls repeated for half an hour. I captured some audio and posted to eBird.

Over breakfast, I faced a dilemma on where to bird before packing up. With 31 species in Fayette County and 21 in Westmoreland, I was unlikely to finish either. I opted for Fayette on the chance I might have a great day and finish it. I started at Greenlick Run Lake, adding 11 species. The best was Common Loon. Others included Eastern Bluebird (using a parking lot light as a birdbath) and Brown Thrasher (06.25).

I moved on to Bridgeport Reservoir. I initially drove to the wrong side, putting me in Westmoreland County where I added 11 species, getting to 34. Then, I drove to the Fayette County side. As I walked along looking in the trees for birds, my trajectory was taking me right at the guy below (06.26). Fortunately, a kid there fishing alerted me just in time; that big snapper would not have been good to step on.

I added 6 species for Fayette County, to reach 48. I shifted to Jacobs Creek Wetlands, where I added 5 in 30 minutes. I figured I could do one more stop before breaking camp and driving home. I opted for another section of the Great Allegheny Passage, this time in Connellsville. It was a very nice walk, but not many birds to be seen.

+++

I spent 3 days at home catching up, booked one more state park, Keystone State Park in Westmoreland County (June 29-July 2), and got ready for the next trip, to Pine Grove Furnace State Park in Cumberland County. I had 23 species there from the day trip in January when I chased (and saw) the Snowy Owl.

On June 16, I was packed with the trailer ready to go but had to wait for the HVAC guy again. This time, however, it was for installation of the correct thermostat, one that supports full daily/weekly programming and internet controls. I was able to get on my way early enough to arrive about 3:00pm, which was check-in time.

+++

The drive to the State Park turned out to be *diabolical*. Without towing, it would not have been bad. But the route (like a previous trip) took many winding and hilly rural roads. It was a stressful drive with a trailer in tow. Then, I got within 6 miles of the State Park and encountered a closed road due to a bridge replacement. The detour took me the wrong direction, then the detour signs disappeared completely.

It took some time to find a place to pull over with the trailer to check the map. Once I was able to do so, I figured out a route that would work. But it was very roundabout. I ended up arriving at the campground almost an hour later than I should have. The only plus was that the set-up was easy because the site was perfectly level (06.27). It was also a very attractive setting in the trees.

Given the time (5:11pm), I stuck to locations in the State Park. Not for the first time, it was impossible to learn what anyone else had been seeing; I got zero cell signal. So, I just found some trails and spent an hour and a half walking about 1.3 miles through some woods and into an open area along a stream. I found good birds. The very first was a

Scarlet Tanager. A pair of Yellow-billed Cuckoo was also great. I added 22 species to reach 45 for the county, not bad considering the late start. I had little luck with bird photos but could not resist a photo of the trail sign and a shot of the Park's namesake furnace (**06.28**).

+++

It was a bit harder to crawl out of bed on the morning of June 17 due to the previous day's trip, towing the trailer along narrow, winding, hilly roads, together with the bridge outage that added an hour to the drive. It was about 7:00am and 44°F when I got to the first site, Caledonia State Park in adjacent Franklin County (**06.29**). Given my Scottish heritage, it was a great park to visit!

I spent 1.5 hours walking a 2 mile loop. Initial new species were a Great Blue Heron and an immature Broad-winged Hawk (06.30).

Overall, I progressed from 12 species (seen in May) to 27 by about 8:30am. After that, however, the pace slowed to a crawl. An hour-long walk in Michaux State Forest netted just 4 additions. The best two were an Ovenbird and a Pine Warbler. The best photos were of a Blue-gray Gnatcatcher (2nd for the county, but 1st good photo), a non-bird (but flying creature) — a Cicada, and the Pine Warbler (06.31).

I continued to have trouble choosing and finding sites because of poor cell coverage. The previous evening, I had to drive 14 miles to find signal to send a text to Fran. Most of the day in Franklin County, I was frustrated by being unable to use eBird to find hotspots. It's amazing how reliant we (I) now are (am) on technology for our (my) outdoor pursuits, particularly for birding. Lacking information, I tried a site labeled as an "Ecopark". It had a small trail but the site was tiny and in the middle of a built-up area. I did add Mallard, Carolina Wren, Brown-headed Cowbird, and House Wren.

From there I tried Greencastle Reservoir, adding 7 species, including Red-headed Woodpecker. I then stopped at a retention pond where waders had been seen. I found none; but added Cedar Waxwing. I stopped for lunch at a community park, 6-8 miles from Welsh Run (a place that some of Fran's ancestors are from and that we used to pass through on trips to North Carolina before I-99 was built). After lunch, I burned an hour walking the park's trails, but found zero new species.

I then spent 2 hours at an interesting place, the Renfrew Museum and Park. I walked 2 miles, adding 10 species to get to 56. Additions included Cooper's Hawk, Chimney Swift, and Indigo Bunting (**06.32**).

Perhaps more interesting than the birds at the Renfrew Museum and Park were remnants of the past that are encountered when walking the site's trails, what the web page describes as a "walk back in time." Among those artifacts, I encountered a reconstructed Lime Kiln and a set of stone mill wheels (**06.33-L&R**).

After adding 3 species at two additional stops, I ended the day with 59 for Franklin County. It would be a challenge to hit 67 before packing up the campsite the next day to leave. Back at the Cumberland County campsite in the early evening, I heard an Eastern Whip-poor-will (#46 for Cumberland), a nice end to the day.

+++

I got started early in my effort to finish Franklin County, leaving the campground at 6:03 AM. It was another cool morning at 46°F. The challenge for the day was to find 8 species before I had to pack up and head home. I was hoping to get it done quickly so that I could add a few in Cumberland County as well.

The start was not a good omen. I went to Caledonia State Park hoping for woodpeckers that I was missing plus a Belted Kingfisher. I spent

1.5 hours walking a loop, adding just 2 species — Downy Woodpecker (but no other woodpeckers) and a Veery to reach 61 species.

I then tried a site for grassland birds. I was missing Song Sparrow, and both Eastern Meadowlark and Savanna Sparrow were also possible. The site was a rural road. I drove, parked, walked, and repeated. Covering about 4 miles over an hour and a half, I picked up Red-tailed Hawk, the Song Sparrow, and one Eastern Meadowlark (#64).

I moved to a state forest site, but when I arrived, they were reconstructing the road. So, I headed for a different hotspot. I did not find that hotspot, so just birded the forest road. I spent a bit of time trying to identify what I thought was a Vireo, but unsure which. It was probably a Red-eyed Vireo, but some of the calls sounded more like Blue-headed Vireo. I still needed Blue-headed Vireo, but never saw the bird so did not list it. I did get a Brown Thrasher on the road (#65).

As I left that site, descending down a forest road with the windows open, I heard a warbler call in the bushes. I stopped and tried to locate it. I thought it sounded like a Yellow Warbler, but I wasn't 100% sure it wasn't a Chestnut-sided Warbler. The habitat was a bit better fit for the latter. I never did find the bird, so that was another one that got away. Not for the first time, I was wishing my sound memory was better.

Next, I drove to a Heron Rookery eBird hotspot. Black-crowned Night-heron had been seen there a few days before. I found lots of Great Blue Heron, somewhat hidden in the leaves (06.34-L&M), I reported 16; I think there were probably more. While there I saw a Baltimore Oriole (not new), and a Great-crested Flycatcher (06.34-R), number 66.

It was after noon, so I gave up on the Night-heron. I opted to try Caledonia State Forest one more time, hoping for Pileated Woodpecker and/or Belted Kingfisher. My thinking was that both species should be easy to find because they are loud and distinctive. By the time I arrived I decided it was getting too close to check-out time, so I pulled through the parking lot and headed back to the campsite.

I got to the campsite about 1:15pm. I packed up and was on my way by 2:00pm. I could've spent 30-40 minutes at the state park and maybe found my 67th. Instead, I ended up with 66 species for Franklin County and 45 for Cumberland County. I would obviously be coming back. I had a very nice campsite, so my plan was to try for the same one for a return trip. The location was ideal to add the final species for Franklin County, complete Cumberland County (where the park is located), and then work on Adams County (just about 5 miles down the road).

+++

Nearly halfway through the year, I was sorry that I had not thought earlier to capture interesting signage about place names. Part of my research over the past decade had been on geographic information retrieval (GIR). Tools we built retrieved geographic information from text by recognizing place names and references, extracting the names, and geolocating them. In the work, I and colleagues encountered many interesting place names that were part of what made GIR hard.

One sign seen during the just completed trip was for the Village of STATE LINE (06.35). This is the kind of place reference that can be challenging for automated methods, since "state line" is more typically a reference to a boundary than to a village.

After a day at home to catch up, I decided on a day trip to Cameron County where I had 53 species from May. Based on eBird, many common species I needed were likely. Adding 14 species seemed doable in a day trip. Among the target species for the day were Scarlet Tanager, Hermit Thrush, Hairy Woodpecker, Yellow-bellied Sapsucker, and (oddly) European Starling.

The day turned out to be a tough grind. I arrived late, just after 8:30am, starting at the Quehanna Wild Area Hoover Farm site. In one hour, I picked up only 2 new species (Hooded Warbler and Northern Flicker). I decided to head to Sinnamahoning State Park but stopped along the way at an intermediate site where (spending another hour) I picked up Yellow-billed Cuckoo and Cliff Swallow. The birds were scarce and not cooperative for photos. I went on to the Sinnamahoning State Park and added a couple more, Scarlet Tanager and Green Heron (**06.36**). But the whole day of birding netted just 6 new species.

Overall, the day's result was depressing, particularly since eBird reports for the day before listed 24 species I needed. These included the 6 found, plus 18 more. Cell signals were poor in most of the county, as typical for rural places, so I did not see these reports until I got home. Even if I had, they might not have helped since a couple of the sites with multiple species were nearly an hour farther from home, thus not practical in a day trip. I was sitting at 59 species for the county and hoping that a single additional trip would be enough.

+++

I was booked to camp at Racoon Creek State Park in Beaver County on Tuesday for 3-nights. But, on Monday I went in for blood work ordered by my GP at my physical (the first in-person check-up in about 18 months). I had been surprised to lose 16 pounds since the past visit, leaving me 6-8 pounds lighter than at any time since graduate school in the mid-to-late 1970s. I'd also had another complaint that prompted the GP to add extra blood analysis. The results came back that day and most tests were normal except the readings associated with blood counts; multiple of those were out of range.

Not surprisingly, I searched online, trying to interpret the results. Causes ranged from slight infection to Leukemia. I had a couple other symptoms that show up with Leukemia and related blood diseases, plus had one completely different concern for which the GP did a follow up referral. I sent the GP a message about my other symptoms. I was worried and did not want to be away if the GP recommended immediate follow up tests. So, I canceled my camping trip.

It took a couple days for a follow up note from the GP. The tentative good news was that (in his opinion) cancer was unlikely — results and symptoms were consistent with ordinary low-level viruses. The symptoms' source remained uncertain as did a reason for my weight loss. The GP ordered a couple extra analyses on the samples they had.

When I met initially with the GP, he and I were surprised at my weight loss. A possible explanation (other than disease) that we discussed was my somewhat drastic lifestyle changes due to COVID-19. While many people gained weight during the pandemic (at least based on news stories), my lifestyle changes could be cause for the opposite. For years prior to the pandemic, I had eaten almost every lunch out, either when at work or on the weekends when Fran and I went to Café Lemont for lunch on Saturday and Sunday (after morning birding for me). Plus, Fran and I typically ate dinner out once or sometimes twice a week. Since March 2020, however, we had zero meals in restaurants and got takeout only a few times. Our home meals (both lunch and dinner) are very healthy ones, with much smaller portions than in restaurants. Additionally, I had been averaging over 12,000 steps/day during my quest, up about 2,000 steps/day from the prior year.

Given the wait for follow up blood tests plus an in-person test the GP had ordered, I also canceled my trip for the following week (to Keystone State Park in Westmoreland County). If subsequent test results showed nothing serious, I would book a trip for part of that following week — there are usually a couple camping sites open mid-week somewhere and I had many counties I had not been to that I could pick from.

On Friday, June 25, I was still waiting for follow up from the GP. Since I did not know if I would receive any news before the coming Monday, I decided to do a day trip. I could make a bit of progress on the quest (to partially offset the cancelled camping trips); and it might also take my mind off the health issues. I picked Wildwood Lake Park in Dauphin County, a place I could get to in an hour-plus.

+++

The next morning, I arrived at 9:00am and did a 3 hour, 4.7 mile walk around the lake. The park is in an industrial area with major highways nearby, thus it was noisy. But that did not seem to bother the birds, including multiple Great Egret, nesting Ruby-throated Hummingbird, and Green Heron (**06.37**). Watching the Ruby-throated Hummingbird feed its chick was a real highlight; several folks were on the boardwalk watching when I walked by, or I might have missed it.

I added 12 species that day, OK but fewer than needed. Still, I did see good birds and had a nice walk around the lake. The trail was busy with walkers, joggers, and a few other birders and/or photographers. Beyond birds and people (and dogs) the park had a lot of signage about history. One example was a sign (**06.38**) detailing the heyday of the now unused Pennsylvania Canal running next to the Lake.

There also was an art-in-the-park event underway with multiple installations, including *It's Just a Phase* (**06.39**-L) — photo included with permission of the artist, Kristin Ziegler — for more see: http://spacepastepress.com/ for more of her latest work. There are also specific efforts to support the birds, including a Chimney Swift Tower (**06.39**-R).

+++

It was June 27; nearly half the year gone. I planned to stay home; I was still worried about health issues and waiting for updates. But I saw an eBird report of nesting Yellow-crowned Night-heron in Harrisburg, Dauphin County. I was surprised to learn that they were nesting in the city. So, I decided to head back to the county, this time going into the city to the "stakeout" hotspot. Yellow-crowned Night-heron would be a Pennsylvania lifer for me.

I checked eBird and found a couple of additional promising sites in the county that were not too far from where I was heading in Harrisburg. My primary target was the Yellow-Crowned Night-heron, but I wanted to make the trip worthwhile by putting a bigger dent in the county list.

Finding the hotspot was tricky since I don't know Harrisburg well. Google took me down a set of narrow, one-way streets. Once there, I saw no parking spots. I had to park a couple streets away and walk back. That turned out to be a good thing. When I got to the hotspot, I had no trouble finding and photographing the Yellow-crowned Night-heron family, both adults and chicks (06.40-L&M).

I returned to the car near the river, finding a Night-heron fishing. I got a photo just after the Yellow-crowned Night-heron grabbed a morsel (a Spinycheek Crayfish, I think). He/she (the Night-heron, not the Crayfish) looks quite pleased (06.40-R)!

Down by the river, I also added a White-winged Scoter (a surprise) as well as Brown-headed Cowbird. From there I moved to Italian Lake Park, also in the city. The Park and the surrounding neighborhood were attractive, with interesting sculptures including a fountain sculpture (with traditional nudes) in the park's pond (06.41).

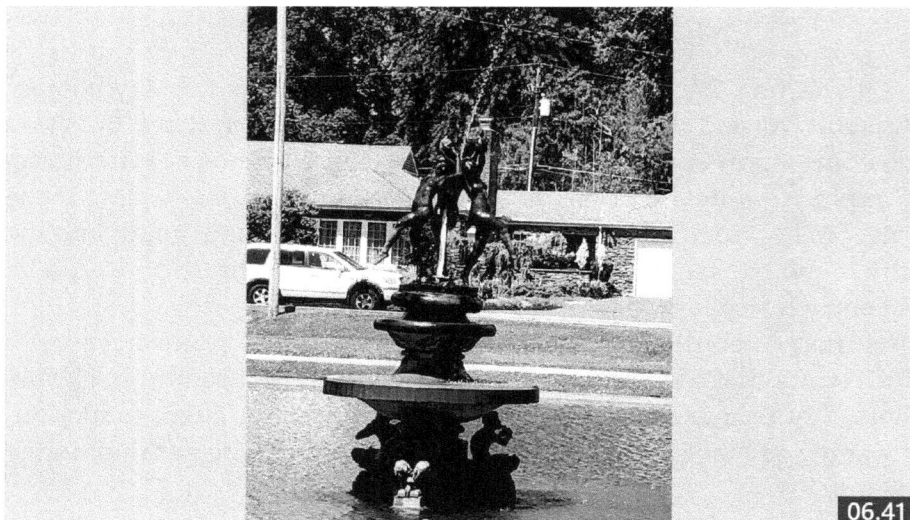

I later learned from a Penn Live story (Deb Kiner, 10/30/17) that the fountain was produced by Italian sculptor Giuseppe Donato as a commission from Milton S. Hershey in 1909. Hershey refused to pay the $30,000 bill. A court case won Donato partial payment, but Hershey refused to display the sculpture (perhaps due to the price, perhaps due to the nudes?). It was donated to the city, kept in a warehouse for nearly a decade, displayed at two locations, then installed at Italian Lake Park in 1971. Nearby, at a private residence, I also noticed a rather unusual Keystone sculpture made of vintage Pennsylvania License plates.

Across from the park was a less attractive site — a closed High School (06.42). The school building was in more obvious disrepair when seen up close than in the photo. In a blog I found later, the school and grounds were described as "History Rotting Away" (https://thesnapper.millersville.edu/index.php/2021/10/18/history-rotting-away-william-penn-high-school/)

06.42

While at and around Italian Lake Park, I picked up 3 species including Chimney Swift (not found at Wildwood Lake Park despite the Swift Tower). From there, my last stop of the day before heading home was State Game Lands 290 — Haldeman Island where I was previously thwarted by road maintenance. In about an hour, I picked up 7 species (including Horned Lark and Yellow-billed Cuckoo) to get my Dauphin County total to 53 — progress, but a long way from the 67 target.

+++

On June 30, I heard back from my GP about test results. His opinion was that there was no reason for concern. A few of the bloodwork tests that had been out of range on the first test looked better on a follow up. Plus, in his view, the overall set of results suggested that there was no serious health problem. It appeared that my weight drop (150->134lbs) was the result of my lifestyle changes. The other piece of good news was that a Lyme Disease test (done due to a tick I found attached after a long day of tromping around in brushy habitat) showed only prior Lyme Disease, no current infection. I had Lyme Disease twice before —

birding is a dangerous hobby. I was quite relieved at the news and that my Geo-Big Year was not being derailed by health issues.

June 30 was my last official day as an active Professor at Penn State. On July 1, I would be Emeritus. I went to the office that day to drop off my faculty ID and turn in remaining keys. That act made retirement feel quite final! While there, I snapped a photo of the hall sign for one of the rooms occupied by the Center I had run from 1998 to 2020 (**06.43**).

+++

With the end of a month and a quarter, it was time again to analyze progress on the quest. As before, I generated a map update (**06.44**).

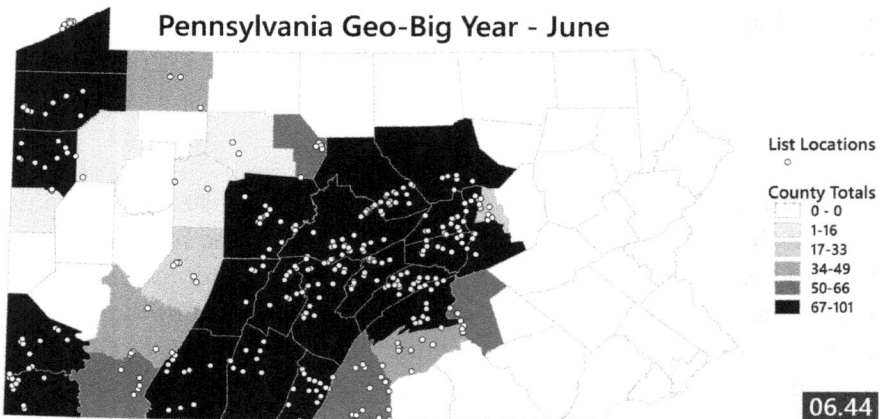

Progress had been made, but not enough. The map and bar chart below (**06.45**) show that I had reached the target in 20 counties, less than

1/3. This was not a good sign for my chances to complete the quest. On a more positive note, I had birded (at least somewhat) in just over ½ of the counties (34). A few factors made me feel the quest remained possible. The biggest was that I would be officially retired the next day. Plus, my health appeared to be OK, the trailer had been working out for solo travel, and fall migration was still on the horizon.

Counties
Adams
Allegheny
Armstrong
Beaver
Bedford
Berks
Blair
Bradford
Bucks
Butler
Cambria
Cameron
Carbon
Centre
Chester
Clarion
Clearfield
Clinton
Columbia
Crawford
Cumberland
Dauphin
Delaware
Elk
Erie
Fayette
Forest
Franklin
Fulton
Greene
Huntingdon
Indiana
Jefferson
Juniata
Lackawanna
Lancaster
Lawrence
Lebanon
Lehigh
Luzerne
Lycoming
McKean
Mercer
Mifflin
Monroe
Montgomery
Montour
Northampton
Northumberland
Perry
Philadelphia
Pike
Potter
Schuylkill
Snyder
Somerset
Sullivan
Susquehanna
Tioga
Union
Venango
Warren
Washington
Wayne
Westmoreland
Wyoming
York

06.45

Third Quarter
Summer Slipping Toward Fall

Days start to shorten
Temperature gets hotter
Birds plainer each day

I began to suspect that our camping trailer was a lemon – unfortunately there are no lemon laws for camping trailers. After hearing positive news from my GP on June 30, I was ready to push on with the quest as the year's 3rd Quarter began. I booked 2 nights at Gifford Pinchot State Park in York County (for July 1-3). When I went to hook up the trailer on July 1, in preparation to head off to the State Park, the jack would not work.

My choice was to proceed with the trip, resorting to the manual crank to raise and lower the jack (and trailer), or to cancel the trip. Since hooking up and unhooking solo was enough of a challenge with a working jack, I opted to cancel so that I could focus on a fix for the jack. I called the company that made the jack. Based on the response (complete lack of surprise at what happened and willingness to replace the jack), it seemed that the jack had a design flaw. The flaw was a "flexible" plastic cover over the control panel. It apparently was prone to leaking (07.01). Electric motors do not like water very much. The manufacturer agreed to send a replacement jack that I could install myself. Or, if I chose to get a dealer to do the installation, they would cover

30 minutes of labor. I used the wait time to reflect on travel strategies for the second half of the year.

07.01

Fran and I had discussed the best plan in relation to the trailer and any travel together. Given the discomfort she had on our last camping trip, Fran thought it was unlikely she could try camping again. The combination of the bouncy ride in the Ford Expedition (particularly when towing on a windy day) and the marginally supportive bed made that form of travel the opposite of enjoyable for her. As a result, I had already started to think about selling the trailer after my Geo-Big Year ended. Beyond this quest, I had little interest in continued solo travel with a trailer of this size and an inefficient, large tow vehicle. The latest issue with the trailer, made it clear that the car/trailer purchase was an expensive (failed) experiment. I decided to sell the trailer right away and trade in the Expedition as soon as practical after that.

That decision posed a challenge for completing the quest while coping with a continuing pandemic. Fran and I decided that one option worth trying together was to book vacation cabins or cottages that accepted dogs and had a kitchen. Being dog friendly was a must, since Skoti is a rescue with anxiety issues. We never kennel him. A kitchen was essential, both to make travel during the pandemic safe (by avoiding eat-in restaurants) and to make it practical for Fran to effectively manage her Type I diabetes (that she has had for 50 years). She has found that consistent meal plans for breakfast and lunch are a key. Thus, we needed facilities to prepare both meals. As a trial-run for this travel option, we scheduled a trip at a small vacation cottage on the edge of the Poconos in Monroe County that was dog friendly and had a (very small) kitchen. We booked the cottage for July 6-9.

+++++

JULY

With no camping trip, and a gap before the Pocono trip, I decided on another Dauphin County daytrip. I was at 53 species. Based on past results, I did not expect to reach 67 that day. But I hoped to add enough species to then need only one additional trip.

I started at Detwiler Park, doing a different loop walk. It was slow going. I covered 3.5 miles in 2.5 hours and added just 5 species with no good photos. From there, I moved to a section of the Appalachian Trail (07.02-M&R). Views were nice (07.02-L) and the trail had bird activity.

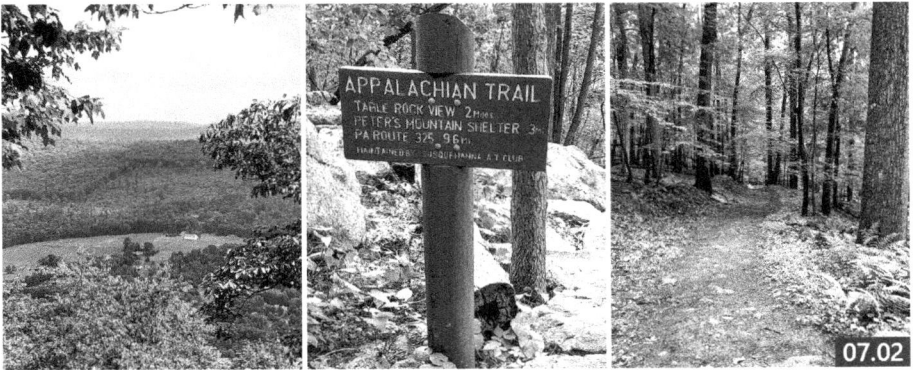

I walked 0.6 miles out and back in one direction and was able to do a 1 mile loop in the other direction. Over about 2.5 hours, I did add only a few species, but they included some good ones: Black-throated Blue Warbler, Cerulean Warbler, and Black-and-white Warbler. I managed photos of the latter two (07.03).

This Appalachian Trail outing was my first time using the Merlin Audio app in the field. I was surprised with how good it was (or at least seemed to be) in recognizing calls or songs from multiple species at once. While I would not trust it as the only ID evidence, the app was helpful in alerting me about species to look carefully for, which I might otherwise have bypassed due to multiple birds singing and calling at the same time. The Cerulean Warbler was one of those. The Merlin app alerted me to it (ultimately them). I then worked hard to find the first of five, with the photo above showing one of the males.

+++

Before starting home from Dauphin County on July 2, I got an email alert for a message from my GP. I logged in to check. After reviewing all my symptoms and test results, he pronounced me *fit* (for my age). I still had concerns about a few symptoms, but I set them aside as chronic inconveniences. With the health issues resolved, I could focus on birds. It was clear that I needed to pick up the pace for any chance at the 67 x 67 goal. Plus, the task of selling the trailer and trading in the Expedition would increase the challenges by cutting into available time.

On my way back from Dauphin County I planned to stop at Lerch RV in Milroy, PA, to ask about installing the jack and about whether they buy trailers and or do consignment sales. But it was late in the day on a Friday, so I decided to start with an email. I had already emailed the questions about possible purchase or consignment sale to Ainsley RV near Altoona as well as to the dealer we bought from in West Virginia. I was hoping at least one would have a reasonable policy about marketing used trailers.

I initially thought about selling privately. But, while still pursuing the quest, it was impractical to deal with requests to look at the trailer. Perhaps more importantly, given the continuing pandemic, I did not want to risk dealing with prospective buyers who refused to wear masks. The alternative to selling privately or through one of the smaller dealers, was to sell through (or directly to) Camping World. They are a big nationwide RV company with outlets all over the place. The closest dealer was in Pittsburgh, and I assumed I would not get a good price, so I set that option aside as a last resort.

As I was working on finding a way to sell the trailer, I was also thinking about how to bird the state's more distant counties without it. One plan was to book hotel rooms or cabins rather than trying to camp. If I picked accommodations with a mini-fridge and microwave, I could travel with my own food and continue to avoid the COVID-19 risk of eating indoors with others.

If I relied on hotels, I could trade the Expedition in on a fuel-efficient AWD hybrid. I was initially a bit uncertain that I wanted to rule out camping trailers completely. I started to look at the smallest options (with kitchen and wet bath) that might work for solo trips. I found units that could be towed by a few of the mid-sized plug-in hybrid SUVs, specifically the Audi Q5 PHEV or the BMW X3 xDrive30e. A quick check online and at the local dealers found that the pandemic's supply chain disruption left virtually no cars in stock. Plus, BMW decided to stop importing the X3 PHEV to the U.S., so the last ones available were those already on dealer lots. Online search found zero within 250mi. One of my colleagues had recently bought an Audi through a dealer in Columbus, Ohio, the closest with availability (but his was not a PHEV which would be harder to get).

The limits of the smaller Audi and BMW models prompted me to look at the BMW X5 plug-in hybrid, which was going to continue in the U.S. It could tow the small trailers and the ride would be great. The big negative was (not surprisingly) cost compared to the X3 (or the Audi Q5). Thus, an X5 would make no sense to invest in unless I was sure I wanted to get another (smaller) trailer.

+++

Since I had a couple days before our trip to the cabin in Monroe County, I decided to do a July 4 day trip back north to Cameron County. The landscape on the way there was draped in interesting clouds/fog that ringed a hilltop in the mid-distance with a backdrop of wind turbines on the ridge behind that (07.04).

I was at 59 species for Cameron County — in sight of the 67 target. I saw Wild Turkey enroute, but in Clearfield County where I saw them back in April. As before, my first stop was the Quehanna Wild Area

Hoover Farm site. I had a decent start to the morning with addition of Blue-headed Vireo, Hairy Woodpecker, Yellow-bellied Sapsucker, and Purple Finch, the latter two below (07.05).

I made 5 additional stops in Cameron County, with my species total inching up. A Raven (calling) was number 67; I included audio of it in my eBird list. That was the first time that my 67th species was an audio "sighting" confirmed with a recording and sonogram (07.06).

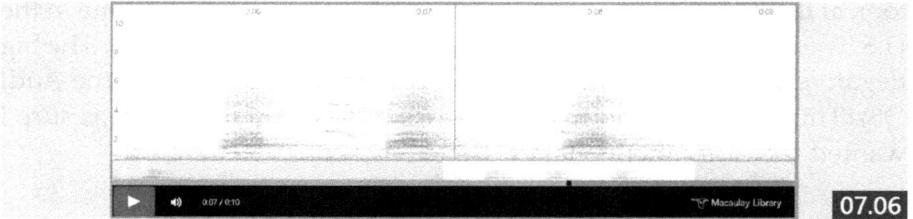

It was not even 11:00am. I moved to adjacent Elk County (where I had 7 species). On the way, I added 3 species in Cameron County, reaching 70 with a Killdeer. Then, over about ¾ of an hour in Elk County, I added 6 species. These included Blackburnian Warbler, Northern Parula, and a Veery. Facing a 2-hour drive home, I called it a day.

+++

On July 6, I got a response from the closest RV dealer. They offered to buy the almost new trailer but offered only 60% of what we paid for it. I sent back a detailed itemization of the features it had, indicating that the price offered was quite a bit less than I was willing to sell for. I asked them to review the many options our trailer had and again asked if they do consignment sales.

+++

On July 6, Fran, Skoti and I drove to Stoddartsville, Luzerne County for our first outing together since the Bedford camping trip. While the historic sign was nice (**07.07**), Stoddartsville was not much of a place, just a few buildings that have been re-created or renovated.

The cabin was small but comfortable. The best feature was its location on a ledge over the river. There was a nice patio (**07.08-L**), the living area had a fireplace that we did not try (**07.08-M**), and the kitchen was very small but functional (**07.08-R**).

After a Chinese takeout dinner, we took a walk. When Fran and Skoti returned to sit on the patio, I continued down the untraveled road. I found 19 species, including a Scarlet Tanager, an Ovenbird, and a Ruby-throated Hummingbird.

+++

On our first full day in the area (July 7), I posted 7 lists in eBird, all from sites in Luzerne County. I began the day by spending about 3.5 hours at Bear Creek Preserve. I walked a 2.5 mile loop that took me through mostly wooded terrain (**07.09**). The morning's hike added 16 species to get to 37. It was an interesting mix including multiple warblers, Eastern Towhee, a Yellow-billed Cuckoo, Field Sparrow, and Great Blue Heron (three of them).

07.09

The best photos (in order) were Ovenbird (I saw one the day before but got no photo), Black-and-white Warbler, Chestnut-sided Warbler, and Common Yellowthroat (07.10).

07.10

I joined Fran and Skoti back at the cabin for lunch on our river-side patio. That afternoon, I visited Francis E. Walter Dam (twice) and Penn Lake. I reached 54 species, including a Rose-breasted Grosbeak (07.11-L) that had a bath in a stream, then posed while drying off and one of the more attractive Brown-headed Cowbirds I have seen (07.11-M). That evening, Fran, Skoti, and I took a walk after dinner. I added Hairy Woodpecker to reach 54 for Luzerne County (07.11-R).

07.11

The next day (our last at the cabin), my objective was to complete Luzerne County and make a dent in Monroe County. I ended up spending the entire day in Frances Slocum State Park (07.12). The park is named for a woman from a Quaker family who, after being abducted by Delaware warriors when she was five, assimilated into the Miami peoples, married, had children, and lived out her life with them until her passing at 74 years of age. Despite the namesake, Fran (short for Frances) decided not to accompany me to the park; instead, she stayed at the cabin with Skoti doing some reading, photos, and sketching.

Frances Slocum State Park
07.12

The best bird of the day was a Yellow-throated Vireo, (07.13-L). But several others also posed nicely, including: a female Baltimore Oriole, an Eastern Phoebe, and a Brown Thrasher, in order (07.13).

07.13

I reached 66 species by 11:10am. At that point, I went back to join Fran and Skoti for lunch, hoping for number 67 from our cabin's river side patio. Fran had seen a Belted Kingfisher fly by earlier, so I stuck around for nearly 2 hours hoping to see it. We had an enjoyable lunch with birds around, but no Kingfisher – nor anything else new.

I decided to start Monroe County, again hoping for an easy number 67 in Luzerne County near the cabin during dinner. I went to the Thomas Darling preserve and did a 2.1 mile walk. The trailhead was indicated by a nice marker (07.14-L). The trail was a bit rough, with some roots and rocks, and some plank-based sections to help avoid wet feet (07.14-R). That made it hard to look for birds, I could mostly listen. I only ended up with 17 species to start Monroe County.

Back at the cabin, our pre-dinner walk produced a brown creeper, number 67 for Luzerne County!

+++

The evening of July 8 was our first in-person restaurant dinner since March 2020. The COVID-19 rate in Pennsylvania (particularly where we were) had finally decreased to the point at which health authorities were saying in-person dining was OK. While we were still generally cautious, we decided the risk was low enough. After all, it would not seem much like a vacation trip without a dinner out.

We ate at the Boulder View Tavern in Lake Harmony, PA. We were surprised to find live music – also a first for us in over a year. We heard the Strawberry Jam Duo, who played 60s and 70s classic rock – as if they knew we would be there that night.

+++

July 9 was checkout day, and 11:00am checkout time. I let Fran sleep in and went out to do a couple hours birding at a nearby site in Monroe County, Game Lands 127. Birds were scarce initially, but I did see a young bear (07.15-L). By about 9:00am, I reached 30 species, thus not a bad start. These included an Ovenbird, Great-crested Flycatcher, and Red-winged Blackbird —left to right after the bear (07.15).

As we packed, I was still hoping for a Bald Eagle or Kingfisher at the cabin. But no luck. So, I ended with exactly 67 for Luzerne County. Fran left a note to the hosts on our way out (07.16).

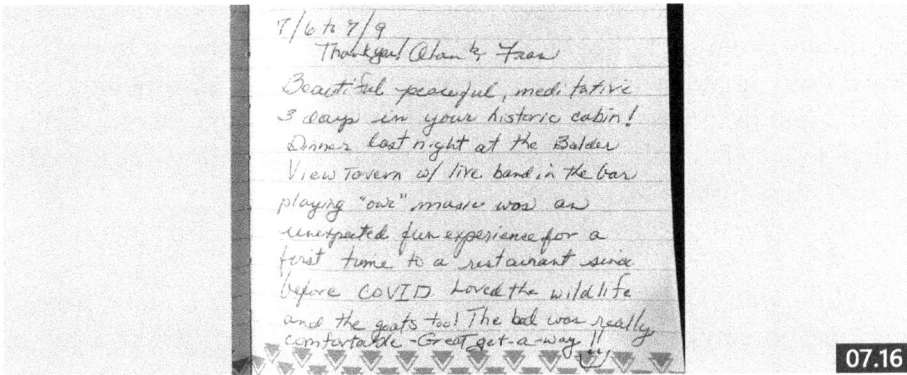

We headed out about 10:45am. On the way home, we stopped at Hickory Run State Park in Carbon County, a new county for the quest. While Fran sat in the shade, I tried to walk Skoti and bird at the same time. We did a piece of the "Shades of Death Trail" (07.17-L). The trail, with its name "attributed to the thick forests and rough terrain experienced by the early settlers," is listed in park literature as a favorite of birders. I ended up with 11 species in about one hour. After my brief walk with Skoti, we all stopped at the Visitor Center and found an interesting large map that one could walk across (07.17-R).

The weather was looking threatening, so we decided to head on home. I picked up 4 species as we exited the park, for 15 as my Carbon County start. We saw zero new species from the car in any other un-completed county during the drive home.

+++

On July 9, I contacted the RV dealer near Altoona again since I had not heard back after an initial reply that they had received my first inquiry and would talk with the boss. They never bothered to reply to my follow up attempt to get a response. I could only assume they had no interest in buying the trailer or selling it on consignment. On that same day I called the manufacturer to ask if they ever buy back nearly new trailers for resale, but they do not.

+++

While waiting for a reply from the RV dealer we bought from, I decided on another day trip to Dauphin County (July 11) to attempt finishing that one off. After my previous trip I was at 61 species. I expected to reach 67 by lunch time. Doing so might allow me to head over to Montour County. We had dinner plans for our anniversary, so I had to be certain to get home in time. As usual for most counties, the last few species for Dauphin County were hard.

I spent the whole morning walking around Wildwood Lake Park. I slowly added species as I walked the loop. I was not seeing many new birds but did find another really intriguing art sculpture, "Lotus on the Land" (07.18-L) – photo included with permission of the artist, Lorayn McPoyle. The art nicely reflected adjacent nature (07.18-R).

I had picked up Northern Mockingbird (07.19-L) at a stop on the way to Wildwood Park, so had 5 to go on arrival. As I circled the entire lake, I got a nice photo of a juvenile Wood Duck, not new, but so close it barely fit in the frame (07.19-R). On the walk, I added a Great-crested Flycatcher, Canada Goose, Rock Pigeon, and Blue-gray Gnatcatcher, reaching 66 as I completed the loop. While I ate lunch at a picnic table, I watched and listen for additional species. There should have been Barn Swallow or Belted Kingfisher, or Yellow Warbler, but none appeared.

I decided to go over to Front Street along the river, since both Barn Swallow and Ring-billed Gull had been seen there. At one stop, I looked at lots and lots of swallows, but all seemed to be Northern Rough-winged Swallow. This was the first county in which they were more prevalent than Barn Swallow. The eBird bar chart for Dauphin County does show a slight overall propensity for Northern Rough-winged Swallow over Barn Swallow (07.20), but not in early July. It should not have been that hard to find Barn Swallow.

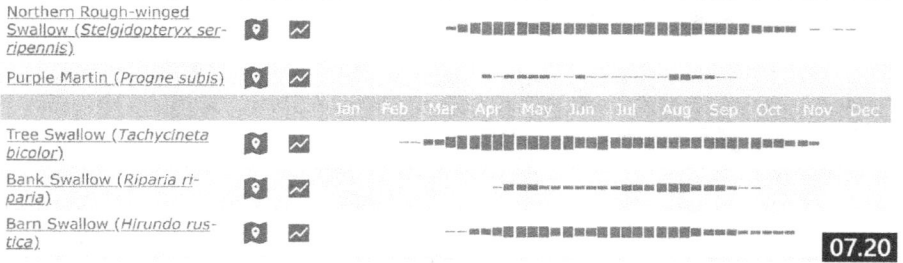

			Jan	Feb	Mar	Apr	May	Jun	Jul	Aug	Sep	Oct	Nov	Dec

Northern Rough-winged Swallow (*Stelgidopteryx serripennis*)

Purple Martin (*Progne subis*)

Tree Swallow (*Tachycineta bicolor*)

Bank Swallow (*Riparia riparia*)

Barn Swallow (*Hirundo rustica*)

07.20

After seeing a gull fly over toward the water, too quickly for an ID, I moved down the street to get a better view. I ultimately found a group of gulls on the far side of the river, but close enough to see. They were all Ring-billed Gull. That got me to 67.

Since the Peters Mountain Appalachian Trail site was not much out of the way and it was too late for a different county, I stopped there on my way home. I added a Yellow-throated Vireo plus a Common Raven to reach 69. On the drive down the mountain, Barn Swallow finally appeared – 17 of them! Thus, it was a successful day with Dauphin County completed and a few to spare.

+++

We booked dinner at Pine Grove Hall in Pine Grove Mills on the evening of July 11. The restaurant, in a historic building, had (a year before) replaced its predecessor with one more focused on locally sourced fare. This would be our second meal out since COVID-19 started, and the first at this new (to us) place. We booked for a few days before our anniversary because that date was unavailable. In past years, we had celebrated our anniversary with a day at the Arts Fest (https://arts-festival.com/), then dinner at Spat's. But, with the pandemic, the Arts Fest was only virtual, and Spats lost their lease and had to close. So, our trip to the Poconos and this dinner out would be our celebration.

Beyond COVID-19, it was a somewhat unsettled anniversary because of retirement plan uncertainty. Fran's health issues removed her desire to travel. But my vision of retirement was all about travel. Obviously, I expected to do birding trips, but as a Geographer I also had looked forward to other travel adventures. As we approached our anniversary (number 38) we needed to regroup and figure out what we would be doing with ourselves. Short-term I still planned to finish the PA Geo-Big Year quest, mostly solo. Beyond that, little was certain.

As we discussed the future, one thing became clear. I would not get a smaller trailer; I don't really enjoy camping by myself. Thus, the only reason to have a trailer would be for Geo-Big Years, and it seemed like my first Geo-Big Year might be my last.

On the camping trailer sales front, I did not hear back from the closest dealer until July 12. The answer on price was negative, they would not budge. They recognized from the option list I sent that our camper was worth substantially more than their offer, but they said there was no market here in central Pennsylvania for a relatively small but high-end camping trailer. They followed up with a response to the consignment question; no to that too. I had now ruled out the nearest options for selling the trailer (plus the manufacturer). I was still hoping to hear something positive from the dealer we purchased from.

While waiting for the RV dealer reply, I focused on replacing the Expedition. I stopped at the BMW dealer to inquire about an X5 xDrive45e. The dealer offered a good price for the Expedition, but no discount on the X5. The end-cost was worse than anticipated. Plus, the X5 was bigger than I wanted, its towing capacity was no longer relevant, and ordering would require a multi-month wait. So, I ruled BMW out.

That left the Audi Q5 plug-in hybrid as the most attractive option. While less efficient than a Toyota RAV4 Prime, its interior is more comfortable (meaning Fran might find travel tolerable) and it could probably be bought in Pennsylvania (Maryland is the closest place to acquire a RAV4 Prime). The local dealer had one Q5e available, but not with the features I wanted. The salesperson seemed to have no experience swapping with other dealers so I continued to search online.

On July 13, I finally got a reply from our West Virginia RV dealer; the owner and his son had both been on vacation. They were willing to buy our trailer back. Their offer was about 75% of what we paid, making it a very expensive 17 nights of camping that the trailer ultimately got used for. But, based on all the information I had, this was a typical price for a "used" camping trailer and clearly better than the 60% the other dealer offered. It did not seem worth the hassle to attempt a different sales route. So, we decided to go ahead and sell to the dealer.

One glitch in selling back to the West Virginia dealer was that the trailer title was in both of our names. To avoid Fran needing to travel with me to West Virginia and back, we went to the local title place (and paid a fee) to convert the title to list me alone.

With near certainty that I would be able to sell the trailer, there was more urgency to find a car solution. On July 13, I contacted our local Toyota dealer to make sure I was right that they could not acquire a RAV4 Prime. They could not, and they had no RAV4 hybrids in stock. They were willing to order a RAV4 hybrid, but it would be a multi-month wait. So, I kept exploring other options.

+++

I got frustrated sitting at the computer, looking up cars, so I opted to do another day trip, back to Cumberland County (July 14). I had not chased many rare birds thus far, but accounts of Roseate Spoonbills at the Big Spring Laughlin Mill hotspot prompted a chase. When I arrived, no Spoonbills were visible. The best vantage point appeared to be on private property. Since I was alone and saw no one to ask permission from, I was about to give up and leave. Then, some other birders showed up. They were local and said the property owner welcomed birders. I followed them to the edge of the stream and was rewarded by a view of the pair of Roseate Spoonbills in a tree, with a Great Egret a bit above them. I got rather distant photos of one perched Roseate Spoonbill and one Egret when it moved to the stream (07.21). I also added Northern Rough-winged Swallow at that site.

My Cumberland County total was 50 species as I left the site. I made 3 more stops, reaching 60. Additions included Baltimore Oriole, Wood Thrush, Belted Kingfisher, and Wood Duck. With a minimal chance to reach 67 that day, I headed for home at about 2:00pm.

+++

During my day between outings, I continued to explore the Audi Q5 PHEV. I learned it has no spare tire. While increasingly common with new cars today, I did not want to be without a spare in a car I would use on rugged forest roads in places with zero cell coverage. I dropped Audi from consideration.

Given extreme scarcity of new cars on dealer lots and the long wait times, I expanded the scope of my search to include Hyundai Tucson and Santa Fe hybrids. But the Tucson also has no spare tire and the Santa Fe was a bit bigger than I wanted (it would not fit in the small garage at our OBX house). Plus, none were available locally, and ordering one would mean a months-long wait. So, I added the Toyota Venza, which comes only as a hybrid, to my search.

While dealing with the trailer sale and car search, I was still trying to make progress on the quest. So, I booked two hotel nights in Butler County in the west. Since Fran was not venturing out due to the continuing pandemic, we decided I should use her RAV4 hybrid for the trip. If I could complete Butler County quickly, I planned to work on Lawrence County, where I had 7 species from my first trip west.

+++

On July 16, I headed to Butler County, expecting to arrive about 10:00am. On prior trips with the trailer, I made purposely late starts to arrive at the mid-afternoon check-in time. Without a trailer, I would be able to start birding immediately.

Having spent so much time arranging the trailer sale (including the title change so Fran could avoid the trip to West Virginia), plus dealing with a fraud case on our credit card, I was not well prepared for birding in Butler County. My best option was to check eBird reports to pick a starting point. I selected the Todd Nature Reserve, see map (07.22-L), getting started a bit after 10:00am. It had some nice trails (07.22-R).

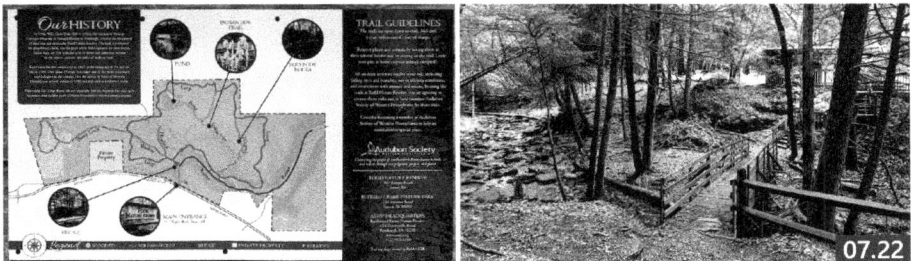
07.22

I walked nearly 2mi in about 2 hours and netted 21 species. Nice ones included Scarlet Tanager, Black-throated Green Warbler, Hooded

Warbler, Acadian Flycatcher, Broad-winged Hawk, and Yellow-billed Cuckoo. Overcast skies and woods were not conducive for photos. I added 7 species while shifting to the Thorn Reservoir and 8 more there to reach 36 by mid-afternoon.

Next, I went to Preston Park, a site with interesting history. Based on information from Butler Township, within which the site sits, Dr. Frank Preston and his wife Jane Preston situated Dr. Preston's glass research facility ("Preston Laboratories") within an 88-acre English garden woodland designed as a place to "live, work, and enjoy nature." The site was clearly birder-friendly. One interesting feature I encountered was a life-sized guide to shape and size of birds likely to be seen soaring overhead (07.23).

The site included great habitat detailed on a map that I later learned was created by Bev Evans (a former Masters advisee of mine). Along a stream, I saw both Mallard (several) and Wood Duck (also several), plus a fox looking for an easy meal (07.24). I started late and it rained off and on during my hour walk. So, I added only 4 species to reach 40.

I ended the day at only 41 species. That evening, I had my first solo restaurant meal of the quest, at the Hardwood Café (07.25-L), ending with a decadent dessert (07.25-R).

The next day, I was hoping to finish off Butler County by lunchtime. But the slow pace of the prior day continued. I started at Moraine State Park at about 6:30am. It was a day of off-and-on rain, sometimes heavy. The rain kept me in a roofed observation platform for the first 45 minutes, from which I picked up Green Heron and Belted Kingfisher (07.26-L). Overall, I spent about 4.5 hours walking 3 miles at various sites in the State Park. I reached 59 species a bit after noon. These included a family of Northern Flicker along the Sunken Gardens Trail (07.26-M) and a male Rose-breasted Grosbeak (07.26-R).

I posted 7 additional lists that afternoon. One interesting site was the Jennings Environmental Education Center where I spent about 1.5 hours (but picked up only Field Sparrow). They had several photo stations set up prompting visitors to take photos of specific views and contribute them to a repository (07.27).

By 5:25pm I was at 66 species, 1 short. It was pouring rain and had been for over an hour and the first break in rain was predicted to be 6:30pm. So, I decided to stop at the hotel for a quick dinner (of microwaved leftovers). After dinner, I scanned the skies from the parking lot looking for Chimney Swift (one of the two most likely based on eBird Target Species). I soon spotted 2 Chimney Swift overhead (I also saw a Bald Eagle – not new but a bit surprising from the hotel lot).

07.27

+++

The next morning, after checking out early, I planned to focus on Lawrence County. As usual, I checked eBird to figure out a good starting place. There was a report of Dickcissel at the Volant Strip Grasslands, with Sandhill Crane also nearby. So, although I originally planned to head east (in the direction of home), these birds drew me west. I was still looking for my Pennsylvania lifer Dickcissel and Sandhill Crane would be a year bird. Henslow's Sparrow (another year bird) was seen at the Grasslands too. I got to the Volant Strip Grasslands early (about 6:45am) as the sun was still peeking over some clouds (**07.28**).

07.28

Shortly after I arrived, the Merlin audio app signaled Dickcissel, but I could not hear it. The audio saved by the app was not sufficient to ID (at least for me). Another birder arrived, spent some time there, then moved down the road a bit. He came back after a few minutes saying he was *fairly*-certain he saw a female Dickcissel. We went to that location, but nothing showed. I ultimately gave up on Dickcissel, after seeing and hearing a couple Henslow's Sparrow, plus Bobolink, Red-winged Blackbird, and Savannah Sparrow, latter three below (**07.29**).

From there, I went off in search of Sandhill Crane. The other birder provided directions to a former strip mine where two had been seen. Initially, I saw only a Great Blue Heron (07.30-L) and was about to give up, thinking that the Cranes had moved off to feed in fields for the day. Then, I noticed movement in tall grass at the far end of the pit — Sandhill Crane! I got a reasonable photo of the pair (07.30-R).

Across stops at 5 sites, I reached 53 species in Lawrence County. Another stop at the Volant Strip Grasslands, trying for Dickcissel was again unsuccessful, although I did see a male Bobolink this time (07.31-L). Among additions for the day from other sites were Field Sparrow and Cedar Waxwing (07.31-M&R) along with Rose-breasted Grosbeak, Green Heron, Yellow-billed Cuckoo, and Hooded Warbler.

After the Hooded Warbler (at McConnells Mill State Park) it was about 2:30pm. With no chance to reach 67 that day, I decided to head for home to arrive in time for dinner at a reasonable hour.

+++

I spent 3 nights at home, taking time to process photos from the trip and investigating car purchase options. I made no further progress on the car – just spent frustrating hours online looking for dealers with any of my options. It had become clear that pandemic supply chain issues had hit the auto industry hard and that it might take months (or years) to recover. I was also still waiting to get the updated title for the trailer. We were able to file for the title change at the local title place, but the title itself comes from the state. Pandemic slowdowns were also impacting how quickly that could happen.

In the meantime, I booked one night in Chambersburg, PA. My plan was to finish Franklin County (1 needed) and Cumberland County (6 needed), then make progress on Adams County.

+++

Before I left home, I checked eBird and found that White Ibis (a PA lifer) had been reported at a site in Cumberland County. I decided to make that my first stop even though the route would take me further east than planned on this trip. I arrived at the site reported in eBird at 9:49am and found 5 White Ibis still present (**07.32**).

Finding the last 5 species (after the White Ibis) for Cumberland County proved to be a challenge. I was hoping for a Belted Kingfisher, Ruby-throated Hummingbird, or Double-crested Cormorant since all had been reported at the White Ibis site, but I had no luck on those or anything else new. A local birder told me of a nearby site where I did manage to add Acadian Flycatcher.

Moving west, toward Franklin County, I stopped at Winding Hills Nature Trail, hearing and seeing a Willow Flycatcher (**07.33-L**). Next, I tried Mt. Holly Marsh Preserve where I walked 1.25 miles and picked up Louisiana Waterthrush (#66) and Raven (heard, #67). At the same location, I added Hooded Warbler for number 68 (**07.33-R**).

07.33

On completing Cumberland County (finally, on my 4th visit), I proceeded to my hotel in Franklin County. After dropping my stuff, I went searching for number 67 there. I tried a site with a farm pond visible from the road. At first, I saw nothing new. But, as I continued to scan, I saw Cliff Swallow (#67), then a couple Vesper Sparrow with white outer tails clear in flight (#68). As I was stowing my scope, a Belted Kingfisher flew over the pond (#69). I had hit my target and beyond, so was ready to start working on Adams County.

I headed to the Long Pine Run Reservoir in Michaux State Forest. In 45 min., I added 7 species, the best of which was a Common Loon. I also saw a Scarlet Tanager feeding at the side of the road, a location where I have seldom seen one. Due to the scarcity of birds, I decided to give up for the day and go find dinner.

+++

I debated (with myself) about whether to have dinner inside a restaurant or get takeout due to COVID-19 resurgence. Since I was vaccinated, with the Pfizer vaccine, I decided a restaurant was an acceptable risk. I picked a Japanese restaurant in Chambersburg, PA, where I guessed (correctly) that staff would take more care about COVID-19 than in some of the typical PA options. The service was quick, so I was back at the hotel by about 7:30pm. I listened to a bit of the Cleveland baseball game while planning the next day. Cleveland won 5-2 to keep their record above .500.

+++

The plan for July 22 was to try a new site in Michaux State Forest, then shift to the Gettysburg area for different habitat. At the first stop (walking 1.5mi in 2 hrs), birds were scarce. I added only 11 species for Adams (the best were Black-and-white Warbler and Hooded Warbler). This pace would not get me to 67 before I needed to head home.

Next, I went to the Gettysburg National Military Park (NMP), another unusual birding spot that reminded me of birding at the Flight 93 Memorial. The Gettysburg NMP, of course, has many more monuments and other artifacts on display (more than 43,000, based on park information) and was also considerably busier (about 700,000 visitors in 2021, down from a peak in 2002 of more than double that).

I spent most of my time at two sites, Little Round Top-Devils Den and Spangler's Spring. The best find was a Pennsylvania lifer, Blue Grosbeak. I got only a mediocre photo (07.34-L). I also added Belted Kingfisher and Baltimore Oriole (07.34-M&R). Birding was slow and I headed home with just 43 species in Adams County.

+++

After a day at home, I decided on another day trip (July 24), back to Montour County where I had 18 species from my brief foray in May. I birded at 4 sites and reached 43 species by 10:30am. The best bird of the morning was a Dickcissel (the Pennsylvania lifer I missed in multiple counties previously). I did not manage photos. But I did capture audio that I posted in eBird. Some other grassland birds seen were American Goldfinch, Bobolink, and Grasshopper Sparrow (07.35).

I then decided to try the Montour Preserve and spent 3 hours walking trails, including one circling the reservoir. I added 15 species to reach 58. These included Bald Eagle, Blue-gray Gnatcatcher, Great-crested Flycatcher, Louisiana Waterthrush, and Spotted Sandpiper. The best photo was a cooperative, adult Red-headed Woodpecker (07.36).

+++

While I was birding Montour County, the updated trailer title arrived in the mail. It would be great to finally have the trailer saga over. It was an expensive boondoggle. On July 26, with the updated title in hand, I towed the camping trailer to the West Virginia dealer. The sale process was quick. I ended up getting about $500 less than I had been quoted by phone, but at that point I was disinterested in arguing or taking a chance that the deal would not go through, so sold it.

With the trailer sold, replacing the Expedition became more urgent. Given lack of success finding hybrids, I considered a straight electric car, with a plan to drive Fran's RAV4 hybrid on trips beyond its range. On July 27, I drove a Chevy Bolt, the only all electric car in stock locally. It was nicer than I expected, but not as comfortable as the RAV4. The bigger negative was lack of an AWD option. Our driveway is long, curved, and steep; thus, AWD is necessary in winter. On July 28, I checked on the Ford Mustang Mach-E. None were in stock, and the dealer could not provide a delivery date (meaning months of wait).

A big factor in car scarcity seemed to be a worldwide computer chip shortage. A *New York Times* story (April 23, 2021) said a new car "can easily have more than 3,000 chips." I almost convinced myself that the spare tire problem (of the Audi Q5e and others) could be coped with by using an *inReach* satellite texting device. But *inReach* has an ongoing monthly cost and tire repair in remote places might be impossible.

The computer chip shortage (and lack of cars on dealer lots) was just one pandemic impact on my Geo-Big Year (and on everyone's lives generally). In late July 2021, COVID-19 rates were rising and masking up indoors was again advised. This increased my stress about staying in hotels. My experience at the first couple I tried was that almost no one (guests or staff) wore masks.

With the trailer gone, I began to investigate getting a tent and air mattress to avoid hotels in counties with high COVID-19 rates. I had last tent camped in 1982 when we lived in Colorado. I was unsure how my 69-year-old body would fare, but it seemed worth a try (and a less expensive experiment than the trailer and Expedition). I would need a much better air mattress than the backpacking one I used to have!

On July 28, as I checked for the umpteenth time on car options, I saw that the Lewistown Toyota dealer had apparently taken delivery of 8 Toyota Venzas. I called the dealer, and they had one with features I wanted on their lot. So, I immediately drove to Lewistown for a test drive. It was a nice car in many ways, but it had some features I knew going in that I would not like; touch screen rather than knobs for all controls, a fixed moonroof, and limited space in the hatch. On the plus side, the seats seemed more comfortable than in Fran's RAV4 hybrid. It also had a few additional electronic safety features, which were nice. The biggest plus, of course, was that *they had one available*. In July 2021, few dealers had anything delivered that had not been pre-sold.

I considered the Venza on the 35-minute drive home. It was not my first choice, or second, or even fifth, but better choices were unavailable. I decided to buy and alerted the sales agent. We completed the deal 2 days later – happy owners of a new hybrid Venza (**07.37**) and happier former-owners of a gas-guzzling Expedition. It was the first time in my life that I traded in a car and received money back – another plus, along with fuel efficiency, of getting rid of the Expedition!

07.37

While the vehicle transactions were happening, I booked a "cabin" so that Fran, Skoti, and I could do a 3-day outing together (Aug. 1-4). It was in Wayne County, the far northeastern corner of Pennsylvania. According to the Vrbo listing, it was supposed to be pet friendly. But after I booked, which ended up going through Expedia (that I learned later had purchased Vrbo), I was sent a contract that said no pets. I went round-and-round trying to deal with terrible customer service from the management company that was handling the property.

Although there was no indication of a specific fee on the Expedia website I booked with, the management firm said I owed $99 +9% tax to have a pet. They had no customer "service" by phone, so I had to argue back-and-forth through email, ultimately agreeing to the charge. But they kept sending me a contract to sign that said no pets. They sent it six times in the space of 30min. I ultimately called Visa to contest the charge. The next morning, I got an email from the property group apologizing for the wrong contract and asking me to sign what they claimed to be a new version. But the new version was identical!

+++

With one day left in July, and a new car, I decided to do a day trip to Elk County. I had only 13 species from a brief foray on July 4th, so there were many species to be seen. The difficulty with the cabin booking delayed my start. I almost stayed home, but I decided to go anyway since I needed a break from all the hassle.

I got to the first site a bit after 10:00am, where I added 3 species. I then did a 3 mile, 2 hour walk around the Moshannon SF--Beaver Run Impoundment. It was a nice setting (07.38) with a good variety of birds.

07.38

I was at 33 species when I completed the walk about 1:00pm. I did not manage many photos; the best was of an Osprey landing on its nest (07.39). Other good birds at the site included Blue-headed Vireo, Rose-breasted Grosbeak, Yellow-throated Vireo, and Yellow-bellied Sapsucker. The biggest surprise, however, was a Bonaparte's Gull. I saw it flying but did not manage a very good photo (I did include three marginal images in my eBird list).

I spent another 1.5 hours in Elk County before heading home. It was slow going because it was hard to navigate around the county. As typical in rural sites, cell coverage was nearly nonexistent. Thus, eBird's report plotting feature did not help and navigation devices would not work in many locations. I ultimately decided to give up for the day and head home with just 40 species for the county.

+++

When I got home, an updated copy of the rental agreement for the cabin in Wayne County had finally appeared in email. Fran and I decided to sign the contract, pay the extra pet fee, and do the trip – hoping for the best on accommodations from a dubious property management group. We were booked for the next day, August 1, so had a lot of travel prep to do in a hurry.

The day trip to Elk County marked the end of July. Thus, it was also time to get another map-based look at progress (or lack of it). It had been a stressful month with the trailer sale and car purchase, both of which were surrounded by mega-uncertainty. So, it was unsurprising to see the state of the map (07.40). I had made progress, with many central and several western counties done. But differences from June were too small. The big gaps remaining in the west, along the northern tier of the state, and for all of the southeast were quite daunting.

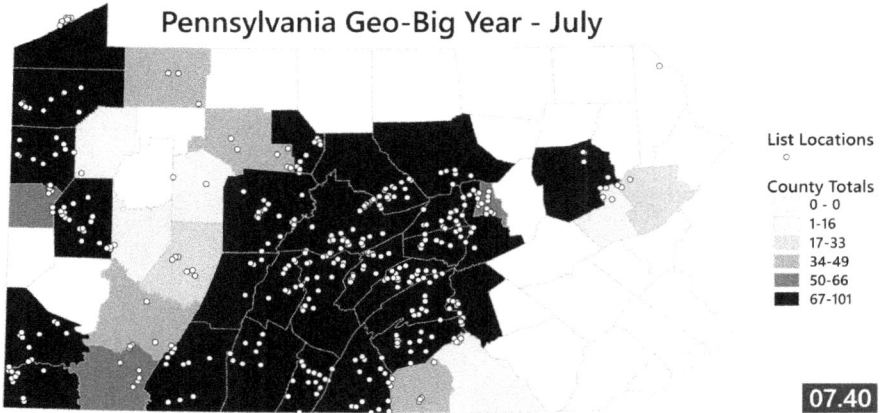

Pennsylvania Geo-Big Year - July

List Locations
○

County Totals
0 - 0
1-16
17-33
34-49
50-66
67-101

07.40

My hope as August commenced was that having settled the trailer sale and car replacement, things might go more smoothly. Plus, fall migration was around the corner to look forward to.

+++++

AUGUST

August 1 had us on the road to Pleasant Mount, PA. Check in time was 4:00pm. The drive was uneventful, but slower than anticipated. Although we arrived late, they were still servicing the "cottage," which turned out to be a manufactured structure, essentially a small house trailer. The plus was that it was clean (once they finished) and reasonably well equipped. The negative was the queen-sized bed crammed into one tiny bedroom, with about 1 foot of space at the foot and along one side of the bed. It was a real challenge to climb in and out of bed as well as to avoid banging one's head on the overhanging cabinet that took the place of a closet at the foot of the bed (I was unsuccessful).

The complex was a former horse farm. It had tennis courts (in poor repair) and some trails winding around the property, but no horses. We brought dinner from home, so got that ready after I unpacked the car and we did a short walk around with Skoti. The setting looked good for birds, and I started my Wayne County list with 9 species, mostly from the porch as we had dinner.

+++

The next morning, I got up early, walked Skoti, and had a quick breakfast. I was off before 6:30am and generated 3 ad hoc lists on my way to the first planned site for the day. When I reached that site, Belmont Lake, I was at 20 species, including American Kestrel; I saw 4 in one tree, two shown below (08.01).

08.01

A half hour at Belmont Lake (08.02-L) added 5 species. That was followed by an hour and a quarter on the O&W Rail Trail, yielding 10 more to reach 35, including Purple Finch and Gray Catbird (08.02-M&R).

08.02

Between 10:00am and 3:30pm, I made multiple stops, including several at different sites in Prompton State Park, reaching 47 species. These included Broad-winged Hawk, Great-crested Flycatcher, Black-and-white Warbler, and Chestnut-sided Warbler (08.03).

08.03

Over the rest of the day, I added 5 species to reach 52; the last was a Wild Turkey (08.04), seen as I drove down a rural road having just said (to myself, out loud), "I should see some turkeys here".

+++

That night, we opted to eat indoors at a restaurant, our 3rd in-person dining together in over a year. We picked the "top" place in the area, at the Hotel Wayne in Honesdale, PA. I do not eat mammals (since the late 1970s). So, my options are fowl, seafood, or vegetarian. From the available options, we both picked duck. I feel slightly strange as a birder eating duck, but it has been a favorite dish since I was a kid.

The restaurant, in an old hotel, had ambiance. And we had a room to ourselves – they spaced people out and it was a big place. While the meal was not unusual, the duck was nicely done.

+++

The next morning, I had a very slow start. As it approached noon, I was still 4 species short for Wayne County. I started a 3-mile loop at Lake Wallenpaupack. It was generating few new species. I was focusing on just finishing the loop and moving on when I heard a call that I was uncertain of and tried the Merlin app. It alerted me to a Spotted Sandpiper. Since I had not recognized the call on my own, I did not list it initially, but started searching. I eventually found one walking along the Lake's far shore.

I remained 1 species short and tried a wetland visible from the roadside. I scanned around looking for Wood Duck but saw none. I thought I was hearing Swamp Sparrow but then noticed a couple of lumps on a log. I focused on them and took a not very good photo. But it was definitely Wood Duck, a pair (#67).

I then refocused on the Swamp Sparrow, which I confirmed. While looking, I heard a loud "squeaking," Sandhill Crane. I accidentally closed the Merlin App while trying to get my camera out, so I ended up not saving audio. But I did get distant photos of two Sandhill Cranes taking off from the swamp and flying toward the northeast (08.05).

Most other photos for the day were of species I had seen the day before. Among these were a female Rose-breasted Grosbeak, a Song Sparrow, and an Eastern Wood Pewee (08.06).

I was at 69 species for Wayne County after the Wood Ducks, Swamp Sparrow, and Sandhill Cranes at the wetland, so moved on to Lackawanna County. I had 16 species to start the county, including Scarlet Tanager, Baltimore Oriole, and Yellow-throated Vireo. Back at our accommodations, a walk after dinner yielded a Yellow-bellied Sapsucker and Least Flycatcher to raise the Wayne County total to 71.

+++

On August 4, we packed up and were off by 9:00am. We headed for a Nature Conservancy Preserve; lack of 'facilities' prompted us to switch to the Archbald Pothole State Park. The park had nice trails. But our walk through the woods (me, Fran, and Skoti) was disrupted by mosquitos. I then tried walking Skoti on park roads (to get him a bit of exercise before the drive home), with Fran following in the car. But Skoti got too excited when Fran passed us. So, he ended up riding, while I walked. The park was marginally productive; I found Brown Thrasher and Indigo Bunting, both ones missed in Wayne County. As we left Lackawanna County for home, my list was at 28.

+++

After a day's break, I took a one-night solo trip to McKean County (Aug. 6). On the way, I got off I-80 at the Penfield, PA exit. That brought back long-ago memories about going to a nearby site, not to bird, but to hang glide, twice with an instructor and twice with Fran (who came along in case of a mishap). On one trip, I did have a mishap, breaking a glider wing, but fortunately no bones. I fixed the hang glider – it remains *hanging* in the garage where it got "parked" 25 years ago.

The trip also highlighted how geographically illiterate Siri was (as of August 2021). I asked Siri how far it was to McKean County. She answered: "it is 161 miles to Pennsylvania." I was in the middle of Pennsylvania at the time. Siri clearly did not know (and could not figure out) what a "county" is. Thus, she gave me the distance from where I was to the capital of Pennsylvania, or at least that is my best guess on how her completely unhelpful answer came about.

In McKean County, my first stop was a rails-to-trails site in Mt. Jewett. The trail head was interesting with a historical plaque (a section shown below), a train engine bike rack, and a colorful mural (08.07).

Mt. Jewett

In 1881, the name Mount Jewett was chosen by General Kane in order to entice Hugh Judge Jewett, the president of the Erie Railroad, to invest in the development of the local railroads. The Erie line carried bituminous coal from the DuBois and Punxsutawney areas to Salamanca, New York, then to the Great Lakes. At its heyday, Mt. Jewett was a bustling town with several sawmills, a basket factory, a window glass company, a leather tannery, and a small airport.

I contacted Angela Cornelius, the mural artist, for permission to include my photo of her work here and on the book's web site. She not only granted permission, but also provided information about the community-focused art she was doing and leading others (including children) to do. For more, I encourage the reader to check out her site https://visitanf.com/cornelius-creative/.

While culturally interesting, the trail yielded only 10 species in an hour. The best two were a Gray Catbird, which was flying straight up to catch a butterfly, and a Broad-winged Hawk, which landed and perched in a tree near the trail (08.08-L&TM). Overall, birding was slow going across the entire day. I birded 5 additional sites between about 11:00am and 8:30pm reaching just 34 species by the end of the day. Some cooperative birds were American Redstart at the Willow Bay Recreation Area and Common Yellowthroat at the Richard E. McDowell Community Trail (08.08-TR&BM). The last was Ring-billed Gull, also at the Richard E. McDowell Community Trail (08.08-BR).

The most interesting site for the day, but one yielding just 4 new species, was Kinzua Bridge State Park, home (as the web site says) of "the reinvented Kinzua Viaduct ... once the longest and tallest railroad structure at 2,053 feet long and 301 feet high, ... partially destroyed by a tornado during 2003." It is a bit mind-boggling to imagine what it was like as the tornado ripped through the forest and bridge. The scope of destruction remains clear from the pedestrian walkway built upon what remains of the support towers for the bridge. Despite few birds, I enjoyed the stroll on the walkway. Images below show the full walkway from the parking area (08.09-T), the scene from the start of the walkway toward the end of the viewing platform with tower ruins to the left in the valley below (08.09-BL), a view of the crowded viewing platform at the end of the walk and the gap made by the missing bridge (08.09-MR), and the ice cream enjoyed after the walk out to the end of the walkway and back (08.09-BR).

One factor in the low species count for the day was lack of warblers, at least ones I managed to ID. In addition to the American Redstart and Common Yellowthroat, the only other warbler species I turned up were Magnolia Warbler and Hooded Warbler, both at Willow Bay Recreation Area. As with other sites on this trip, non-bird features of the site provided as much or more interest than the (very scarce) birds. This included finding out about the North Country Scenic Trail (apparently more than twice the length of the Appalachian Trail -- https://northcountrytrail.org) and realizing that I could easily end up in the wrong state (08.10-L&R).

+++

The next morning, my first site (after Eastern Bluebird and House Sparrow enroute) was the Ormsby Swamp Conservation Area. Progress was slow, with 9 new species in 3 hours. They included two more warblers (Blackburnian Warbler and Black-throated-Green Warbler, neither very photogenic) along with a White-throated Sparrow, Dark-eyed Junco, and juvenile Swamp Sparrow (08.11).

The next stop was Hamlin Lake Park, a community park in Smethport, PA. It is a nice park with a lot of water. I added only 4 species (of birds). Two were particularly photogenic, Common Merganser nicely reflected in a pond and a pair of Green Heron having an altercation with one charging the other (08.12-L&R).

The other new bird species were Eastern Kingbird and Killdeer (**08.12-L&R**). Additionally, I added a new mammal for the year, a Mink, which was a surprise in an urban park (**08.13-M**).

I picked up 5 more species (of birds) with short stops. These included Rose-breasted Grosbeak and American Kestrel. With my total at 54 species, I started the roughly 2.5-hour drive home.

+++

At that point, I had 28 counties completed – less than halfway to the end goal. I did have several other counties started, including Warren County where I decided to head next (with 37 species from the trip back from Erie in May). Given that start, I expected a one-night trip would be sufficient to finish it off. Optimistically, my plan was to return through McKean County and try to finish that as well.

+++

August 9 was a foggy, humid morning and it was going to be a hot day. I considered changing to an eastern county (predicted to be cooler) but stuck with Warren. Geographically, I was trying to fill in gaps in the west before focusing on the east. The logic was that counties nearer the ocean (east and particularly southeast) would be more productive than others late in the year.

One geographically interesting feature of the drive to Warren County was the intersection below – where north is in both directions, North 948 to the left and North 66 to the right (08.14).

I arrived at my first stop a bit before 10:00am. Birds were scarce. I added only 7 species by noon. By about 4:30pm, I had reached 55 species. Three more hours added just 3 more. My success at photography was comparable to that at finding new species. Just a few of the new species were photogenically cooperative; these were Hermit Thrush, Osprey, and the last species of the day a Merlin found at dusk at Beaty Park in Warren (08.15).

+++

The next morning, I was up and out by 6:00am. I had two interesting encounters on the way to the first site. The first was seeing a large painted quilt replica on what turned out to be a Grange Hall, the Watson Grange (#1068, according to the sign). The quilt replica was apparently part of the "Pennsylvania State Grange Heritage Quilt Trail." When Fran and I moved to Pennsylvania, she became a fabric artist (after working as a Registered Dietitian in Virginia and Colorado) – going back to her first degree in fine art. While Fran creates original designs, mostly landscapes (see: quiltedvisions.net), she appreciates the craft of traditional quilt designs and much of her fabric art uses construction methods borrowed from quilting. So, I texted Fran a photo, then had to explain it was painted rather than fabric out in the sun (08.16).

08.16

The second interesting encounter was an addition to my county list – Wild Turkey. The first ones seemed to be contemplating whether the speed limit applied to them (08.17-L). The next was so close it did not fit in the photo frame (08.17-R). I ended up seeing 14 Wild Turkeys on my way to the first stop that morning.

08.17

With an early start and Wild Turkey before my first planned stop, I thought reaching 67 for Warren would be easy. I was wrong. I began at a site in Allegheny National Forest, where several species I needed had been reported. I quickly found an Eastern Towhee, but Blue-headed Vireo and Hairy Woodpecker were the only other new species in an hour at the first stop.

I decided to try Hearts Content Recreation Area. That turned out to be a bust. There was a trail, but it was quite buggy, and a guy was running a noisy weedwhacker in the parking lot. I gave up quickly (without generating a list) and moved to the Buckaloons Recreation Area, the site I had success at in May. It cost $5 (as before), but this visit was not as successful. I added just 2 species, Tufted Titmouse and Northern Parula (to reach #64).

With 3 to go, I headed east toward home. At the Kinzua Dam Public Access, I picked up 2, Turkey Vulture and Killdeer. But I couldn't find number 67. While not new species, I did get nice photos of juvenile Dark-eyed Junco and Barn Swallow (08.18).

Still 1 species short, I returned to Chapman State Park, the most active location in eBird for species I had not yet seen. When I arrived, I heard a Red-breasted Nuthatch call (#67). I then did a quick loop but had no additions. Just before I got back in my car, I heard a high-pitched call – a Golden-crowned Kinglet. That is a species I often miss due to my now limited ability to hear high pitches, but this one was very close. It was 3:30pm. With no chance to get the 13 more species I needed in McKean County, I settled for having finished Warren County and headed for home.

+++

I spent a day at home planning. I decided on a day trip next, to Montour County, where I had 6 to go and a Yellow-crowned Night-heron was seen the previous day. Having never had that species in Pennsylvania before the family of them earlier in Harrisburg, it would be great to pick one up in a second county. No other rarities had been showing up in Montour. But it was one of the last counties that was practical for a day trip.

+++

August 12 was going to be a hot day. It was 73°F at 7:05am and a heat advisory had been issued for later in the day. Getting to 67 species in Montour proved harder than anticipated, which I guess at this point I should have anticipated! I ended up walking about 5 miles in the heat, including the trail around the lake at Montour Preserve. I gradually added Brown Thrasher, Ruby-throated Hummingbird, Green Heron, Black-and-white Warbler, Pileated Woodpecker, and finally Purple Martin (#67 – a single individual flying with a group of Barn Swallows). My photos of the day were all marginal, so none are included here. I posted a few, including one of the Purple Martin, with my eBird lists. As I checked sources to confirm the Purple Martin, I was surprised to find that the prototypical Purple Martin photo in the Merlin app was my own photo from Duck, North Carolina!

+++

A new Intergovernmental Panel on Climate Change (IPCC) report had just come out, making it clearer than ever that human impacts are destroying the planet. That (again) had me feeling conflicted about my Geo-Big Year. On the one hand, birding is an avocation with concern for the environment at its core and I was contributing data in sparsely covered places. Plus, the birding and other environmental organizations Fran and I belong to direct resources to environmental conservation. But, all travel generates a carbon footprint and travel for birding is not necessary (except perhaps for one's mental health). Still, trading in the Expedition and trailer had made my travel "footprint" much smaller. I was getting 42mpg with my new Venza, better than advertised and a huge improvement over the Expedition's 19mpg without the trailer and 10 mpg when towing. Of course, the Chevy Bolt I looked at would have had an even smaller footprint. But, at present, the Bolt and other electric vehicles have limited range and the rural places I was birding had few or no charging stations. While many of the state parks have installed charging stations, park visitors often ignore the signs and park gas cars in the spaces – a reflection of the politics of rural Pennsylvania.

+++

For my next outing, I opted for a Saturday-Sunday trip. I avoided weekends previously because parks are busy. But we needed my car at home while Fran's was in the shop Monday-Wednesday (or Thursday). I put a 10-inch scratch in the hood of her car when trying to steer around a misplaced recycle bin, grazing the neighbors' mailbox. The fix was $120/in, due to the Blizzard Pearl paint.

As I planned more trips, the COVID-19 rate had increased again. Although Fran and I both had our shots we knew vaccinated folks who had contracted COVID-19. At our age, we were staying cautious. So, tent camping was back on the table. I looked at many tents online. One good option seemed to be the Kelty Rumpus six-person tent. While I would be on my own, I was not going to backpack and wanted something I could stand up inside. The Kelty option seemed to be available, but I was not certain enough to buy before my trip; I opted to decide on my return.

Along with tents, I compared air mattresses. The ones that looked good ran about $300. There was not much beyond the tent and air mattress I would need. I had suitable plates, cups, pots, small cutting board, and more, purchased for use in the trailer. I needed to check the viability of my old sleeping bag and camp stove. If I purchased just a tent and air mattress, I calculated that I would need to camp for 8-9 days to break even on the cost in comparison to hotels with fridge and microwave for meal prep.

+++

For my short Saturday-Sunday trip, I picked Forest County. It was one of the few counties without a high COVID-19 rate that was also accessible for a one-night trip. On August 14, I decided to start at Cook Forest State Park. That was probably a mistake. The park itself was quite busy by 9:30am on an August weekend. I took a trail through the woods. It ended up being a little over 3 miles and I added only 7 species (to the 8 I had from a previous short foray). The environment was attractive despite the lack of birds as seen in a view of the river running through the park (08.19-L) and of the woods from a trail (08.19-R).

08.19

After lunch, I drove along some forest roads, ultimately reaching Buzzard Swamp near the hotel (**08.20-L**).

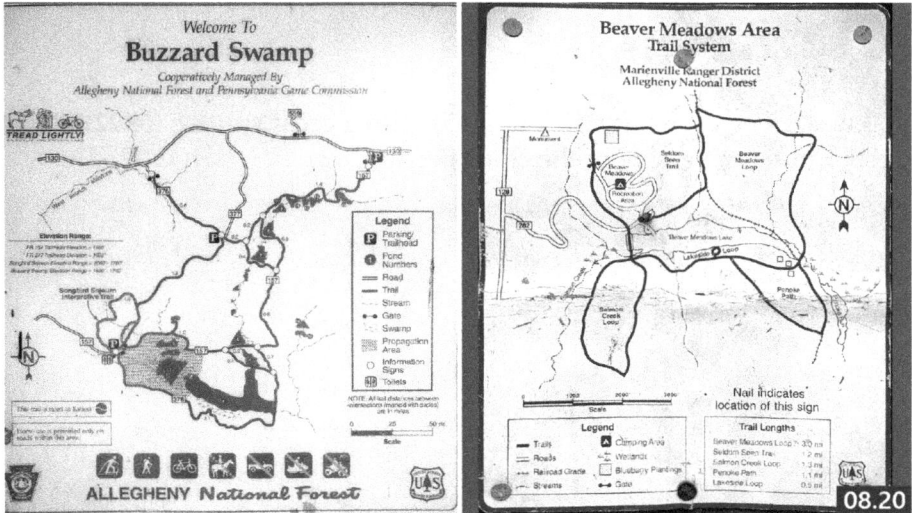

08.20

Buzzard Swamp was a slightly more productive spot with a Green Heron and Great Egret, but I ended up making the mistake of doing a long loop walk – again. The loop was about 4 miles and I think I only saw 18 species, 10 of which were new. The ones I got decent photos of included Chipping Sparrow with late breakfast, Barn Swallow flying by, and Dark-eyed Junco posing nicely (**08.21**).

08.21

When I left the swamp about 4:00pm, I started a search for dinner (since I had not packed one on this trip). The small town that my hotel was in (Marienville) had no grocery stores and the Italian restaurant where I was going to buy a takeout pizza was closed for a couple of weeks. So, I had to drive to a nearby town in Clarion County to buy a pizza. Once I did that, brought it back, and ate it, I went to a nearby state recreation area, Beaver Meadows (**08.20-R**). The site had a reservoir that I walked around partially. But I saw zero new species. On the way back into town I got a House Sparrow next to one of the restaurants, ending the day with just 31 species.

+++

I was greeted on Sunday (Aug. 15) with a great sunrise (**08.22**), obviously more impressive in the color version.

My first birding stop was at an unusual place, Lighthouse Island in Tionesta, PA. It is a 22.5-acre privately owned island, but with a public boat launch, fishing pier, and a one-mile walk/bike trail. The site includes a replica Statue of Liberty, a big sign for Freemasons, and a bunch of very patriotic stuff.

The most unusual feature (reflecting the island's name) is the Sherman Memorial Lighthouse (**08.23-T**). The "lighthouse" is an octagon shaped tower, 50ft high and 16ft wide, with a 25ft lantern room on top. A plaque proclaims it was built "as a beneficial landmark for the Tionesta community, and to serve as a place to preserve the heritage of the Sherman family". The lighthouse serves no navigational purpose, nor has it ever done. Another interesting feature of the site was a replica "crib dam" (**08.23-B**), with details about its construction and use. It was constructed by what was then the Department of War (later the Army Corps of Engineers). This dam was built to enhance commerce using Tionesta Creek (a back channel of the Allegheny River) by raising the water level to move logs to lumber mills.

08.23

Beyond history I added 9 species on the loop trail. These included Double-crested Cormorant in the river (a pair) and in nearby reeds, one Great Blue Heron (08.24).

08.24

In addition to the lighthouse, replica Statue of Liberty, crib dam, and more around the site, there was a sign, which seemed like good advice in the middle of the pandemic, see selfie (08.25).

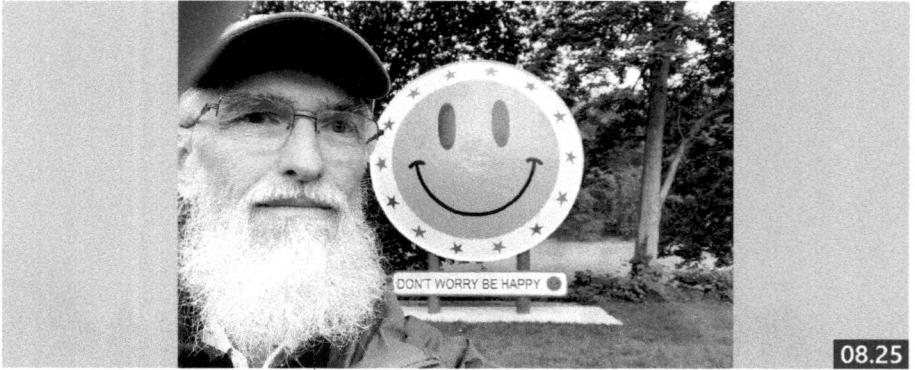

From Lighthouse Island, I went to Tionesta Dam, then to a marsh area. I added species very slowly, picking up 9, including Magnolia Warbler, Ruby-throated Hummingbird, and Blackburnian Warbler (08.26). I had late lunch near the marsh but saw no new species.

After lunch, I returned to the dam hoping for a Merganser or Bald Eagle; but had no luck. I started back to the Buzzard Swamp but realized it would take too long. So, I opted for Cook Forest, a bad choice since I added only 1 new species, a Common Raven heard calling. I headed for home, ending the day with 51 species.

+++

During the overnight trip, I thought more about tent camping. COVID-19 rates kept rising and vaccinated folks were catching it. That made hotel stays seem even riskier. Where I had stayed, few hotel staff wore masks and virtually no guests did. Some hotels had plexiglass barriers at the check-in desk, but not all. That, and limited hotel options in rural counties solidified my decision to give tent camping a try.

When I got home on August 15 and checked, the Kelty tent I wanted was sold out. So, I ordered the slightly cheaper Coleman Dark Room Skydome 6-Person Tent. A couple days later I then added an Exped

Megamat 10 Insulated Self-Inflating Sleeping Pad, hanging tent light, ground cloth, and a couple other necessities. I pulled out my sleeping bag, last used in 1985. After checking that it was generally OK, I went to a laundromat with machines big enough to wash and dry it. I also pulled out my ancient Coleman stove (purchased in 1977) that uses white gas pressurized manually with a built-in pump. I bought fuel and tried to fire it up – surprisingly, it worked.

A couple days later, the tent and air mattress arrived. I set the tent up in the basement as a trial run. I had not realized from the advertising that the tent top was mesh; shown below at my first campsite (08.27). The full rain fly (once added) provides privacy and darkness (as advertised), but the mesh makes it a summer tent only. I assumed that would be fine (maybe even desirable) on my first trip with warm weather predicted. But it was not ideal for cool weather in the fall. I might later buy a second (4-season) tent for colder weather.

08.27

At that point, I was not too confident about how I would fare with camping. I ended up with a sore back on my last hotel stay … not a great omen for sleeping on the ground. I thought, not for the first time, that it was no fun getting older.

In addition to preparing for the first tent trip, I started to re-learn how to generate choropleth maps with a Geographical Information System (GIS), to produce more polished maps than with the web tools I had been using to track progress for myself. Although I am a geographer who taught cartography, I had not used a GIS since about 1998. My teaching focused on building mapping apps from scratch. To document my Geo-Big Year, however, I needed the data processing tools of a GIS. I opted for QGIS (the top open-source GIS) since I had been a proponent of open-source software throughout my career.

I downloaded QGIS and by August 18, I had generated my first (crude) progress map. It used a diverging color scheme with counties below half-way to the target shown in brown, 0 species - dark brown, 1-16 species- medium brown, and 17-33 species - light brown. Counties at or above half-way were shown in shades of increasingly darker greens, depicting 34-49 species, 50-66 species, and 67 or more species, respectively. That first map had no legend or title and was not designed to reproduce in monochrome. It is shown below (**08.28**) with a minus sign "-" in each of the brown (less than half) counties.

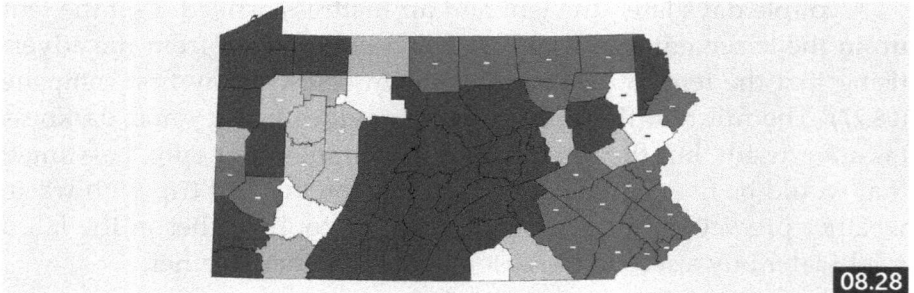

I still had a day at home before my next trip. So, I added a layer of Pennsylvania eBird hotspots to the map (coordinates obtained from eBird at the Cornell Ornithology Lab). Once data were in the system, I figured out how to distinguish hotspots I had visited from those I had not and then display those locations on top of the choropleth map. While my first maps were incomplete, and not suitable for reproduction, I was convinced that QGIS could do the job.

+++

On August 20, I set off for my first tent camping trip. I booked one night as a trial run to see how well I coped. I was amazed at how full the car was with just tent, air mattress, sleeping bag, cooking utensils, food, and other supplies. Temperature was expected to be in the mid-80°F range when I arrived, so setup would be uncomfortable. My campsite was at Clear Creek State Park in Jefferson County, close to Forest County. I planned to make progress on both counties.

With a tent rather than trailer, I could bird before checking in. I arrived at Kyle Lake (just off I-80) at 9:00am. I had a good start with 12 new species. None were unusual, but I was happy with Double-crested Cormorant (**08.29-L**), Belted Kingfisher, and Pileated Woodpecker. My other decent photos were of Black-capped Chickadee and an unusually attractive juvenile European Starling (**08.29-M&R**).

08.29

My second stop was Mosquito Creek Road. The road was named appropriately – I birded mostly from the car. In 45 min. I added just 1 new species, Cedar Waxwing. I spent the rest of the morning at Cloe Lake, reaching 36 species by 1:00pm with Wild Turkey (**08.30**).

08.30

Next, an hour at a State Game Lands, added just 3 species. I did confirm, however, that if a tree falls in the woods and someone is there, they hear it! A tree came crashing down near the trail I was on.

Driving between sites, I saw a couple of Punxsutawney/ Groundhog signs. Groundhog Day is one of Fran's favorite holidays and we both enjoyed the Groundhog Day movie (more than once). So, I captured photos and texted them to Fran (**08.31**).

08.31
3/4 mile
PUNXSUTAWNEY
MUNICIPAL AIRPORT
Groundhog
Plaza

I stopped to check-in at the campground to set up before any rain. Putting the tent up went better than I expected, 19 min. to get the main tent up and another 15 min. to add the rainfly. Photos show an image of the road into the campground, the campsite with my car prior to tent setup, and the tent fully erected (**08.32**). Adding the rainfly without a helper proved tricky; it was good that the day was calm.

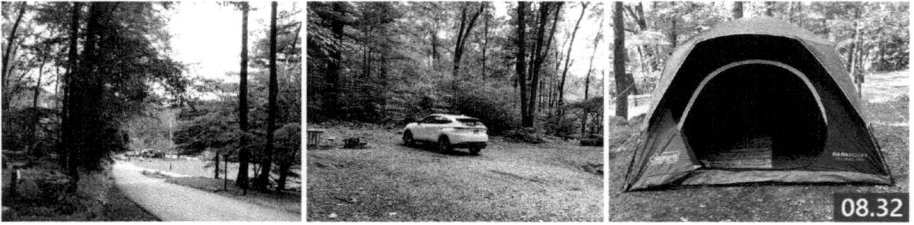

Since I was at the campground, I prepared an early dinner with the goal of post-dinner birding. I had stir-fry cooked on the ancient Coleman stove. I'm still amazed that it worked.

As with most rural counties, many places I went in Jefferson County, including the campground, had poor or zero cell coverage. So, planning strategies on where to bird as well as communicating with Fran was difficult and sometimes included driving a few miles to a hilltop where there was cell signal.

After dinner I opted to bird the state park I was staying in, even though I could not check on what had been reported. In nearly 2 hours, I added only 1 new species, Dark-eyed Junco, getting me to 40 species for the county. I decided to give up for the day and grab an ice cream since it was about 80°F. They had some very interesting seating outside (08.33); I had no idea what prompted the western theme, but I decided to sit at an ordinary picnic table rather than on one of the saddles.

+++

I woke after a reasonable night's sleep on my new air mattress, which was quite comfortable. It took about an hour to break camp. I got started on a morning walk about 7:00am. It was the hottest walk of the day because it was hilly, with a rise of more than 400 feet in one section, and very humid. The birding was not very productive; I added just 8 species in about 3 hours, walking nearly 4 miles. But the scenery was good (08.34-L) and labeled — Irish Rock (08.34-R).

After the walk I drove down a forest road and encountered a hunting cabin with an interesting name — Frozen Toe Lodge (08.35); it made me wonder about the history there.

The day got drier and less uncomfortable, but across several sites I added just a few species. I reached 53 by 2:45pm, with a Mallard, Rock Pigeon, and Green Heron, all added in a small park next to the county seat with I-80 passing overhead. Photos included ones of a molting Scarlet Tanager and a Brown Creeper (08.36-L&M). The Green Heron was the best photo for this trip (08.36-R).

I tried one more site (about 30min. away) on the way home. Just as I arrived it started to rain. I got out, put on my raincoat, and started down the trail despite the rain. But the rain kept getting harder, so I turned back. I got to the car as the rain turned to a deluge. The beginning of the drive home was not very pleasant.

+++

All in all, the tent camping trial went reasonably well. The least positive factor was the shared facilities and lack of concern about COVID-19 by most (if not all) of the other park visitors. If it wasn't for COVID-19, I would have taken a shower on the first evening because it was a warm day. But since the COVID-19 rate had been going up quickly all around the state, I suffered without a shower. It was good that I was alone!

I took advantage of the days at home to continue work on my QGIS maps. I set things up so that I could quickly update my monthly map after each trip.

Between trips, I also had my "annual" appointment at the Optometrist. COVID-19 restrictions had canceled my 2020 appointment. In the interim, I started to have issues with one eye, and was concerned about cataracts. The news was worse than expected. My right eye had developed *macular puckering*, a condition with tissue growth around the retina that distorts its shape. While this does not always impact vision much, in my case it was doing so. Worse yet, a surgical fix typically yields 20-40 vision, thus worse than I had. This was particularly scary since my vocation is as a cartographer / data visualization researcher (and I planned to continue research as an Emeritus Professor) and my avocation is obviously birding. My Optometrist suggested I schedule a follow up appointment in six months to assess the situation.

In the meantime, I planned to proceed as if this was my last opportunity to complete a birding quest. I picked Columbia County for my next trip, this time opting for a 2-night hotel stay rather than camping (due to predicted warm nights). It was a county I had not visited. The goal was to reach 67 in one trip; then try adjacent Schuylkill County.

+++

I arrived in Columbia County, along the Susquehanna River, at 9:19am (Aug. 24). My route took me through a covered bridge (08.37-L) to a bend in the Susquehanna River, which was spilling over its banks (08.37-R). It was predicted to be very hot, so, I wanted to make good progress early before birds took shelter. This first site turned out to be one of the best I had experienced during August.

I spent about an hour and twenty minutes along the river, reaching 33 species. Water birds included a Mallard, Green Heron, and Great Egret (08.38) along with Great Blue Heron, Double-crested Cormorant, Spotted Sandpiper, and Solitary Sandpiper.

I also had good birds in trees and bushes lining the shore including Downy Woodpecker, Cedar Waxwing and Eastern Bluebird (08.39).

Things slowed down as the day wore on. When I stopped for dinner (5 sites later at 5:00pm), I was at 44 species. These included Red-winged Blackbird, Barn Swallow, and American Kestrel seen at a small wetland. Since I brought leftovers from home, dinner was quick. The room was my first with a dishwasher. But I had no reason to use it, since I had just one dish. I washed that dish and was back out by 6:15pm.

The day ended at the Bloomsburg airstrip where I got Killdeer and Eastern Meadowlark, to reach 48 species. Back at the hotel, I listened to baseball; Pittsburgh was up 4-0 and Cleveland down 4-1. Pittsburgh hung on for a 4-2 win. Cleveland closed the gap to 1, but then lost 7-3.

+++

The next morning, I added a Fish Crow at the hotel parking lot and was at my first site, State Game Lands 226, before 7:00am. I walked 3 miles in 3 hours, adding 13 species to reach 61 before lunch. I had little success with photos, the "best" were ones of a female Bay-breasted Warbler, a Blue-gray Gnatcatcher, a male Baltimore Oriole, and a female Rose-breasted Grosbeak (**08.40**).

Beyond birds, the landscape held interesting features. These included a road sign reflecting interests of the locals, a historical marker commemorating a corn crib (must be a story there), and a nice trail at Jakey's Hollow Natural Area (**08.41**).

It was a slow afternoon, as typical when I was over 60 species. At 3:00pm, I was at 65. It took another hour to reach 67, at Briar Creek Lake, with a Brown-headed Cowbird and a Northern Mockingbird. I also added Least Flycatcher. Too late for another county, I went back to the hotel and fixed dinner. After dinner, it was still 87°F, so I went to an in-town park to sit by the river – seeing zero.

That evening, I listened to baseball again while planning the departure day. I decided to focus on Schuylkill County, one I had not yet started. In that night's baseball, it was Cleveland that managed to win (7-2) while Pittsburgh squandered a 2-0 lead in the fifth to lose 5-2.

+++

The morning of August 26 started well with a quick hotel exit. My first Schuylkill site was an eBird hotspot called "Air Products Wildlife

Sanctuary" that had a nice range of species reported. But I found it was not open to the public. Web sources said it was managed by the Little Schuylkill Conservation Club, with a focus on raising fish for release in streams. The eBird reports must have been posted by Club members with site access. From the road, I could see one pond and did manage 5 species, including Wood Duck, Canada Goose, and Great Blue Heron.

I moved on to Tuscarora State Park and stopped at the visitor center to pick up a map. The place was inundated with birds. I reported 18 species (10 new), including Red-bellied Woodpecker, Northern Flicker, Baltimore Oriole, and Common Yellowthroat. I then did a mildly productive, long loop walk. The best additions were Belted Kingfisher and Green Heron. My best photos were of a Red-eyed Vireo about to eat what looks like a ladybug, a group of Rock Pigeon (including an anti-social one), and a Gray Catbird showing off its rust colored undertail coverts (**08.42**).

I reached 35 species by 10:30am. One of the Hawk Mountain sites is in Schuylkill County, and I considered heading there. But when I looked up details, I realized that reaching the North Lookout would take a mile walk each way in the sun. So, I stuck with my plan to do Hawk Mountain in October and headed to a nearby state game lands.

Directions from eBird took me to a spot with a very overgrown path. I saw a few birds, but the only new species were Eastern Towhee and House Finch. The latter was probably the best find from the perspective of ultimately reaching the county target; I often missed House Finch by sticking to the least urban sites.

As I drove to the next site, I found a better access point to the game lands. But it was hot, and the habitat looked identical, so I drove on. I saw Graylag Goose (several) in a farm pond; presumably domestic, so I did not list them. The next farm pond, however, had a Mute Swan – posing nicely (**08.42-L**). I also got a reasonable photo of a Black Vulture flying overhead (**08.43-R**).

08.43

I ended up at another lake where a local foundation funded a nice walkway (08.44-L). from which there was a view of a little waterfall (08.44-R). But the site was unproductive in the middle of the hot afternoon. As I walked, the Merlin app signaled Brown Creeper, but I could not hear it and could not find it, so did not list it. I did add 3 species: Mallard, Carolina Wren, and Carolina Chickadee. By the time I left the lake for home, at 2:45pm, I had reached 44 species for the county.

08.44

+++

Covid cases seemed to be raging. But it was too hot to camp, so I chanced another hotel night for my next trip. Depending on the COVID-19 situation, and if/when Fran and I could get a booster shot, I figured I might need to put the quest on hold after this trip, until this wave of COVID-19 subsided or focus on days and places I could camp.

After deciding to risk a hotel, I needed to pick a destination. Virtually all Pennsylvania counties were in the high-level for COVID-19, so none seemed safer than others. I picked York County. I checked eBird for PA year-birds reported; there were two: Snowy Egret and Little Blue Heron. Both had been seen at the William H. Cain County Park – Lake Redman Boardwalk. That would be my first stop.

+++

The drive to William H. Cain County Park in York County took about two hours. I resisted the impulse to do intermediate stops. I planned for a morning at the park, then check-in at the hotel (to put food in the mini fridge) before heading to other locations.

The Boardwalk at the Park was great. I arrived at 9:30am and managed to see the Little Blue Heron, 4 white phase with one in flight (**08.45-L**) and the Snowy Egret (**08.45-M**) - marginal photo. I also had a Green Heron taking off (**08.45-R**), plus Great Egret and Wood Duck. Starting with 6 species in the county, I was at 34 by the time I left at 1:15pm.

I moved to Spring Valley County Park. It was on the York County Birding Trail (**08.46-L**) for which I found a map: http://www.yorkaudubon.org/york-county-birding-trail-map.html. Walking about 2 miles, I added 12 species, including Yellow-billed Cuckoo (**08.46-M**) and Ruby-throated Hummingbird (**08.46-R**). Overall, I had a good day. I got to 50 species with a return to the Lake Redman Boardwalk, adding Common Yellowthroat, Bufflehead, and Great-crested Flycatcher.

+++

I quit for the day about 6:00pm and went back to the hotel to fix dinner. The room was spacious and had nice places for my meal (08.47-L) and subsequent cleanup (08.47-R).

+++

The next morning (Aug. 30), I went to multiple sites in Codorus State Park. Starting about 6:45am, I spent about 5 hours walking about 4 miles, gradually adding species. On one trail, I passed a Chestnut Research Orchard, part of the larger effort by the American Chestnut Foundation dedicated to restoring the Chestnut tree (08.48).

I reached 67 species with Pileated Woodpecker, after adding Blue-winged Warbler for 66. I then added a Veery and an Ovenbird pair to reach 69 in York County. Poor light yielded marginal photos. The best were: Pectoral Sandpiper (camouflaged), Spotted Sandpiper (with spots faded away), and number 67, the Pileated Woodpecker busy working on a tree (08.49).

With a couple hours left I tried Adams County where I was at 43 species. The sky looked threatening (**08.50**), but rain held off.

I stopped at two sites, Long Arm Reservoir and State Game Lands 249. I added just 7 species, reaching 50 species. The only decent photos were of a Turtle and a House Wren (**08.51**). I headed for home to work on the summary of progress for August and plan for September.

+++

August slipped by quickly. It was time to check progress — the map was discouraging (**08.52**). Two previously blank counties were completed, a couple others were finished, and several new ones were added to or started. But 19 counties were still blank and 16 others had more to go. I clearly needed to pick up the pace with only four months left.

Pennsylvania Geo-Big Year - August

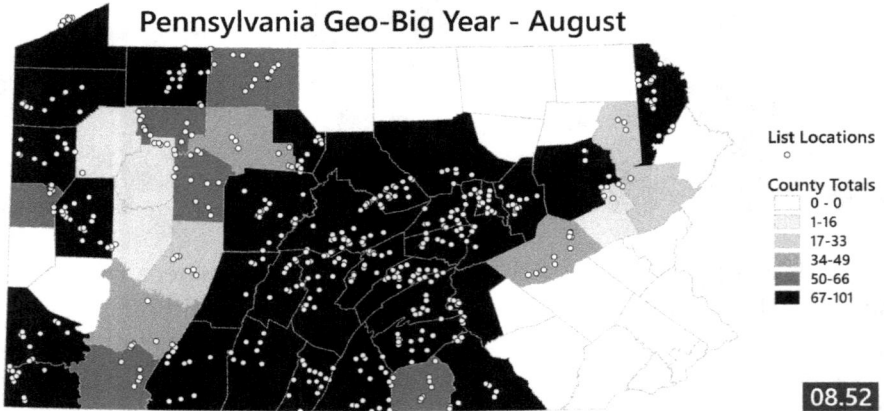

List Locations
○

County Totals
- 0 - 0
- 1-16
- 17-33
- 34-49
- 50-66
- 67-101

08.52

+++++

SEPTEMBER

During a couple days at home, I worked on plans to fill gaps in the map. I decided to focus on the far west holes first, then work on the remaining western counties. For my first September trip, I scheduled two nights of tent camping at Raccoon Creek State Park in Beaver County. It was one of the places I canceled due to my health scare earlier in the year. Now, I'd be in my tent rather than trailer. I tried to book for three nights but had to settle for two, just before Labor Day weekend.

+++

The forecast was spectacular for camping with highs in the mid-70s with nights at about 50°F. While evenings would be cool, my sleeping bag was a serious one, thus more than enough. But, 20 minutes into the trip I realized that I had forgotten my air mattress. While the sleeping bag would keep me warm, I could not face sleeping directly on the ground. So, I reversed course, heading home to get it. That turned a three and a quarter hour trip into a four-hour trip – not a great start.

It was noon when I arrived at the Independence Wetland in Beaver County. During lunch at a picnic table, I saw Red-tailed Hawk and

Common Yellowthroat and heard a Belted Kingfisher. Then, on a brief walk, I added Downy Woodpecker, Ruby-throated Hummingbird, and Eastern Bluebird – (09.01).

I went on to Raccoon Creek State Park where I was camping. I set up the tent (09.02-L) and prepared dinner (09.02-R).

Tent camping and eating meals outside have advantages; during dinner, I picked up a few species, including Bay-breasted Warbler (09.03-M). I then went to the lake and got Great Egret, Green Heron, Spotted Sandpiper, and Cedar Waxwing (09.03-L). A big surprise was Eastern Kingbird (2 of them), listed as rare in eBird. I posted a poor image of perched Kingbirds in my eBird list and 1 flying away here (09.03-R). I finished the day with 41 species. About 1:55am I woke up to hear a Barred Owl for number 42!

+++

The next morning (Sept. 3), I was up early, but tired after a poor night's sleep. The tent site had a slope. When I set up, my choice was a flat damp area or dry slope – I opted for the slope. During the night, my sleeping bag kept sliding down the air mattress every time I moved. I had the air mattress overinflated, adding to that problem. To make matters worse, the temperature dropped to 49°F. Plus I forgot my pillow, a towel was a marginal substitute. All in all, I woke up stiff and cold. Bringing oatmeal instead of yogurt turned out to be a great idea!

I started at the State Park's lake (09.04-L) and picked up Killdeer, Canada Goose, and Great Blue Heron, and its tracks (09.04-R).

From the Lake I went to the 314-acre Wildflower Reserve (09.05-L). It was a very nice place to bird. It was obvious, however, that they had flooding very recently. There was a lot of brush knocked down, branches scattered around, and trails slick from mud (09.05-M). But ... some wildflowers did not seem to be bothered (09.05-R).

I added 11 species at the Wildflower Reserve, reaching 57 for the county, but I was there for nearly 3 hours and walked 2.35 miles, see map—rev. 11/04/20 (09.06). Thus, my pace was quite slow. From the Reserve, I went back to the Independence Marsh looking for the final 10. I picked up only House Wren, Bald Eagle, Common Grackle, and Red-shouldered Hawk to reach 61 when I left there at 1:45pm.

Wildflower Reserve Trails: 4.5 miles of hiking   09.06

Art Witt Trail: 0.26 mile, yellow blazes, easiest hiking
This short trail meanders through a forested, open forest at the entrance of the Wildflower Reserve. This trail is dedicated to Art Witt, the first person to complete 10,000 volunteer hours in Pennsylvania state parks.

Audubon Trail: 0.44 mile, white blazes, more difficult hiking
Audubon Trail s elevated high above the flowing waters of Raccoon Creek, with many places to stop and admire the valley below. During spring, this is a good trail for birding, and in autumn it is great for fall foliage. One end of the trail intersects Henrici, Jennings, and Old Field trails.

Beaver Trail: 0.22 mile, purple blazes, easiest hiking
Beaver Trail passes through an American sycamore forest along the banks of Raccoon Creek. There are several nice spots to view wildlife.

Esther Allen Trail: 0.12 mile, green blazes, easiest hiking
This short trail connects Old Wagon Road with Jennings Trail. It honors Esther Allen for her volunteer work educating park visitors about the botanical treasures of the Wildflower Reserve.

Hickory Trail: 0.16 mile, pink blazes, easiest hiking
Much of this trail follows along the bank of Raccoon Creek. A very short spur trail leads to a scenic spot along the creek. This trail honors the Hickory Club, an outdoor association, which preserved a large section of the present-day Wildflower Reserve.

Jennings Trail: 1.54 miles, blue blazes, more difficult hiking
This is the longest trail in the reserve. It offers a little bit of everything, traveling past the historic Hungerford Cabin, scenic views by Raccoon Creek, spectacular wildflowers, excellent fall foliage, and many great locations for wildlife observation and birding. The trail allows access to many of the shorter trails within the reserve. It honors botanist, O. E. Jennings, for his many contributions to the Wildflower Reserve.

Henrici Trail: 0.51 mile, red blazes, more difficult hiking
This trail allows hikers to explore a forested valley of the reserve, featuring an abundance of ferns. The eastern section is covered by wildflowers in the spring. This trail honors Max Henrici, who strongly advocated the preservation of the reserve and played a leading role in the development of the trail system in the Wildflower Reserve.

Meadow Trail: 0.56 mile, light green blazes, easiest hiking
This trail begins and ends in a hardwood forest with a large meadow in the middle. In August and September, the meadow is filled with late summer wildflowers. It is also a great location for watching butterflies and hummingbird moths.

Old Field Trail: 0.65 mile, orange blazes, easiest hiking
This trail traverses a field undergoing forest succession with several sections that follow the banks of Raccoon Creek. Old Field Trail connects with Henrici Trail on both ends.

Old Wagon Road: 0.19 mile, light blue blazes, more difficult hiking
This short, elevated trail descends to the floodplain along Raccoon Creek from the interpretive center. It connects to Esther Allen Trail and ends at Jennings Trail. It features lovely fall foliage and spring wildflowers.

Audubon Trail

Pressing on toward the target, I headed to a preserve a little bit further north, the Rocky Bend Nature Preserve. I got a few good birds, but I was almost ready to give up on that site with only 65. As I started to drive out, I saw what I thought might be field sparrows, which I was missing. I also saw a Green Heron (not new) land in a tree. I parked again and walked to the spot where I had seen birds, but they had taken off. I decided that what I saw might have been a group of female Indigo Bunting, since I had seen several when I first arrived.

The extra ramble produced nothing new, but since it was late I decided to stick with the site. I looked up and saw a Chimney Swift (#66). I scanned the skies and saw 6 more, then European Starling – an unsatisfying number 67, but number 67 none the less.

I hoped to add extras at the campground but had no luck. I saw a couple of Great Egret, 1 Great Blue Heron, 1 Spotted Sandpiper, and 1 Green Heron, none new. Photos were hard to come by that day. The best included a male Red-bellied Woodpecker with its tongue sticking out, a female Indigo Bunting, and the first Chimney Swift that flew over (09.07).

09.07

I went to bed early and got up at 5:00am. I immediately heard a Wood Thrush (#68). It was checkout day. I packed up camp and saw a House Sparrow on the way out (#69).

I headed to adjacent Lawrence County where I had 53 species from two previous trips. I started at a site viewable only from the road, Three Rivers Gravel Pond. I added 6 species, including Spotted Sandpiper, flyover Common Merganser (a group), and Pied-billed Grebe. With that start, I expected to finish Lawrence County by lunchtime and then stop in Armstrong County on the way home. Well, "best laid plans" ... as the saying goes. After the quick start, progress ground to a snail's pace. Between 9:00am and noon I added only 2 species. At that point, I headed to Shaner Ponds (where I had Sandhill Crane in July).

On the way, I stopped at the Wampum-New Galilee Marsh, which seemed to have no public access. Scanning from the road, I was surprised to find 7 Common Gallinule there (09.08-TL). When I arrived at Shaner Pond, I found Sandhill Crane again, plus a Green Heron (09.08-BL). Both were on my county list already, but nice birds. I added one new species, Virginia Rail.

At 62 species, I tried another wetland, hoping for a Great Egret. I walked about a mile and a half there and was about to give up. I rounded a corner where I planned to turn around and a Great Egret flew up and overhead (09.08-R). I also picked up a Double-crested Cormorant. The walk back was hot and tedious. I took a different path, it petered out, and I had to trudge through some brush to rejoin the main path. At that point it was about 3:00pm and I still needed 3 species. I checked eBird for the location with the most species seen recently. The top site turned out to be somebody's home, as I learned when I got there.

09.08

I got to the site about 15 minutes later. I saw that it was a private residence, but several feeders were visible from the road. I felt a little weird standing by my car, peering into a strangers' yard with binoculars. Since they had many feeders and had posted to eBird daily, I hoped they would understand if they saw me. I quickly added House Finch, then focused on the hummingbird feeder. Within 5 minutes, I was rewarded by a Ruby-throated Hummingbird. I kept looking for Hairy Woodpecker, Baltimore Oriole, or Chipping Sparrow, all reported there. I saw a Downy Woodpecker … and then another Downy; I kept trying to turn the second one into a Hairy but that was not to be.

I checked eBird again for the next best location. It was essentially a mud puddle in a field. Multiple shorebirds had been seen. When I arrived, 12 minutes later, all I saw were Killdeer (not new). I counted 25. Then I saw one lone small Sandpiper. I took a bunch of photos and kept watching. Eventually, between my scope and photos, I was able to confirm that I was looking at Least Sandpiper, 2 for number 67 (09.09-L). Their legs were slightly muddy, but I eventually saw yellow. Before leaving, I added a Semipalmated Plover, number 68 (09.09-R).

I reached my target just after 4:00pm and I decided to quit and head for home. Google Maps said I would arrive at about 7:00pm. Since Fran and I usually eat between 5:00pm and 5:30pm, I texted that I would be late and that she need not wait for me — but she did wait.

+++

It was great to finish off Beaver and Lawrence counties. That meant I had *sealed the western border* of the state. While a big hole remained in the west, Allegheny County (Pittsburgh), I decided to focus on the north with McKean County (at 54 species) and Forest County (at 51).

There were no convenient options for tent camping. So, I booked one night at a hotel in Forest County close to the McKean County border. The hope was to finish both counties in a one-night trip. My wishful thinking also included picking up a few species in Clarion County, where I would go for carry out pizza, plus doing a stop in Elk County on the way home. If things went exceptionally well (if I scored lots of migrating fall warblers quickly) perhaps I could finish three counties.

While I was optimistic, rapidly shortening days and the quickly shrinking migration window had me worried about completing my Geo-Big Year. I would need to have some luck. The scope of the challenge prompted me to think about fallback plans; the low bar was to bird in every county. But I was not ready to give up on the 67x67 objective. That was the motivation for this overnight trip; I thought I had a chance, even if small, to finish off three counties in two partial days.

+++

I never seemed to get started from home as early as planned. It was 7:30am as I started out. And, I had forgotten to get gas the day before, due to hours online with bill paying and appointment scheduling, then processing prior trip photos until 9:00pm. So, I had to stop to gas up.

I began in McKean County. My first stop was discouraging. An hour and a half, walking 1.3 miles at State Game Lands 62, yielded just 4 new species. All were potentially photogenic birds who chose not to be photographed: Chestnut-sided Warbler, Bay-breasted Warbler, Scarlet Tanager, and Ruby-throated Hummingbird.

The pace remained slow the rest of the day, with difficult birding conditions due to wind making it almost impossible to hear songs or calls. It was also almost impossible to take photos, birds seemed to be sheltering in the bushes, and it was difficult to distinguish bird movement from wind movement. In all, I posted 7 more lists, walked nearly 6 miles, and managed just 5 more species to reach 63. These included Field Sparrow in State Game Lands 62 plus a Northern Shoveler and a Double-crested Cormorant at Hamlin Lake Park in Smethport (09.10). Number 63 was an Ovenbird on a trail in Kinzua Bridge State Park, my only addition in a trek of more than 1.5 miles.

My last stop was a mile walk around the *Forest Lawn Cemetery* in Kane, PA; I added zero species but did notice an interesting sculpture at the entrance – a wolf on a big rock howling (perhaps at the moon). When I went into town to pick up a carryout Chinese dinner, I saw another wolf sculpture. I became curious.

+++

That evening at the hotel, I went online to learn why there were multiple wolf sculptures in town. In the 1920s, Dr. E.H. McCleery (a local physician) started to acquire wolf pups from the western U.S. and bring them to Kane, PA where he developed a captive breeding program designed to help save the *lobo* wolf. For more on this, see: *Pennsylvania Heritage*: http://paheritage.wpengine.com/issue/winter-2019/

After learning about the wolves, I planned the next day. I was discouraged about not finishing McKean County but decided to stick to my original plan for day two, which was to start at the Buzzard Swamp in Allegheny State Forest, Forest County, since it was the closest site to the hotel. I set the alarm for 5:00am.

+++

I was out of the hotel by 6:05am. The "Swamp" was attractive in the early morning (09.11) and I had a reasonable morning there. Starting with 51 species, I was at 62 by about 10:00am. I also added 6 species in Elk County where the "Swamp" extends across the county line, a line I crossed over and back on a loop walk.

When I got back to the car, I planned to move on, but heard more activity. I spent another 20 minutes and added 3 species to reach 65 before 11:00am (including a Brown Creeper). Through the morning, I had moved from 51 to 65 species, with additions including a female Rose-breasted Grosbeak, a Yellow-bellied Sapsucker, and a female Cape May Warbler (09.12).

09.12

On the road out, while still in the State Forest, I saw movement that suggested Ovenbird (a species I still needed). I stopped, parked, and walked along the road looking for the bird. While doing so I heard a Hairy Woodpecker, number 66 (09.13-L). I then saw the Ovenbird for number 67 (09.13-R).

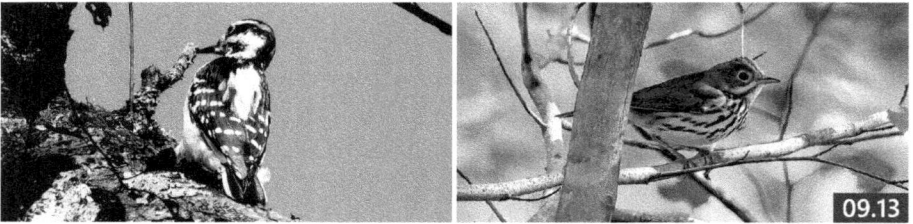
09.13

Having finished Forest County with the Ovenbird, I returned to McKean County. I stopped at the Mount Jewett rails-to-trails site first, but had no luck there. I then went to Kinzua Bridge State Park again and this time walked down the path to the bottom of the valley. I took multiple photos of the bridge ruin along the walk (09.14). As perhaps reflected in the images, it was a quite steep, long walk down; but I was rewarded with 3 species, Indigo Bunting, Cape May Warbler, and Common Raven (heard). That got me to 66 species.

09.14

I then tried again at the Ormsby Swamp Conservation Area for Wood Duck and Great Blue Heron (both reported there recently) but had no luck. I put on my muck boots and walked out a little way; but I ran into a stream that I could not cross. I'm not sure how the people that have reported from there were able to see much. I did get a photo of a pair of Broad-winged Hawks flying together overhead that I posted on my eBird list. This was not a new species, however, so I remained one short for the county.

Running out of options and time, I went back to Smethport and Hamlin Lake to look for Great Blue Heron or other water birds; but once more, no luck. As I moved among sites, I was scanning the skies, looking for Red-tailed Hawk, Cooper's Hawk or Sharp-shinned Hawk, or maybe a Chimney Swift. I wasn't having any luck.

I planned a route home with a chance for Common Grackle (reported near a road-side market) and/or a stop at a Game Lands where several warbler species I was missing were reported the day before. As I drove, I kept scanning the sky looking for Red-tailed hawk. I finally saw a pair of them. That was number 67. I skipped the Game Lands and headed for home.

+++

At this point, the odds of achieving my 67x67 challenge were rapidly diminishing. But I continued to press on. It was clear that the next month could be the key. Migration was underway in earnest; so, it was prime time to rack up species quickly.

I was happy to have finished two more Northwest Counties. Adding a few species in Elk County was also nice. Before heading back to Elk County, I directed my focus west, starting with a one-night trip to Indiana County. I had only 19 species there, most from the January day trip to chase but not find the Clay-colored Sparrow, and I was optimistic that with migration I could finish the county. The plan was to then schedule a four-night trip the next week to counties a bit further west and north of Indiana. I had seven other counties to the west, beyond day-trip range, to finish.

During my two days at home, I spent time looking for places to camp in Venango or Armstrong County. I found nothing. It was going to be tricky to decide the best strategy for where to head when. It was a complex, multi-criteria decision-making problem that required consideration of birding site location, recent and likely bird sightings, weather predictions, travel distances and times, and location and availability of camping sites or hotels. I had studied computational methods for such decision-making in graduate school (1976). As far as I was aware, however, there were no approaches (yet) that could handle optimization problems of this complexity combined with huge amounts of uncertainty (e.g., related to uncertainty that specific species will be in specific places at specific times, and that a birder of my skill level will find/ID the species if they are there/then). Building such a system might become a post-quest challenge to try; for now, I'd just guess.

+++

I got started early on September 10 for my one-night Indiana County trip, arriving at Yellow Creek State Park by 8:45am (09.15).

My first species was Wild Turkey (09.16-L) — always fun. I birded sites within the park until nearly 3:00pm. By that point, I had gone from 19 species to 47. I added several warbler species, including Black-and-white Warbler (09.16-M), American Redstart (09.16-R), Nashville Warbler, Black-throated Green Warbler, Hooded Warbler, Common Yellowthroat, Blackburnian Warbler, and Tennessee Warbler.

During the afternoon, with 5 more sites, I pushed my total to 58 that included Ovenbird, female Magnolia Warbler, and Cedar Waxwing

(09.17). Other good species were Ruby-throated Hummingbird (not at a feeder) and Indigo Bunting.

+++

My hotel was the most rundown I had stayed at. I was happy I booked only one night. I ate dinner (leftovers from home) and listened to baseball with Pittsburgh (who rallied to win 4-3 over Washington) and Cleveland (who led early but then lost 10-3 to Milwaukee).

With 9 species to go for Indiana County, I expected to reach the target early the next day. I explored site options, and I picked Blue Spruce County Park where I had some success in February. I realized that the next day would be 9/11. That prompted me to think about the birding at the Flight 93 memorial back in June.

+++

The morning was a cool and foggy one, 47°F when I arrived at Blue Spruce County Park. It was a big park, with many options. I ended up on a trail along a run that was quite productive. I added 9 species to reach 67 by about 9:45am. Additions included female Scarlet Tanager, Chestnut-sided Warbler, Philadelphia Vireo, Bay-breasted Warbler, Black-throated Blue Warbler, Yellow Warbler, and Cerulean Warbler. I was uncertain whether the Cerulean Warbler would be accepted since it was unexpected so late in the year and my only photo was terrible. So, I continued looking for a "spare". I found Chimney Swift flying over the reservoir, then on my way toward Jefferson County saw a couple American Kestrel. My description of the Cerulean Warbler plus the poor photo proved to be sufficient documentation to accept the report. Thus, number 67 was the Philadelphia Vireo, and my final total was 69 for Indiana County.

I headed to Jefferson County about 11:00am. I was hoping that would be enough time to finish it off since I had 53 species. By 2:45pm, however, I added only 3 species to reach 56. One impediment to progress was a stop at Cloe Lake. A washed-away bridge (09.18) made my planned walk impossible, so I did not stick around there. That situation cost me about an hour.

I ultimately got to 60 species before heading home. The afternoon was particularly hard going due to wind. The last half hour or so the wind died down and I added Cape May Warbler and Field Sparrow. Photos were all marginal, also due to wind.

As I started for home, I was worried about Penn State Football traffic. I asked Siri the score early in the game and she said Penn State was up 14-0 over Ball State. I assumed that a lot of people would leave at halftime, so I stopped worrying about traffic. I did worry about health of those attending, however, since Penn State imposed no mask or other restrictions while we were still in the middle of a pandemic.

+++

It was disappointing to finish only one county on the trip. My plan to finish the west first was not going well. It was obvious that fewer, longer trips would result in fewer miles driven and less time driving, thus more time looking for migrants. On the other hand, it was easier for Fran and Skoti if I had shorter trips. Since COVID-19 began, I was doing all grocery shopping (at 6:00am when our local store opened for "seniors"). And, I could take Skoti on more frequent, longer, and brisker walks than Fran could. That said, Skoti did enjoy the slower walks with Fran on which he could sniff more!

Along with balancing time on the road and home plus worries about finishing the quest, my deteriorating vision had started to impact my birding. I no longer had the visual acuity with glasses that I used to. Situations where I might have identified a bird without optics now required a good look with binoculars, the binoculars seemed a bit harder to focus when in low light, and views through my scope at maximum magnification needed better light than they used to. All of this meant that I had come to rely on the camera more and more. The image-stabilized body and lens on my Olympus OMD-E1 Mark III with 300mm Pro lens was somewhat like carrying an image-stabilized hand-held scope. If I got a photo, I could zoom in and often confirm an ID. The problem with this strategy, of course, was that it was still early fall, leaves were still on the trees, and the birds that are trickiest to identify in fall are small and moving quickly among the leaves.

+++

Reviewing my progress map, gaping holes in many parts of the state prompted me to deviate from a plan to finish the west first. Lackawanna County drew my attention as the only gap in a southwest-to-northeast corridor of completed counties. I had 28 species in Lackawanna County from the trip with Fran and Skoti a couple months earlier. And, it was a county with a conveniently located state park and available campsites. I booked two nights with a plan to finish the county, then head north to Susquehanna County (where I had zero) or south to Monroe County (where I had 30). Pike County (also zero) was next to Monroe County and both counties had been getting interesting migrants. So, I would monitor eBird and watch for anything rare popping up and use that to decide which county to focus on after Lackawanna.

I hoped to finish off multiple counties on this trip. We were almost halfway through September, with migration peaking soon. Review of the Pennsylvania bar charts for warblers shows the fall peak in mid-September or early-October (09.19). The few migrant species that peak later tend to have lower numbers, thus are less likely to be seen at all on a 1 or 2-day trip to a county.

While stressing about the future, I was also monitoring weather for the coming trip. On Wednesday, when I would break camp, thunderstorms were predicted. Depending on if/when that happened, I might decide to head home or to wait out the storms, since they might bring down migrants. If I did the latter, I'd book a hotel for a night or two – camping during a thunderstorm or at a wet campground was not my idea of a good time.

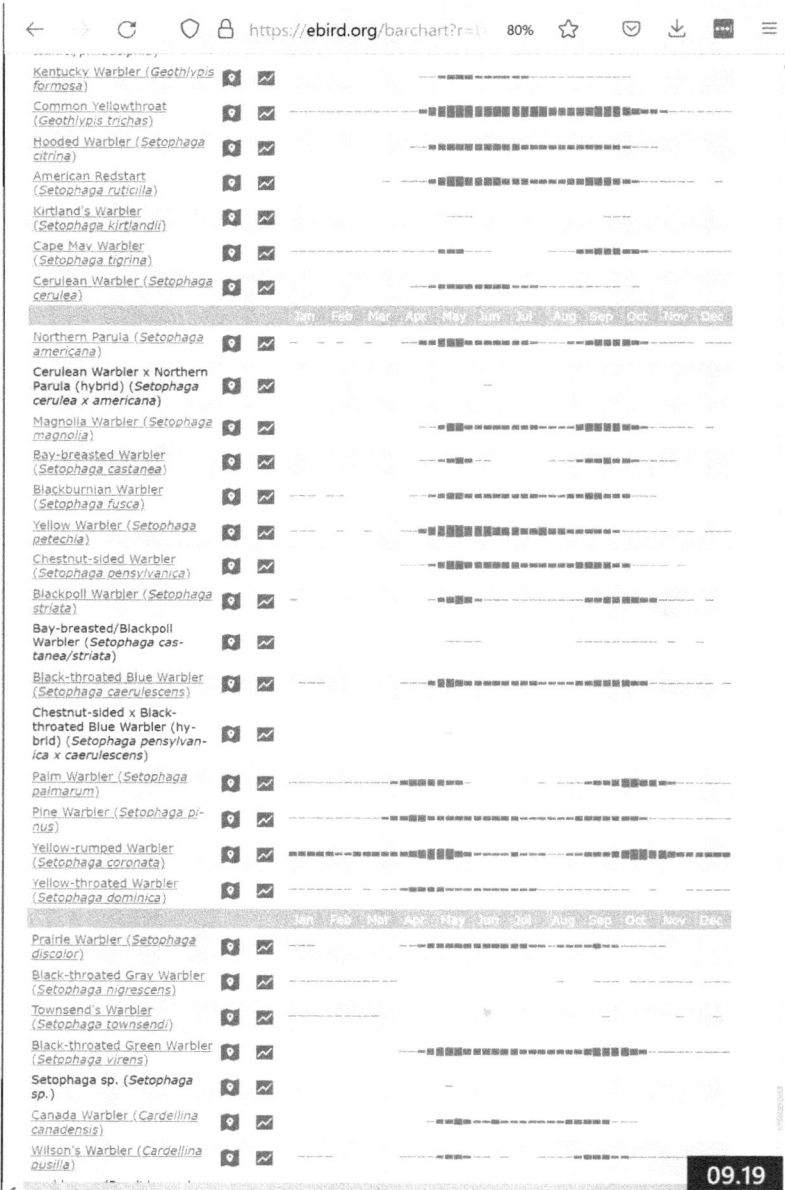

+++

I got off on September 13 at 7:15am for the 2.5-3-hour trip to Lack-awanna County. The navigation system told me to continue following I-80E for 99 miles. The number of miles I was driving was getting me down (again). If I had heard earlier about Steve Howell chalking up 32,940 miles doing a 2020 traditional, North Carolina big year, I might not have started (see Epilog for more).

I had a rather slow day. I began at Archbald Pothole State Park (a place visited with Fran and Skoti in August). I added 9 species including Palm Warbler, Ring-necked Pheasant, and (with photo) Eastern Phoebe (09.20-L). Other stops included the Gravel Pond, Fords Lake, and Lackawanna State Park where I camped. By day's end, I was at 48 species (additions included Bald Eagle and Yellow-rumped Warbler (09.20-M&R). The next day needed to be better.

+++

Setting up camp was quick, at what turned out to be a nice site (09.21-L). Before dark, I sat down to my dinner of left-over stuffed eggplant and potatoes, plus avocado and bread – it tasted as good as it looked (09.21-R). Sunset was at 7:15pm; the days were quickly getting shorter, making the quest that much harder.

During the night, I had the sensation of something small walking across my body. At first, I thought I was dreaming, but it kept up. I eventually found a visitor in my tent (09.22). Taken in the semi-dark, the photo looked like an impressionistic painting.

On September 14, I started in the State Park, spending about one hour total on parts of two trails. I was surprised to find a balloon launch (09.23-L); but, it was a bit foggy for anyone to fly that morning (09.23-R).

In the park, I picked up 5 species, including my favorite bird, a Green Heron; but I still needed 14 more. So, I decided to go back to Archbald Pothole State Park (based on species reports over the past few days). It was slow for quite a while. I talked to another birder, who had seen a Connecticut Warbler, which would be a year bird for me. I spent quite a bit of time looking, with no luck.

I ran into that birder again while he was scanning a flock of mixed warblers. I missed some species he saw, but I picked up 3 species: Blackpoll Warbler, Bay-breasted Warbler, and American Redstart. I kept working the area and saw another Palm Warbler. Then, as a last-ditch effort, I decided to go through the woods, despite mosquitoes. The bugs had eased up a bit, so I was able to do a loop path along a ridge with a view down on some trees rather than up. Another mixed flock of migrants dropped in. I added multiple vireos and warblers, including Philadelphia Vireo, Cape May Warbler, Black-throated Green Warbler, Tennessee Warbler, Pine Warbler, Magnolia Warbler, and Blue-winged Warbler. I also saw Scarlet Tanager (not new) and had a brief look at a Ruby-throated Hummingbird. That got me to 67 species by 11:30am. I thought I had only 66, so went looking for number 67.

I decided to hunt for Canada Goose and Double-crested Cormorant. I assumed either or both would be easy to find. Driving back to the state park to try, I saw Canada Goose (a gaggle) near a large pond (#68 that I thought was 67). I parked to scan the pond and a Pileated Woodpecker flew by (#69). At the state park I then saw 3 Double-crested Cormorant (#70). My best photos for the day were of species I already had, Brown Thrasher staring intently (09.24-L) and Scarlet Tanager, smiling for the camera (09.24-M), or an extra beyond the target, Pileated Woodpecker, seeming to beat its head against a tree (09.24-R).

09.24

It was mid-afternoon when I finished off Lackawanna County. I decided to make a start on Pike County and headed to Lake Wallenpaupack, the closest site to where I was at the time. I got to my first stop there about 3:00pm, with my first species a Wild Turkey – a great start. But I only managed to reach 9 species by the time I needed to head back to camp to fix dinner.

+++

All afternoon I debated whether to give up my second night at the campground and find a hotel. Rain was still predicted and packing up when everything was wet would be a drag. Plus, it was 81°F with high humidity after I finished dinner. That was sufficient motivation to book a hotel and pack up. It took me about an hour to break camp, not too bad. I booked (for 2 nights) near Stroudsburg in Monroe County. It was the first place (other than the rustic cabin Fran and I stayed at) that I had a fireplace, albeit electric, which I did not need or use (09.25).

09.25

In hindsight, I should have moved to a hotel that morning. I had to cover most of the same ground to get to the hotel that I had done to return to the campground from Pike County. My hotel in Monroe County was close to Pike County, so I decided to return to Pike County first the following day.

+++

I was up early as usual, off to the Delaware River Gap National Recreation Area. I found it foggy, humid, and full of mosquitoes. I put on bug repellent, supplementing my insect shield clothes. I did not get bitten, but the mosquitoes were extremely annoying, buzzing around my head. Still, I got a good start, adding 14 species including Bald Eagle, Warbling Vireo, Yellow-throated Vireo, and a Yellow-billed Cuckoo.

Next, I stopped at the Pocono Environmental Education Center where I picked up 12 more species including a female Black-throated Blue Warbler, a Scarlet Tanager, and a Wood Thrush (09.26). At that point, I was at 35 species and added Belted Kingfisher at a nearby lake (that was otherwise not productive).

Between 10:15am and 3:00pm, progress was slow. Six eBird lists from different sites added just 8 more species. These species included an Ovenbird (09.27-L) and a Red-tailed Hawk with snake (09.27-M). I also got a photo of a male Black-throated Blue Warbler (09.27-R).

I spent the rest of the afternoon at Promised Land State Park – quite a name. The Park's web page said the name traces to The Shakers, who tried to farm and build a life there unsuccessfully and are said to have sarcastically labeled it "the Promised Land." If true, it changes my image of The Shakers, who I would not associate with sarcasm.

My progress toward 67 in Pike County continued to be slow. But I did have one big find for the day, Trumpeter Swan, found shortly before the sun started to set (09.28-L). Before that, I also captured a nice photo of an adult Bald Eagle as it was about to land on a stump in the shallows of the lake (09.28-R).

+++

I finished the day with just 49 species. It would be a challenge to even finish Pike the following day before heading home.

Back at the hotel, I fixed my second serving of stuffed eggplant and potato leftovers. They were great, again. The hotel suite was nice, but the lack of concern about COVID-19 exhibited by most other guests and the staff was disconcerting. Only I wore a mask. I was on the third floor and used the stairs to come and go, avoiding others.

+++

On September 16, I was checked out by 6:09am and headed to Peck's Pond in Pike County looking for warblers reported there. It was a gray morning, with rather poor light and nothing on the pond (09.29).

I managed only two new warbler species at the pond, Yellow-rumped Warbler and Cape May Warbler. The addition of a Spotted Sandpiper got me to 52 species, but that took more than one hour. I was starting to worry about even finishing the county.

At that point, I tried to figure out where to find the 15 more species I still needed. I thought about returning to Promised Land State Park, but I had limited luck there the day before (other than the Trumpeter Swan). So, I looked for other locations. I noticed Shohola Wildlife Management Area, which had a big reservoir. It looked promising. Nothing had been posted there in the past week, but many species were possible. I decided to give it a try.

I spent about four and a half hours at Shohola, posting 6 lists to eBird and walking just over 3 miles. One walk yielded Black-throated Green Warbler and Bay-breasted Warbler (09.30-L&M). At that stop I also saw Magnolia Warbler and Tennessee Warbler. The next stop added Chestnut-sided Warbler and Northern Parula. Another walk (ending just before noon) added Double-crested Cormorant, Field Sparrow, and House Wren (09.30-R) to reach 65 species.

Still in Shohola, I tried another path with nothing new. I drove a bit further, parked, and walked a side road leading to the water. I scanned around and to my surprise I saw Great Egret (5 of them) on the far bank (#66). It was 1:15pm and I was 1 species short (facing a 3-hour drive home). I heard several calls; one was probably a White-throated Sparrow, but I was not confident in an ID based only on the *chip*. There were multiple warblers flitting around, but I never got a good look at any except for Black-throated Green Warbler, which I already had.

I decided to give up on the site and try somewhere else. As I got back to the car, I was surprised to hear a Least Flycatcher. I then saw it and got a few photos of number 67 (09.31-L). I was a bit sorry I had already decided to go home that day because finishing Monroe County, where I had 31, seemed within reach if I stayed. But Fran was expecting me, so I stuck with the plan.

With a bit of time left, I decided to try for extra species in Pike County. I checked a couple urban places where House Sparrow, House Finch, or Rock Pigeon seemed possible; I had no luck. I then tried the north end of Lake Wallenpaupack (a large reservoir I had visited the other end of two days before). Both Eastern Bluebird and House Finch had been reported. I parked at one place, but nothing was accessible, so I shifted locations to where I could walk on the dam/causeway. Multiple people there were excited about a Bald Eagle in a tree. It was my fourth for the day, but I did take photos since it was so cooperative (09.31-M).

I kept looking for Eastern Bluebird with no success despite good habitat. I was about to give up when I saw something fly down to the dam's base. I could not see where it landed, so I walked to a better vantage point. I was surprised to see a guy fishing. I saw no bird and guessed the fisherman prompted the bird to continue along the water's edge to a point out of sight.

I kept scanning the dam's base just in case. My perseverance was rewarded with a real surprise. I found an American Pipit (09.31-R). They were listed as rare in the county for mid-September, but I got decent pictures to support the ID. At that point I decided to head for home.

+++

I took just one day off at home. The quarter was running out quickly. I spent time planning and decided on a day trip back to Jefferson County on September 18, where I was at 60 species. I expected to finish the county in a day trip and perhaps add to adjacent Elk County. I also booked a four-night trip to the northeast right after that, staying in Bradford County between Susquehanna and Tioga County. I continued to skip Sullivan and Wyoming County. Fran and I were considering a trip there (with Skoti) in October.

At this point, I was focused on making as much progress as possible before the 3ʳᵈ Quarter of the year ended. Depending upon success (or not) of the 4-day trip to the northeast, I would pick counties to visit that I had the best chance to complete.

+++

I got up and out on a foggy September 18 by 6:09am. I headed to the Five Bridges Trail, the closest spot to home in Jefferson County. I was hoping fog would clear by the time I arrived about 7:30am.

The trail was a great choice; I finished the county quickly, reaching 67, then 68 and 69 before 9:30am. I had a Yellow-bellied Sapsucker first, then Swamp Sparrow, then a flock of mixed warblers and vireos that put me over the top. These included Black-throated Green Warbler, Philadelphia Vireo – number 67, and Blackpoll Warbler (09.32) plus Bay-breasted Warbler and Tennessee Warbler.

I moved on to Elk County where I was at 47 species from 4 previous short forays. Based on the quick success in Jefferson County, I arrived at my first stop in Elk County thinking it would be easy to finish it that day. I was (again) wrong.

I did well at my first site (Little Toby Creek Trail), adding 7 species in 40 minutes. These included American Redstart, and Eastern Wood-Pewee. But then things bogged down. I only got 3 new species the rest of the day at four stops between 11:00am and 4:00pm. That put me at just 57 species. With no real chance to complete the county that day, I decided to head home. I again remembered that Penn State had a home football game, a night game against Auburn. So, I opted for a route that did not pass the stadium to avoid the usual traffic snarl.

+++

September was slipping away. With less than half a month left, I booked four nights at a hotel in Towanda, Bradford County along the northern border. The goal was to complete at least Bradford and Susquehanna County. I opted to do everything from one base because accommodations are scarce in Pennsylvania's northern tier.

+++

I left the house at 7:19am on September 20; it was 55°F and quite foggy again. The navigation app predicted 9:01am arrival at the first stop; so, I expected the fog to burn off by then.

My plan was to bird Bradford County on day one, then focus on Susquehanna County during day two and three (until completing it), then go back to Bradford. Optimistically, I would finish Bradford mid-day on day four, giving me parts of two days to focus on a third county. There had been no recent eBird postings for the western half of Bradford County (the bit I would reach first). So, I picked the closest hotspot to Centre County as my starting point, Taylor Rd. Marsh.

As I was driving toward Bradford County, Fran called to tell me I left part of my lunch at home (the cheese to go with crackers). I had left more important things at home on other trips, so did not stress about this (much). I could remedy the oversight; but it was unlikely I could find cheese as good as the locally made farmers' market cheese I meant to bring. It dropped to 54°F. And I drove in and out of thick fog on I-80. I had to slow down and did not get to my first site until 9:15am.

The marsh yielded 19 species in 35 minutes; a promising start. The best was a Northern Harrier flying over the fields just after I arrived (09.33-L). After that start, my pace diminished markedly. While parked for lunch, I picked up Wild Turkey and Hairy Woodpecker. My next site netted only 4 new species, including a Dark-eyed Junco (09.33-M). I did not reach 30 species until after noon, with Turkey Vulture (09.33-R).

While birds were scarce, the site was interesting historically. The road I walked down took me to a historical site for *The Village of Barclay* and its cemetery, founded on March 28, 1866 (09.34).

Based on signs, the cemetery was founded through a deed from the Barclay Coal Company to the Bishop of the Dioceses of Philadelphia. It became the resting place for remains of "children who died of diseases and other infirmaries commonly treated today; miners killed in the mines; and others who succumbed to the everyday hazards of life in an earlier time." Many gravestones remain legible and attest to this description. A church was also built on the site, but it closed at the turn of the 20th century and the deed to the land passed through several entities until it ended up with the Pennsylvania Game Commission in 1930. The grounds are described as "fragile" due to a combination of subsidence from underground mining, vandalism, and general neglect.

During the rest of the day, I added species only sporadically. It appeared I would finish the day with 39, but then I remembered a Common Grackle seen while driving. I added that to get my total to 40. That was not what I had hoped for after arriving relatively early, but I was within striking distance of 67 with one more day.

Toward the end of the day, I had some great views of the Susquehanna River (**09.35-L**) and came across another interesting historical site – the French Azilum (near what is now Asylum, PA). A plaque for the latter (from 1930) details some history of the settlement (**09.35-R**).

+++

I had not investigated Bradford County history prior to my trip. Visual evidence suggested that large parts of the county had been quiet,

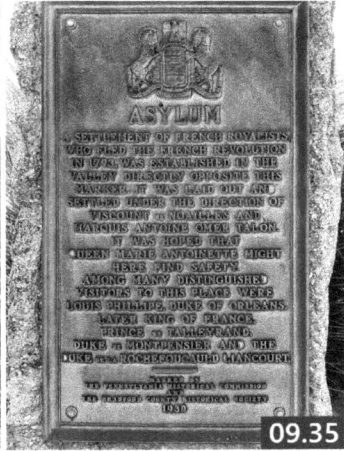

rural places. But … things appeared to be changing quickly. Oil and gas extraction efforts were evident everywhere, including on the roads filled with many kinds of trucks (**09.36**).

My impression was of a once rural place that was drastically disrupted by the current natural gas boom. That, of course, was the perspective of someone who is financially secure. Perhaps many folks living in the area are quite happy for the boom due to the promise of jobs. That said, after driving through the county and staying at a hotel I suspected that the local jobs were mostly in service activities, like hotels and restaurants, with outsiders working at the oil and gas sites. Most vehicles parked at the hotel (and others I saw at field sites) had out-of-state plates, and the hotel was full of folks working in the gas fields. Later during my stay, I captured a photo to illustrate the vehicles of typical clientele at the hotel (**09.37**).

09.37

Back at the hotel, I looked at the migration forecast on the Cornell site. If I was in Indiana or Illinois, I would have been in great shape. Massive migration was predicted there overnight, with Pennsylvania quiet. By the following night, Pennsylvania migration was looking better. I decided to stick to my plan to focus on Susquehanna County the next day, then reassess based on migration estimates.

+++

I could have had a better start on the morning of September 21. The weather looked wonderful, but I overslept. It was 5:42am when I woke up, 42 minutes later than intended. That was probably why I ended up behind a long line of tanker trucks. Both Bradford and Susquehanna Counties are big, making distances between locations long. In this case, I had planned for a 55-minute trip from Towanda where I was staying to my first Susquehanna County site – but the tanker trucks quashed the plan. It was a two-lane road with the trucks going about 35 mph.

Eventually, I arrived at a site called Hollister's (Dump Hill) Pond. There had been many eBird posts from there, but I could not find a good access point (perhaps there is not one). I birded from the road and a parking lot that allowed views into the pond (really a little lake). I ended up with 24 species in about one hour. These included Magnolia Warbler, Black-capped Chickadee, and Gray Catbird (**09.38**), along with Nashville Warbler, Blackpoll Warbler, Belted Kingfisher, Wood Duck, and Spotted Sandpiper.

09.38

I then shifted over to Salt Springs State Park where I spent two hours and raised the total to 39 species. Highlights included Rose-breasted Grosbeak and Common Yellowthroat (09.39-L&R). I was having a decent morning but almost ruined it. I crossed a stream without a walking stick, stepped on a wet rock that (I should have guessed) proved to be slick (09.39-M). I almost slid into the stream. I ended up with only slightly wet toes. I needed to remember that carrying the camera in a shoulder sling and binoculars in a harness impedes balance on tricky terrain.

09.39

Overall, I had a good day, reaching 54 species, the last one being Eastern Bluebird on a wire as I was on my way to the hotel.

+++

Neither the weather nor migration forecast prompted me to change my strategy. On my way out the next morning, I caught a great sunrise that I included in my usual "good morning" text to Fran (09.40) – much more impressive in the color version.

09.40

Fran texted back asking about the "aliens" in the corner. I had not seen them in my hurry to grab the photo before the sun came up fully ... and while "parked" at a stop sign. Zooming in they appeared to be lighted Halloween creatures of some kind (a bit early, since Halloween was 6 weeks off). Photo processing after I returned home uncovered what appears to be a Viking skeleton crew in a very tiny longship with dragon's head (09.41).

From the "aliens", I moved on to my first stop, back at Salt Springs State Park. I added 4 species and got a photo of a Nashville Warbler seen but not photographed the day before (09.42-L). Then I picked up Common Merganser (09.42-M) and House Finch at Quaker Lake. At the next stop, State Game Lands 35, I got a nice image of a Red-eyed Vireo in flight (09.42-R).

Between sites, as I passed a private lake, I happened to see a Ruddy Duck by itself in the middle. That was unexpected and I captured a low-quality photo put in eBird as documentation. I spent nearly 2 hours at Game Lands 35, adding just 3 new species. At about 2:00pm, I decided to change locations completely to the one non-private location where multiple species I needed had been reported. It turned out to be a Township Park. In a low spot with standing water, I picked up Solitary Sandpiper as number 65 and Red-winged Blackbird as number 66. I was looking for Killdeer to reach my target but had no luck.

I started driving toward a site in the southwest part of the county. But I made a wrong turn down a country road. While on that road, I saw a Double-crested Cormorant in a lake. I turned to my left, and across the field I saw a bunch of Wild Turkey. I thought I had numbers 67 and 68. But when I submitted them, they showed up on my Lackawanna County list. I had apparently gone about a mile into Lackawanna County. So, I added my 73rd species to Lackawanna County (the Wild Turkey was new there) but still had to search for number 67 in Susquehanna County.

I kept heading to the original site I was looking for. I got near but the location was ambiguous. I reasoned that it was probably a farm down a dead-end road that looked like a private lane. I was uncertain whether it was OK to drive down that "lane". So, I just drove around some back roads in the area inside Susquehanna County. It was starting to rain so conditions were not good. But at about 5:30pm, I came across a Ring-necked Pheasant for number 67 (I got a marginal photo that I put in eBird).

+++

Having finished Susquehanna County on Wednesday, the goal for Thursday was to complete Bradford County where I had 40 species from the first day of the trip. I was up and out by 6:09am. The prediction was for 1-2 inches of rain, but it was not raining when I left the hotel. On my 23-mile drive to the first stop the rain started. I was (of course) hoping to have enough breaks in the rain to make good progress and that the front would bring in species that wouldn't be around otherwise.

When I arrived at the first site at 6:43am, there was little or no rain. I managed a 1.7 mile walk with rain only heavy enough to be bothersome for the last 10-12 minutes. I added 8 species, a slower pace than I had hoped, but better than it could have been with heavy rain. Additions included a group of Common Merganser and Red-eyed Vireo.

After the first site, I found myself on Easy Street (09.43). Easy Street was not so easy since I began to run into heavy rain. Despite rain, I ventured out at a place called Round Top Park. When I started it was only a moderate rain. I was not getting too wet. I saw a Wood Duck and then walked down a small trail. I started to see activity in some trees. I know there was more than one warbler but all I managed to see was a single Nashville Warbler. The rain then became heavy, so I turned back to the car. At one point it was a real deluge, the hardest rain for any outing all year. If I hadn't already paid for another night at the hotel, I might have just given up and left for home. But the weather was supposed to be decent the next day, so I kept at it, focusing on places that had water that could be seen from the car if needed.

The first of these places was a reservoir at Mount Pisgah State Park. I did pick up water birds there, including Double-crested Cormorant, Pied-billed Grebe, Belted Kingfisher, and Green Heron. Overall, I spent nearly 4 hours at the State Park, walking on multiple trails and getting quite wet. My shoes ended up very soggy as were my socks. I was glad when I finally returned to the car that I had spares of both!

It was just after 5:00pm when I finished up at Mt. Pisgah State Park and my total was sitting at 63 species. It was difficult to figure out where to try next since there were few postings in eBird and no species seen in the past week that I had not already seen. I decided to try a site on the Susquehanna River. On the way there I saw a Red-tailed Hawk for number 64. It took me until about 6:30pm, but I managed to add Tree Swallow, Northern Rough-winged Swallow, and finally an Osprey to reach 67. I then headed to the hotel to fix my dinner.

+++

Having finished Susquehanna County and Bradford County (just), I decided to spend my travel-home day in Tioga County, trying to make progress on closing off the northern tier. It was a brisk 48°F morning when I checked out of the hotel at 6:15am. Skies were clear, the moon still visible, and views (once it was light enough) were good (09.44).

The first site I picked, Tauscher Pond, was about 55 minutes away. I began with just 2 species, but with the good weather I was optimistic that I could reach the target that day – not sure where that optimism came from. Not long after getting to Tioga County I saw a hawk flying. It was smaller than a Red-Tailed Hawk, but a car behind me made it impossible to ID. Despite that miss, things started well with Common Merganser and Canada Goose enroute. Then, I added 15 species at the Pond in just 38 minutes, including a Great Blue Heron flying right over me plus a female Common Yellowthroat and a Gray Catbird (**09.45**), as well as a Belted Kingfisher and a Yellow-bellied Sapsucker.

I moved on to Hills Creek State Park, making steady progress. Among additions were Blackburnian Warbler, Black-throated Green Warbler, and Yellow-rumped Warbler along with a Green Heron (always a favorite). I left there at 36 species for Tioga County.

My next stop was at Tioga Hammond Lakes – Ives Run Recreation Area. The area had clearly had a lot of rain. The reservoir was very high with flooding into the parking area, over sidewalks, and generally submerging sections that were not typically underwater (**09.46**). I ended up wearing my Muck Boots to walk along some of the paths and was rewarded with an interesting mix of species.

I birded two more sites, reaching 49 species. They included 4 more warbler species, Tennessee Warbler (poor photo posted into eBird), Magnolia Warbler, Yellow Warbler, and Pine Warbler (**09.47**). I also added Blue-headed Vireo, Ruby-crowned Kinglet, and Swamp Sparrow.

At that point, it was 1:00pm. I did a bit of roadside birding on my way to Woodland Park where I reached 53 species with an Osprey and a Black Vulture. I tried other places over another 1.5 hours with little success, adding just American Kestrel (#54) before heading for home.

+++

The trip was good, with two previously blank counties done and a dent in a third. I decided to try finishing the northern border by the 3rd quarter's end — Elk (at 57), Tioga (at 53), and Potter (not started).

I hoped to have new glasses for the next trip. I asked that they be sent directly to our house, but they did not arrive. I finally called and was told that my glasses came in some time before. They said they tried to call to let us know but could not leave a message. Apparently, they could not figure out our phone's call screening, which simply requires the caller to press "1" and state who they are. And … they had my email but did not try that. The dual mistakes (not sending the glasses directly and not leaving or emailing a message) were annoying.

Fran picked up the glasses for me on Friday (9/24). I tried them most of Saturday and my vision seemed worse. I found a sharp drop off in clarity for peripheral vision, making the new glasses harder to drive with than my old ones and even harder for birding. With COVID-19, it had been two years since my prescription had been updated, so the problems could be that my eyes deteriorated sufficiently that no glasses will be comfortable to see with. But, in the short run, I decided to return to my old glasses for my next trip and call the eye doctor's office on Monday to see what could be done. Getting old remained no fun.

+++

When I left the house at 6:11am on September 26, it was 55°F – not bad. Elk had been a hard county due to lack of eBird reports for the southern half, which is closer to home. There seemed to be just one local birder posting to eBird, infrequently, but only at sites beyond day-trip range for me. The day prior, that birder saw many species I had yet to see, but at sites more than two hours from home. I opted for closer sites that have a reasonably high probability of species despite zero recent reports. I figured that if I was not successful at the initial (closer) sites, I could work my way further north. I started out hopeful of adding the 10 species I needed by lunch time.

I began at the Elk County Visitor Center, but there were too many families there looking for Elk. Birds were mostly scared off and those present could not be heard over the people chatter. After a half hour with zero additions, I gave up and moved to the Moshannon State Forest Beaver Creek Impoundment where I added 6 species in about an hour and a quarter, including Pine Warbler, Yellow-rumped Warbler, Red-shouldered Hawk, and White-throated Sparrow (09.48-L). I departed that site just after 10:30am with my county total at 63.

I moved over to Deibel Road where I saw Wild Turkey (09.48-M) and heard a Ruby-crowned Kinglet, which got me to 65. Then I heard and recorded a Swainson's Thrush doing its repeated quip. With one to go, I started looking for Dark-eyed Junco, House Finch, Purple Finch, or still missing warblers. I stopped in the State Forest to eat my lunch. I saw nothing while eating, but when I got out of the car to put my camera and binoculars back on, a group of Dark-eyed Junco flew up from the ground behind the car. I counted 8. My best photo was not great, but as species 67 for the county, I've included it (09.48-R).

It was a bit after 1:00pm, so it was too late to shift to an adjacent county. I decided to take a "scenic" (less direct) route out of the county to add a couple extra species. I did not manage to add anything, but the scenery was good (09.49).

+++

I spent a day at home organizing my next short trip. It would be the last trip for the 3rd quarter of the year. Time was rapidly slipping away, and migration was going to be over soon. I stuck to my plan to try finishing the northern tier in September, booking a two-night trip at a hotel in Potter County right next to Tioga County, my two remaining counties along the border.

For this short trip, I still needed to wear my old glasses because nothing had been resolved about the new ones yet. I managed to schedule a phone appointment about the glasses, but the earliest they could do was on the Friday when I returned from the trip. It would've been great to have some new glasses (that worked better than the old ones), but I would just have to make do.

As I planned my trip, eBird reports were again no help, with zero reports for Potter County over the past 7 days and no sightings of anything I had not already seen in Tioga County. This situation (lack of active birders in rural places) drives home the importance of a Geo-Big Year over an ordinary Big Year. A Geo-Big Year forces the birder (me, here) to explore infrequently birded territories. As with state and national birding atlases, geo-birding prompts birders to visit sites that may not be the "best" spots to find rarities or rack up numbers. But it provides data about which species are present in which territories.

One challenge of a Geo-Big Year, of course, is that you cannot be everywhere at once. If you do a geo-birding weekend, where the goal is to see X species at each of Y hotspots, only some hotspots can be visited in the peak early morning hours. Similarly, in a state-focused Geo-Big Year like mine, some counties get visited in the spring, others in fall, and others at off times. The alternative is to generate an even bigger carbon footprint crisscrossing the state multiple times during the year.

+++

I ultimately decided to start in Potter County, where I had zero species . I left the house at 6:45am Tuesday, in the pouring rain and hoping that the rain would stop by the time I arrived. I intended to start at the northeast end of Sinnemahoning State Park. I birded the more southern section back in May when working on Cameron County.

On the way, while crossing through Elk County (naturally), I saw my first ever Elk in Pennsylvania — grazing at the roadside. There were guard rails on both sides, but the road had limited traffic. I was able to stop long enough to capture an iPhone photo (09.50-L); the Elk was too close for my regular camera, which, as always, had the fixed telephoto lens mounted. Here, I pair the photo with a view from later in the day overlooking the valley at Lynam Run State Park (09.50-R).

I had a very slow start on Potter County. Sinnemahoning State Park netted just 12 species in an hour plus. I moved to Cherry Springs State Park (much more frequently visited for star gazing than birding), where I found multiple warbler species, including Magnolia Warbler, Pine Warbler, Yellow-rumped Warbler, and Palm Warbler (09.51).

I left Cherry Springs State Park at 12:15pm with just 23 species, including Eastern Bluebird and Eastern Towhee (09.52-L&M). I added a Belted Kingfisher (09.52-R) enroute to Lynam Run State Park.

I spent an hour and a half at Lynam Run State Park, adding just 4 species. Next, I headed to my accommodations in Galeton, PA, stopping at Galeton Lake in the middle of town. The lake was productive; I added 8 species in 30 minutes, including Spotted Sandpiper, Common Merganser, and Hooded Merganser (**09.53**).

+++

I checked into my accommodations, Nob Hill Motel & Cabins. The place was far from new, but it was clean and functional. I had a separate "cabin" that included a full kitchen (**09.54**).

I went back out to a Game Lands for a last try. I added only Eastern Wood-Pewee, ending the day with 38 species. I returned to the cabin to fix dinner and listen to baseball. I retired early, with Pittsburgh up 7-6 over the Chicago Cubs. They went on to win 8-6; I should have kept listening; wins for Pittsburgh were scarce in 2021! My plan for the next day was to finish Tioga County, then return to Potter County.

+++

Wednesday started slowly -- again. My first two stops yielded just 2 new species (Bald Eagle and Coopers Hawk). Next I tried Leonard Harrison State Park overlooking the *Grand Canyon of Pennsylvania.* It was not an ideal day; the valley was fog-filled (**09.55-L&R**). But I took a 1.6 mile hike on the Overlook Trail anyway (**09.55-M**). Birds were hard to come by; I added just 5 species that included Black-throated Blue Warbler, Blackpoll Warbler, and Red-eyed Vireo.

At 10:15am when I left, I was at 61 species, still hoping for 67 by noon. That was not to be. I posted 5 lists before reaching 67, a surprise Baltimore Oriole, at 5:30pm. Photos were hard to come by. The only decent ones of new species were a Dark-eyed Junco, from Hills Creek State Park, and a Palm Warbler, from the Pine Creek Rail Trail, both bookending a nicely posed Eastern Painted Turtle below (**09.56**).

It was too late at that point to do much in Potter County, so I went back to Galeton Lake in town in case some other waterfowl had shown up. None had so I headed to my cabin for dinner.

+++

I again listened to Pittsburgh baseball. They took a 2-1 lead in the 6th but lost 3-2. While that was disappointing, I had a birding surprise – a Great Horned Owl calling about 9:05pm, putting me at 40 species for Potter County. The goal for the final day of September was, of course, to finish Potter County. Based on progress to that point, adding the 27 species I needed before heading home would be hard.

+++

I got up at 5:00am as usual. After hearing a Great Horned Owl the night before, I was hoping for other owls – but no such luck. I drove into nearby Game Lands 64. The main road was busy; it appeared to be a route to work. I stopped at one site but there was no accessible trail. I listened for a while but only added American Robin.

I found a side road leading to a big pond and marsh. Walking nearly 2 miles uphill got me to the pond, but I found no water birds. Two hours netted just 4 new species (Golden-crowned Kinglet, Ruby-crowned Kinglet, White-eyed Vireo, and Pileated Woodpecker), reaching 45 for the county. My most interesting sighting was a Coyote on the trail.

I returned to Cherry Springs State Park, hoping for something new. I added just 2 species on a 1.5 hour, 1.75 mile loop walk (Field Sparrow and Blue-headed Vireo). I moved to Ole Bull State Park as my last stop before heading home. I did two loop walks (1.5mi and 2.1mi). The park had nice trails and great habitat (09.57) but was extremely quiet. It was nice to be the only human there, but lack of birds was disappointing. I only managed to add 3 species the first walk (Dark-eyed Junco, Downy Woodpecker, and Broad-winged Hawk) and zero species on the second. I was getting very tired of those long walks with few or zero new species; I needed to develop a more efficient strategy.

I headed home just before 4:00pm with only 50 species in Potter County. It was discouraging to manage only 10 additions in nearly a full day of birding with more than 7 miles on foot. I hoped that Potter County would be the most challenging county I encountered. If I ran into other counties this hard, the Geo-Big Year would be unachievable.

+++

With the end of September, the 3rd Quarter of the year ran out. It was time again to review progress. As before, I started with a look at the evolving map of totals by county (09.58).

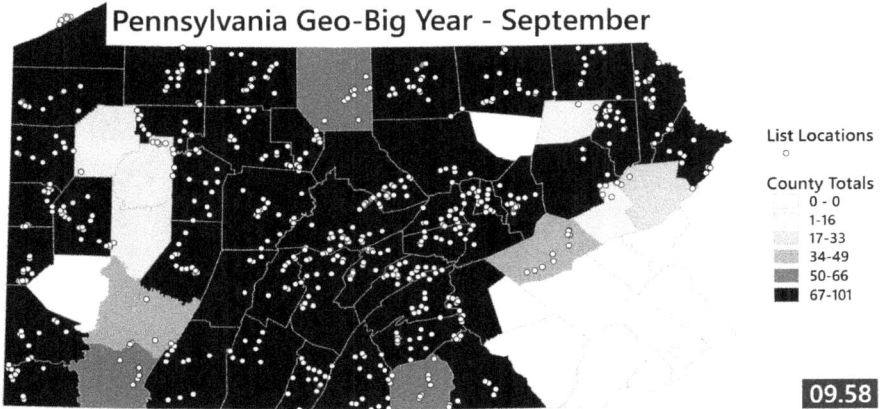

There were clearly major holes in parts of the map that I had hoped to complete by this point. These included six western counties (one of which, Allegheny County, had not been visited at all yet), the stubborn Potter County along the border with New York, a couple aditional northern counties I had not started (Sullivan and Wyoming), Adams County, which was not quite completed, and three counties on the fringe of the southeast that had been started and not finished. Plus, of course, there was the big block of unvisited counties in the southeast.

Things were not looking great, but not impossible. The bar chart generated to document the end of the 3rd Quarter looked a bit less discouraging than the map. It showed only 13 counties, 20%, that I had not at least visited (09.59).

The map more than the chart reflects my general strategy to reach the Geo-Big Year goal. A core part of the strategy was to do the northwest in spring during that migration (I did much of that), try to complete the southwest (not quite done), central (done), and northern/northeastern counties (a few holes left) by the end of the 3rd quarter, and then finish off the Southeast with the remaining months. My assumption on the southeast was that these would be the most practical counties late in the year – post-migration.

At this point, I was confident that I would bird in every county of the state during 2021. I was also reasonably confident that I could reach at least 50 in every county. But I was much less confident that I could still complete the full 67 x 67 quest. Facing the last quarter of the year, I needed to review my overall strategy as well as plan specific details for how to use the remaining bits of fall migration to best advantage.

Counties	09.59
Adams	
Allegheny	
Armstrong	
Beaver	
Bedford	
Berks	
Blair	
Bradford	
Bucks	
Butler	
Cambria	
Cameron	
Carbon	
Centre	
Chester	
Clarion	
Clearfield	
Clinton	
Columbia	
Crawford	
Cumberland	
Dauphin	
Delaware	
Elk	
Erie	
Fayette	
Forest	
Franklin	
Fulton	
Greene	
Huntingdon	
Indiana	
Jefferson	
Juniata	
Lackawanna	
Lancaster	
Lawrence	
Lebanon	
Lehigh	
Luzerne	
Lycoming	
McKean	
Mercer	
Mifflin	
Monroe	
Montgomery	
Montour	
Northampton	
Northumberland	
Perry	
Philadelphia	
Pike	
Potter	
Schuylkill	
Snyder	
Somerset	
Sullivan	
Susquehanna	
Tioga	
Union	
Venango	
Warren	
Washington	
Wayne	
Westmoreland	
Wyoming	
York	

Final Quarter
Winter is Coming (again)

Night coming on early
Birds discarding their colors
What was I thinking?

The first day of the 4th Quarter started with a non-bird blast from the past. I watched a video from my high school's 50th reunion. I did not manage to attend, due to COVID-19 concerns, even though the event was delayed a year because of the initial COVID-19 scare. Reunion organizer and classmate Nancy Leckrone-Kinsey sent the video link. Watching was fun. But it was a shock to see what 50+1 years have done – most folks looked like they were 69 years old!

While highlighting the good time had by folks who attended, the video had a somber part too, recognizing the 33 of 125 classmates who had passed on. Among these were two I had worked with painting and repairing greenhouses. It was my first job (starting at 15) that I did for 6 summers (working for my initial employer) before starting a similar summer business of my own that paid for my grad school.

I was particularly shocked to hear that David, in classes with me from grade school through high school and who I worked with on greenhouses during those early years had passed away at 67. His father and uncle co-owned the greenhouse painting, repair, and construction company I worked for. David was sometimes "foreman" of painting crews I worked on. I still remember the day that 3 friends and I were working on the roof of a greenhouse, listening to the radio, with David as foreman. "Take this Job and Shove It" came on. We turned the volume up, sang along, and did what the song said – making that our last day! Looking back, I feel (slightly) bad that we left David in the lurch that day. As could be expected, David and I lost touch. Based on his obituary, he inherited the business, expanded it, and also built a property management business. The latter was unsurprising. I think he bought his first rental unit the year we graduated from high school.

+++++

OCTOBER

Focusing back on birding as I started the 4th quarter, I was discouraged about my odds to complete the quest after the Potter County trip. But I was not ready to give up. I decided to try finishing off Adams County in the south, an isolated "gray" spot on my map, then focus west. Specifically, I was going to target Venango, Clarion, and Armstrong counties. I hoped (perhaps unrealistically) to complete the set in one 4-night trip. An obstacle was a prediction for rain.

The initial outing of the month began with a poor omen. My plan to head to Adams County on October 2 was set back a day due to effects from a COVID-19 Vaccine Booster shot leading to a poor night's sleep. I just couldn't get up in the morning and slept an extra hour and a half. Adams County would need to wait until October 3. I needed just 17 species there but would go prepared to spend a night if extra time was required.

+++

On October 3, I felt better and got an early start, 5:58am out the driveway. I headed to Long Pine Run Reservoir in western Adams County, arriving at 8:00am. I added 10 new species, including Pine Warbler, Black-throated Green Warbler, Tennessee Warbler, Nashville Warbler, Blue-headed Vireo, and a Yellow-rumped Warbler, the latter two below (10.01). At 60 species before 11:00am, I was on track to complete the county that day.

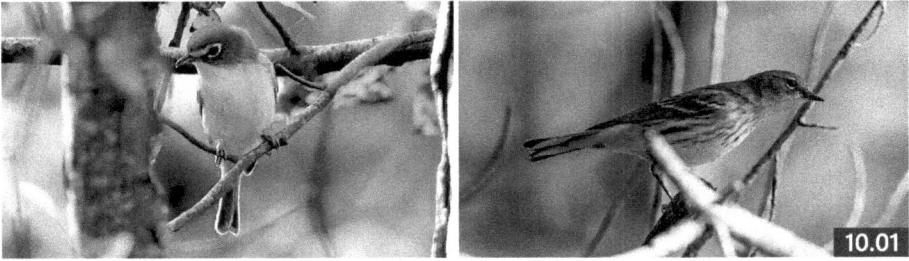

The highlight for the day was a small "pond" at a community park where shorebirds had been reported. I immediately found a Least Sandpiper that had been reported and a Lesser Yellowlegs (10.02-TL&TR). More surprising was a Pectoral Sandpiper and a Dowitcher, which I reported as Long-billed (10.02-BL&BR). I also had both Fish Crow and Savannah Sparrow, three of the latter.

Next, I moved on to the Gettysburg National Monument and got three woodpecker species, Red-headed Woodpecker, Red-bellied Woodpecker, and Yellow-bellied Sapsucker. I also picked up Cedar Waxwing. I had a productive day, reaching 70 species for the county.

+++

The next day at home, I spent time making progress on the sightings map for my quest. I figured out the syntax for color coding hotspot locations based on the quarter of the year in which the last visit happened. The online color map, then, will reflect the seasons I visited parts of the state. I then needed to figure out how to add ad-hoc (non-hotspot) locations from which I posted sightings. I was guessing that about a third of my eBird reports would be in this category. I opted for a different shaped symbol to depict the non-hotspot sites.

While home, I also followed up on my Long-billed Dowitcher ID. Distinguishing Long-billed Dowitcher from Short-billed Dowitcher is hard, and I am far from a Dowitcher expert. So, I sent my sighting (with description and about 10 photos) to multiple experienced birders I knew. A very active Central PA birder responded that my bird had plumage characteristics matching a Long-billed Dowitcher that he and a group identified in Mifflin County the previous month. But, a birding colleague in North Carolina (and Florida) leaned toward Short-billed Dowitcher, due to bill shape and some spotting on the throat that she pointed to. Still, based on the local input from those who had seen the Mifflin County bird, and matches with eBird description of that individual ("Tertials gray/black with narrow rusty edges. No buffy fringes seen as would be on SBDO"), I stuck with my ID and watched for any feedback from the eBird reviewer.

For my next trip, I kept with the plan to fill in some western Pennsylvania gaps, specifically Venango and Clarion Counties with a possible foray into Armstrong County if all were to go well. I had barely started each of these counties.

+++

On October 5, I got out of the driveway at 7:15am, as typical, slightly later than planned. You would think by now I would have learned to plan for "slightly later" … you would be wrong. It was another foggy morning, making the drive slow as well. These were poor signs for trip success. But I began the trip (despite the start time and fog) feeling better about my chances of achieving the quest after the successful day in Adams County.

I was hoping for some remaining warblers since it would be hard to finish the western counties without a few. But texts from birding friends on the Outer Banks in North Carolina showed that warbler numbers were up there, an indication that the peak had already passed in Pennsylvania. This news was unsurprising for the time of year; I had already started to notice the warbler decline on my last couple of trips. Still, one can always hope for stragglers.

The route to Clarion County took me past DuBois, PA. I always chuckle when the Google navigation assistant pronounces the name the French way, rather than as "Do Boys" like the locals.

My first planned stop was at the Clarion Loop Trail in Clarion County. I intended to bird Clarion County until about lunch time, then head to a site in Venango County halfway to my hotel destination in Franklin (the County seat). During the drive, the fog was thick enough to start the automatic wipers on my Toyota Venza. Unfortunately, wipers don't do much to clear away fog. Conditions slowed me down and it was 9:24am (and 59°F) when I started birding the trail. It was a nice, nearly 2-mile walk as depicted on the map at the trailhead (10.03-L), but the hour and three-quarters spent there yielded only 12 new species. Hazy conditions did not support good photos (10.03-R).

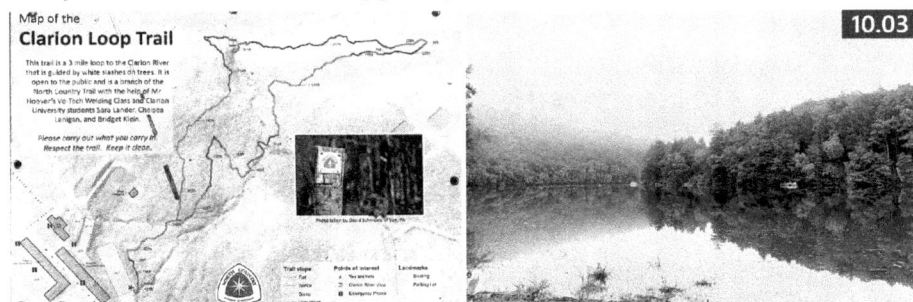

Because the morning had such a low yield, I decided to try another site or two in Clarion County before shifting to Venango. The one I spent the most time at was the Beaver Creek Nature Area. With about 1 mile of walking over a bit more than an hour, I added another dozen species, including Pied-billed Grebe (10.04-L) and Swamp Sparrow (10.04-R). I spent too much time trying to get photos of an odd Pied-billed Grebe with a very long bill (10.04-M). I had never seen one quite like it before.

I then headed for Kahle Lake, on the border of Clarion and Venango Counties. I started on the Clarion County side, adding 32 Killdeer (#34). I got most of them in one photo (10.05).

On the Venango side of the lake, I added 9 species, including a Red-bellied Woodpecker and a Red-tailed Hawk (10.06). I also saw some Killdeer (probably the same group that moved) plus Osprey.

I stopped at 2 more sites in Venango County, Sandy Creek Trail (10.07-L), an attractive place (10.07-M&R) where I added 7 species, then Samuel Justus Recreation Trail in-town where I added 3 more.

All-in-all, I had a lackluster day. I ended with 34 species in Clarion County (started at 9) and 26 species in Venango County (started at 7). The best find of the day was the Osprey seen from the Venango side of

Kahle Lake (based on eBird, it was the county's 2nd for that October). It was tempting to count it for both counties, of course, but I didn't. The most disappointing thing about the day was zero new warbler species.

+++

Slow progress continued the next day. I began at Two Mile Run County Park, Venango County, with heavy fog (again). The fog gradually lifted (10.08-L) and I added 17 species. But it took nearly 7 miles (mostly) walking over four and a half hours. Haze limited photos, the best was of a Yellow-bellied Sapsucker working a tree (10.08-R).

I visited three more sites in Venango County. First was Oil Creek State Park. My initial site there was Blood Farm, where I learned about the 1860s oil boom. Based on historical markers, the Blood family were poor and living in a run-down house when they struck it rich. The Ocean Petroleum Company bought their farm for $550,000 (over $8mil today). I found a pleasant spot for lunch along the creek (10.09-L) and then took a walk on the interpretive trail (10.09-R), but saw few birds with only 5 new species, the best of which was a Blackburnian Warbler.

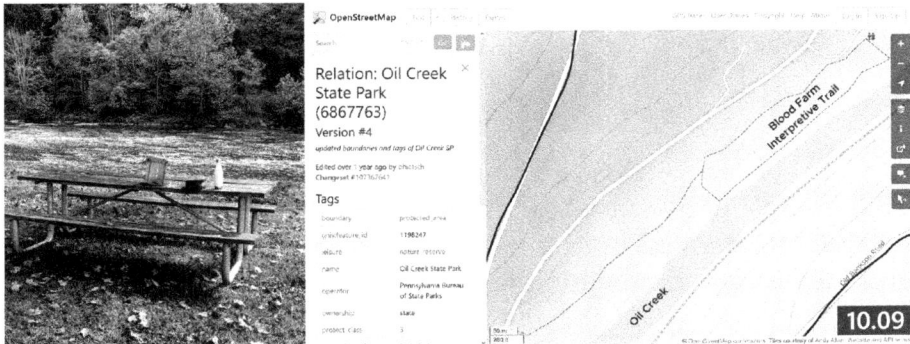

My next stop, Polk Wetland, netted zero new species. As the day slipped away, I picked one last site, the Kerr Tract – Fisherman's Cove where I had a bit of success with 5 new species that included Tennessee Warbler, Rose-breasted Grosbeak, and Blackpoll Warbler (10.10).

10.10

I ended the day with just 54 species in Venango County; finishing the county in just one more day would be tough.

+++

On the way back to the hotel, I passed through a small, covered bridge (10.11-L), one of many encountered during the year. The weather was pleasant, and the hotel restaurant (Liberty Street Ale House) had outside seating. I decided to chance it – if I could get a table outside. I got the last one. My scallop and shrimp dinner was good (10.11-M), but the view from the terrace left something to be desired (10.11-R).

10.11

I had booked 2 nights with the plan to pick another hotel for an additional night or two based on progress. Thus, I would check out of this hotel in the morning. It had been a long couple days to start the trip and I fell asleep listening to the Cardinals vs. Dodgers playoff game; just as well since I did not care who won.

+++

I was up early on October 7, getting to Kahle Lake at 5:05am. The first site was quiet, only adding a Carolina Wren for the county. I tried again at the Polk Wetlands (10.12-L) where I added 4 more in about an hour (Swamp Sparrow, Field Sparrow, Wood Duck and House Wren). I also added House Sparrow while traveling to the Kerr Tract – Fisherman's Cove for another try at a different time of day.

I was at 60 species at 8:00am. By 11:00am, after 3 eBird lists at the Kerr Tract, I had only reached 64 species – discouraging. I checked eBird for species I might find easily. Several that favor populated places were the most likely targets (including Mourning Dove and House Finch). That took me back into town to the Samuel Justice Recreation Trail (10.12-R) where I added both.

I was still 1 short. I returned to Two Mile Run County Park, hoping for a shorebird. It took me about 40 minutes, but I finally found one (10.13), a Green Heron that I watched catch a small fish and then swallow it (seen in the sequence of views below). This was the first county with my favorite bird as number 67!

+++

My initial plan to finish two counties on the trip and make a dent in a third was not going well. As October 7 ended, Venango County was completed, but I was at just 37 species in Clarion County. At mid-day, I tried to book a hotel for another two nights. I was surprised to find zero options. I grabbed a single night at the only hotel having one. I would not have expected a Clarion University football game to fill the hotels; I underestimated their fan base! The hotel I did find was perhaps the strangest I had stayed in. It looked like it was still under construction but was open. My guess was that they were in the process of converting from another brand. A plus was that rooms were extended stay rooms with a full-size refrigerator, not high-end but new.

Dinner was equally odd. I found a place for Mexican carry-out right next-door. It turned out to be inside a Motel 6, which looked deluxe compared to the place I was in. I had plenty of Mexican leftovers, and a fridge that could freeze my freezer packs for the cooler to take it with me to the next hotel or home.

+++

On October 8, sitting at 37 species, finishing Clarion County would be a challenge. My start did not help. It was 6:50am by the time I packed up, left the hotel, then reached my first stop.

The day proved to be a slow grind. I spent my first three hours at State Game Lands 63, walking about two miles. I only added 7 species, including Northern Cardinal, Field Sparrow, Golden-crowned Kinglet, and Ruby-crowned Kinglet (10.14).

I stopped to eat lunch along the roadside at the Curllsville Strips hotspot. It was unclear whether it was publicly accessible. So, I birded from the roadside. The only new species was Ring-necked Pheasant. I tried three additional sites and picked up only 2 more species, Eastern Phoebe and Northern Flicker.

The day's highlight was a non-bird sighting, a spectacular Halloween house (10.15). I texted the image to Fran; she thought it was a table-top sized display rather than an actual house!

10.15

I had not been able to find a hotel for the night. At 51 species, I could not finish Clarion County that day no matter how late I stayed. So, I cut out at 3:00pm and headed for home.

+++

I spent a couple days at home catching up on trip photos and non-birding things. I also thought about options for my next trip. Given the pace I had and the 51 species, it was unlikely I could finish Clarion County with a daytrip. The best plan seemed to be a multi-night trip, perhaps staying in Armstrong County just south of Clarion and trying to complete both counties. I decided to wait a bit on that while focusing on the southwest – Westmoreland, Allegheny, and Fayette.

That next trip seemed like a "make or break" trip. I booked a hotel in the eastern end of Allegheny County to start that county and also target adjacent Westmoreland County (with 34), and Fayette County (with 56). Armstrong County was also nearby. Doing all four on a four-night trip in October was the pipe dream. But I expected to finish Fayette and Westmoreland and hoped for Allegheny County as well.

+++

On October 11, I headed down the drive at 7:15am. I decided to make the first stop of the trip at Powdermill Nature Reserve in Westmoreland County. It was one of the first hotspots with recent sightings that was also along my planned route.

While enroute, I got a text from Fran saying that it was good that I didn't put our birdfeeders up before leaving. While she was making her breakfast, a bear showed up. It looked for the feeders, saw there were none, and moved on. It was the time of year where bears were trying to fatten up and bird feeders were at risk 24x7.

As I drove, the temperature hovered around 60°F, with fog. It was again wet enough (without rain) that the car's automatic wipers kept coming on. It would be a cool damp beginning of the trip.

I spent about 2 hours at the Powdermill Nature Reserve, walking two trails. I added 10 species. The best was a male Black-throated Blue Warbler, my only new warbler for the county that day (10.16-L). The only other decent photo for the site was a Killdeer (10.16-R). After lunch (during which nothing showed up) I made one more stop in Westmoreland County with no new species. At that point, I decided to see if I could finish off Fayette County in the afternoon.

My first Fayette County stop was Jacobs Creek Wetland. I walked 1.6 miles in an hour and a half; this effort yielded 6 new species (to reach 62 for the county). They included a nicely posed Great Egret and a Yellow-billed Cuckoo that I got a great flying photo of (10.17).

I picked up Double-crested Cormorant (#63) at Greenlick Run Lake, but found nothing else on the water (or out of it). I then birded "Duck Pond Rd." for about 30min. (Spotted Sandpiper and Least Sandpiper had been reported). I picked up Red-shouldered Hawk overhead plus both the Spotted Sandpiper (my standby as I approached a target) and Least Sandpiper (for numbers 64, 65 and 66, respectively).

It was after 4:00pm and I had not checked into my hotel, more than an hour away. With 1 to go, I tried Yough River Park, where Mallard were likely, a species I was oddly missing. I found some colorful art in the park —a creative land/seascape at the base of the bridge. My photo (here and color online) is included with permission of the artist, Brandi Bee (10.18-L). And, I had luck on Mallard – number 67 (10.18-R).

I checked into my hotel in Allegheny County and then headed to the nearby Churchill Valley Greenway. With a bit of daylight left, I was able to make a start on that county with 13 species.

+++

Overall, I had a good day. Birding in Westmoreland County was laborious. But I finished Fayette County and started Allegheny County. The Yellow-billed Cuckoo in Fayette County was the best find; looking back now, it was the last for the county for 2021 (eBird shows zero for Fayette County beyond the second week of October for any year).

I had some of Fran's chili relleno for dinner, so fixed that in my room while listening to playoff baseball. It was Boston against Tampa Bay. Neither is a favorite team, but since Chicago-Houston had been postponed, Atlanta had beaten Milwaukee earlier, and LA-San Francisco was late, it was the *only game in town*. Fran and I had picked Milwaukee to root for; all other teams in the playoffs had spoiled past seasons with playoff wins over Cleveland, Pittsburgh, or both. But Milwaukee had lost to Atlanta earlier in the day to fall behind in that series 1-2.

I decided to spend the next day focusing on Allegheny County, starting at 644-acre Frick Park in the heart of Pittsburgh. My hope for October 12, of course, was to have a productive enough day to complete the county before dark. As often was the case now that I was in the 4th quarter of the year, that was quixotic thinking.

+++

I arrived at Frick Park at 7:08am. I spent nearly 5 hours, walking several trails (4.4mi). It was a rather frustrating morning. The park is huge and I didn't know the best spot for warblers. One small group of probable warblers passed through, but I was in the valley, and they were in high trees. I couldn't identify any warblers, just Kinglets (both). For the morning, I had only 21 new species, to reach 34. I added only 2 warblers, Black-throated Green Warbler and Blackpoll Warbler. The latter is below (10.19-BL) along with (shown clockwise from top left) Red-tailed Hawk (flying), Common Grackle, Downy Woodpecker, Golden-crowned Kinglet, and Blue-headed Vireo (10.19).

From there, I drove to a hotspot that in eBird looked great, Imperial Grasslands. The already slow day got slower. There was ongoing construction everywhere. It was not clear how or where other birders had found birds. Almost everything looked like private commercial property. It was even more puzzling that birds would frequent the area.

I gave up quickly, adding just 3 species. I headed for Wingfield Pines Conservation Area, or at least tried to. The eBird directions took me to a point where I couldn't access or even see the site. So, I tried a nearby park, but directions to that did not work either. While still trying to find the second park, I noticed a sign for Wingfield Pines. I turned around and went back and finally found the entrance to the Conservation Area, shown on my photo of the map posted there (10.20). I walked about 3 miles on the trails there in a bit more than 2 hours.

10.20

I added 7 species. Nice additions included a Solitary Sandpiper, Yellow-rumped Warbler (several), and some Blue-winged Teal (10.21).

10.21

Going to the hotel about 6:00pm, I added Brown-headed Cowbird (#47). At one last stop, Duck Hollow along the river, I texted Fran: "Nothing like trying to move between birding locations during rush hour in a city :-(". I found nothing new and headed to the hotel.

+++

Back in my room I fixed dinner and listened to the Milwaukee-Atlanta baseball playoff game. The score went back and forth (2-0 Milwaukee, 2-2, 4-2, 4-4); in the end, Milwaukee lost again to exit the playoffs. Fran and I were left with no team to root for. Spring training seemed very far away.

The next day, my plan was to continue in Allegheny County, trying again to finish it off. I decided to start in a part of the county I had not yet visited, at Harrison Hills County Park in the northeast corner.

As I write this in spring, 2022, I now know that the Fern Hollow Bridge crossing Frick Park, which I walked under twice and drove across once that day in Allegheny County, collapsed about three months later (January 28, 2022). I'm happy I birded Pittsburgh when I did.

+++

October 13 began with reasonable weather. As planned, I went to the Harrison Hills County Park, a large park in the northeast of the county. It was a great place to bird. A couple hours into my time there, I ran into a local birder (Ron Burkert). It was nice to learn about the site and birds seen recently (and expected). Together we saw Palm Warbler and Lincoln's Sparrow. I birded the park until about 3:30pm. Overall, I added quite a few species but not enough. I also did not manage many good photos, the best for new species were of Field Sparrow, Eastern Bluebird, and Gray Catbird (10.22). The latter was number 60.

From the county park, I went to an Audubon preserve, another nice place to bird. It had good trails and diverse habitat. I saw about 20 species in an hour and a half, but only added 1, a Common Raven flyby. I ended the day and drove to the hotel at 61, thus I needed 6 more.

+++

It had been a nice day to be out, and great to meet a local birder. Given the pandemic, opportunities to talk with anyone were few and far between. While birding solo can be fun, it is also fun to share info with and to learn from local birders when in unfamiliar places.

While the day was enjoyable for talking and walking, it was disappointing for birds seen. I had again come up short in the county. Many species remained possible, but most were scarce. Based on recent eBird reports, no single site looked particularly promising. I picked North Park for the next day. It had the most target species in prior Octobers, but only a subset in this week of October. Still, it included several water areas, adding to the odds of less common species showing up.

+++

I arrived at North Park Lake (at North Park) at 7:15am. I started to second guess my site choice, since it seemed busy and noisy with walkers, joggers, bikers, and dogs (plus traffic on roads that surrounded the lake). But, going for a site with water paid off with 3 new species. The first was a big surprise, a Green Heron. Checking as I write this; my Green Heron was the only one in the county for October 2021. I also got 2 expected species, Canada Goose and Double-crested Cormorant. Lighting was poor, but I did manage photos of all three (10.23).

10.23

Next, I headed for a grassland site in the park with various warblers reported the day before. I spent a bit over 2 hours on a loop walk of about 1.3 miles. It was a nice site, as seen in a view down the trail (10.24-L), paired with the sunrise seen earlier from North Park Lake (10.24-R).

10.24

On my walk I first saw Tennessee Warbler, then a Magnolia Warbler (10.25-L), the latter flagged in eBird as rare. After the initial flurry, I was at 65 species, thus 2 to go. I had a dry spell but finally encountered sparrows moving in the brush. I scanned for a White-crowned Sparrow and ultimately saw one but did not manage a good photo. There were also warblers flitting around. I got a Tennessee Warbler photo (10.25-M), and then found number 67, Cape May Warbler (10.25-R).

10.25

Having finished Allegheny County (finally!) before noon, I headed to Westmoreland County. The route took me through a corner of Armstrong County where I stopped at a community park for lunch. I saw 8 species (7 new), putting my Armstrong County list at 10. Since none were unusual, it was probably poor strategy to take the time there.

As I left Armstrong County, in keeping with a *geo*-birding quest, I entered Butler County and took a bridge over the Allegheny River. Part way across, a sign said I was entering Allegheny County. Before the end of the bridge another sign said I had entered Westmoreland County! When I texted Fran about this 3-county bridge, she suggested I count anything seen in all three counties :-) – but I saw no birds. Even if I had, my practice for the year was to count birds in the county I saw them from, even if the bird might be in another county.

Once in Westmoreland County, I drove to Northmoreland Park and picked up Belted Kingfisher, Great Blue Heron, and Pied-billed Grebe. I then spent an hour in the J.H. Walter Nature Reserve. Mid-afternoon is not a great time for a mostly forested site, and I added only 3 species.

My last stop of the day was Mammoth Lake. A 1 hour, 1.3 mile walk added Yellow-rumped Warbler and Palm Warbler plus Wilson's Snipe and Mute Swan; the latter two were cooperatively photogenic (10.26).

I finished the day with Allegheny County done, 54 species in Westmoreland County, and 10 species in Armstrong County. The goal for the next day was to finish Westmoreland County before heading for home. That was going to be tough.

+++

I began my trip's last day at the Otto & Magdalene Ackermann Nature Preserve with a Barred Owl calling. I spent 3 hours there and walked nearly two miles (slowly trying to locate birds I heard calling).

It was an interesting Preserve, with varied habitat, good trails, and nice views, both within and beyond the trees (10.27-L&R).

The preserve also had historical displays with maps, images, and text recounting the extractive industry (including Andrew Carnegie's coke furnaces) that once dominated what is now mature forest. One display included a piece of the map section below, from Beer's 1867 Atlas of Westmoreland County (10.28). The stone quarry, indicated with label, arrow, and outline, supported railroad construction.

In a bit over 3 hours with about 2 miles of walking, I added only 6 species. But, there were a few good ones, including Blackpoll Warbler, Winter Wren, and Magnolia Warbler (10.29).

I left the preserve at 10:30am, with 60 species for the county. The target of 67 seemed within reach. But nearly two hours at Donegal Lake netted zero new species. From there, I birded a stretch of rural road where I picked up Eastern Bluebird and Field Sparrow to reach 62 by about 2:40pm. I consulted eBird's Explore tool. The most promising site was Trout Run Reservoir. But it took 45min. to get there and I added only American Black Duck and Common Raven (reaching 64 species).

It was 3:45pm and I was facing a 2-hour drive home. I opted for one last site, Tubmill Reservoir. There, I found Wood Duck on the water (#65), but it was quiet beyond that. If this was the last western county left, I would have continued until dark if necessary to try for the final 2. But, since I needed to return to Armstrong County just north, plus Clarion County north of that, I decided to head home and get the last two on a follow up trip.

+++

On Saturday, October 16, at home, I caught up on things after the trip and worked on a plan for the next week. I had a Dentist appointment on Monday and an Optometrist appointment on Wednesday. So, I decided on day trips for Sunday and Tuesday, to Potter County and Lancaster County, respectively. Both were marginally practical for day trips (< 2 hours to the closest site).

On the day trips, I knew I'd be thinking about things other than birds. I had received surprising news that could have implications for both finishing my quest and the Christmas bird counts I hoped to do in Dare County, NC at the end of the year. An email arrived from the International Cartographic Association (ICA) telling me that I was selected to receive the Carl Mannerfelt Gold Medal! This is an award with only 13 prior recipients since 1979.

It was particularly humbling to be among such a small group. The most recent prior recipient was Fraser Taylor from Canada, President of the ICA from 1987-1995 and a mentor within the ICA early in my career. Two other past recipients with major impacts on my own research were Arthur Robinson from the U.S. (a leading twentieth century cartographic research scholar) and Jaques Bertin from France (a cartographer / graphic theorist whose theoretical ideas were influential in cartography, information graphics, and visualization more broadly). I met Robinson briefly only once but read virtually all his published work. I almost met Bertin in 1999 when he received the Gold Medal. But I speak no French, so did not try to introduce myself. After Bertin's passing, I participated in an ICA Conference session honoring him and wrote a paper about impacts of his writing (my 2nd on his work).

The news meant I needed to reconsider my decision to skip the up-coming ICA Conference in Florence, Italy in December. While I had attended all but two ICA Conferences (held every other year) since my first in 1989, I had planned to skip this one due to COVID-19 risk plus my Geo-Big Year quest. If I opted to receive the award in person, that meant travel to Italy for a week in early December. In addition to COVID-19 worries and my birding quest, the dates overlapped with the Kitty Hawk Christmas Bird Count (a count I had done for several years). So, this news gave me a lot to think about – in addition to birds.

+++

I pulled out of the garage heading to Potter County at 6:30am on the dot. That was one of the earliest starts I'd managed for a day trip. Potter County had been my hardest county with almost no eBird posts to help. Only two sites had reports in the prior week, with just 4 species seen that I needed. On the positive side, the eBird "Target Species" list had 68 species I needed that were reported (at least once) during some prior October. Thus, there was a lot to be on the lookout for.

I headed to Ole Bull State Park where I had ended my September outing with 50 species. I anticipated species in the morning that were not active on my last visit late in the afternoon. I arrived about 8:30am and walked a loop trail (about 1.4mi). It was cold and wet. I had not dressed for that and my fingers nearly froze. Despite good habitat, I neither saw nor heard many birds in the first half of the walk. At one point, the Merlin audio app indicated Winter Wren. But I did not hear it and pishing drew nothing out; so, I struck out on that one. By the end of the walk, my eBird list totaled just 17 species and only 6 were new (thus I was at 56).

The best part of the walk was coming upon a large group of very active sparrows on the edge of a marshy area; they included Swamp Sparrow, White-crowned Sparrow, and Fox Sparrow. I did not manage good photos of the sparrows but did take one landscape image looking across the marsh (10.30); the color version highlights great fall colors on the ridge in the background.

Next, I drove to Galeton Lake (in Galeton) hoping for water birds I was still missing. There were few birds there, but I did add American Black Duck and Pied-billed Grebe (#57 and #58). From there, I moved to Lyman Run State Park. The real surprise (and the only new species in 2 hours) was a Common Loon (10.31-L). That species was not on the list of 68 target species seen previously in the county in October.

It had been raining off-and-on all day, but it was only about 1:30pm, so I kept at it. I walked a rural road along a stream, where I added Tufted Titmouse (10.31-M). It rained more heavily, so a bit after 3:00pm I started for home. On the way I saw a Bald Eagle and managed an impressionistic-like photo in the rain (10.31-R).

Potter County continued to be hard. Not only did I miss the target on my day trip, but I was unable to even break 60. I was not very confident of reaching 67 with another day trip.

+++

Following an uneventful dentist appointment (fortunately), my next day trip would be different. I was heading to Lancaster County, unvisited to that point. So, all species I saw would be new. I planned to focus on parts of the county closest to home, then try to finish on an overnight trip to a nearby county.

While planning my next outings, I continued to debate (with myself) what to do about the ICA award. From a professional perspective, I felt an obligation to attend the conference to accept the award in person. Plus, the conference had been important throughout my career, providing the chance to hear about the latest research and catch up with colleagues and former students. On the other hand, some colleagues who I have interacted with over the years might skip the conference due to their own age, retirement, and/or COVID-19 concerns. A story in the news made the COVID-19 concern even more real – former Secretary of State for the U.S., Colin Powell, died from COVID-19 complications even though he was vaccinated (most likely due to his reduced immune system due to cancer). I would be continuing to weigh the pros and cons of travel to Florence as I continued with the quest.

+++

On the morning of October 19, I headed to Conewago Recreation Trail and Wetlands as my initial stop in Lancaster County. I was almost fooled by two Mallard decoys, but the live birds I saw were great. There were many Tree Swallows and I also picked up Palm Warbler and Yellow-rumped Warbler. The best bird at the site was a Rose-breasted Grosbeak. I got 37 species before 11:00am. The lighting was not great early, so my only good photos were of an adult male White-throated Sparrow, slightly hidden in a bush, a Swamp Sparrow on a tree limb, and a male Red-winged Blackbird calling (10.32).

Moving between sites I saw a Northern Harrier, then spent an hour and a half at Lake Grubb Nature Park. I added only 4 species, but got good photos, including a Blue-headed Vireo perched photogenically, a Belted Kingfisher monitoring from a stump, a Carolina Chickadee chowing down on berries, a Turkey Vulture drying its wings, a Hairy Woodpecker upside down on a snag tree showing off the shape of the white area on the sides of its neck along with the unspotted white tail feathers, and an American Robin taking a bath (10.33).

Next, I headed to Chickies Rock County Park, arriving about 2:30pm. I was hoping for raptors, but instead saw Double-crested Cormorant and Ring-billed Gull from the cliff overlooking the river. I also picked up a Red-eyed Vireo when walking to the viewpoint. I moved on to a riverfront park where I added only Black Vulture. Before heading home, I picked up Bald Eagle for number 47 – not too bad for an October day trip starting at zero.

+++

For my next outing, I planned a 2-night trip to Schuylkill, Berks, and Carbon Counties, starting with Hawk Mountain, where I had never been. Raptors (and other species) were still being reported there. Hawk Mountain has a site in two counties, so I would have a chance to add to my 44 species in Schuylkill as well as to make a start on Berks County.

In the subsequent week, I planned to head back west to tackle remaining holes in the map. I had three uncompleted western counties, Westmoreland (with 65), Armstrong (with just 10), and Clarion (with 50). Clarion looked like it would be particularly hard, based on the last day I had there. I had spent most of a day adding only 14 species. To have a chance to complete all three counties, I intended to book 3 nights and then, potentially, add a 4th if needed. Failing to complete all three counties in a 4-night trip might be a signal that my quest was out of reach.

+++

On October 21, I headed toward Hawk Mountain at 7:15am. The preserve was about 2.5 hours from home. Starting a bit late was not likely to be a problem for hawks but arriving around 10:00am meant that I'd likely miss some other late migrants.

The drive highlighted issues I had with my new glasses. They were sharper than my previous ones when looking straight ahead. But the periphery was fuzzier. This was problematic when driving and when birding. I was still hoping that the issue was, at least in part, a matter of adjustment, both in position of the glasses on my face and in the angle that I hold my head. I intended to try the new glasses on this trip to see what happens when I bird with them. I did bring the old ones along as a backup plan.

By the time I arrived at Hawk Mountain, paid my entrance fee, and started the trail to the North site, it was nearly 10:00am. The trail to the North Lookout in Schuylkill County goes through a bit of Berks County, and I got my list for that county started with White-breasted Nuthatch and Hairy Woodpecker. Trudging up the trail was a bit of work as a sequence of three views shows (10.34).

Once up the steps, the vantage point is worth it, and it is obvious why this is one of the top hawk-watch sites in the U.S. I spent about 2 hours at the North Lookout along with many other birders (10.35), which included a couple of staff from the sanctuary, and then I came back for 1.5 hours after lunch.

I added 12 species, reaching 56. These included Red-tailed Hawk, Sharp-shinned Hawk, Black Vulture, Northern Harrier, American Kestrel, and Bald Eagle (10.36), plus a Merlin and Common Raven.

Between trips to and from the North Lookout, I spent an hour at the South Lookout (in Berks County). I saw 16 species for that list. These included Sharp-shinned Hawk, Turkey Vulture, Common Raven, Red-tailed Hawk, Bald Eagle, Cooper's Hawk, Northern Harrier, and Black Vulture. The only decent bird photo was a Black Vulture that landed on the rocks just below where I was standing with one of the official counters (10.37). Nearby, there were interesting informational signs about Hawk Mountain and its history.

It was about 5:00pm and starting to get dark, so I hurried down the trail to the car. Enroute to the hotel, I stopped at Landingville Dam and Marsh, but added only White-throated Sparrow.

+++

Friday morning I went back to Landingville Dam and Marsh. It was a good choice. I added Greater Yellowlegs, Swamp Sparrow, Winter Wren, and Rusty Blackbird (the latter a surprise). I was at 65 species, 2 short. I then tried Tuscarora State Park where I found a Ring-necked Pheasant, then Yellow-rumped Warbler, number 67 (10.38-L), along with a Pileated Woodpecker – not new but a nice photo (10.38-R).

I ate my lunch in the park and then searched for the Fish Crows reported that morning. There were none near the lake. But back at the Park Office, I finally heard a Fish Crow call a couple of times (#68).

After completing Schuylkill County about 12:30pm, I had to choose between Carbon County (with 15) and Berks County (with 16). I decided on Carbon County as part of a strategy to work from north and west toward the southeast corner of the state. I went to the most birded state park, Beltsville. At first, I saw nothing. But then I got a cluster of mixed birds including Brown Creeper (10.39-L). Next, I found a group with Kinglets, Sparrows, a Blue-headed Vireo (10.39-M), and a Palm Warbler. Other additions were Belted Kingfisher (10.39-R) and Northern Harrier.

I then went to another site where I picked up 5 more species including a Pied- billed Grebe to reach 40 species at the day's end.

+++

For the last day of the trip, I continued in Carbon County. I was checked out early but Beltzville State Park (my first site) was an hour away. It was nearly 7:30am when I got started. I spent the whole day there except for a brief mid-day foray to Penn Forest Reservoir (where I added zero). I generated 5 lists in the park and walked 5.8 miles. First, I found Canada Goose and a couple of Wood Duck. I should have scoped the many Canada Geese; another birder posted a Cackling Goose – they got a Lesser Scaup as well. Nearly 8 hours of birding netted me only 13 new species, including a Dark-eyed Junco, a Lincoln's Sparrow, and a White-crowned Sparrow (10.40). At 3:15pm, I headed for home.

+++

With days ticking by quickly, I spent one day at home organizing my next outing. I also pondered the potential trip to the ICA Conference. In many ways I wanted to go. Being retired, I would attend fewer conferences, thus have fewer chances to catch up with everyone. Plus, receiving the Gold Medal was a real honor. That said, there were several negatives to weigh against the positives, most important was concern about COVID-19 risk, a risk that even health scientists could not estimate confidently. I needed to decide soon – but did not do so then.

What I did decide on was the next birding trip destination. I opted to try completing the western counties – again. I booked a 3-night trip focused on Westmoreland County, Armstrong County, and Clarion County. I expected to finish Westmoreland quickly since I needed only 2 species. But I anticipated Clarion County (with 50), would be a challenge and thought Armstrong County (with just 10 species) would be as well. I just hoped for the best.

The plan for the initial trip day was to start at Keystone Lake in Armstrong County. In Westmoreland County, the migrating waterfowl were being reported in the afternoon. So, I intended to focus on Armstrong County through lunch and then head to Westmoreland County for my final 2 species there.

+++

I got started at Keystone Lake about 9:00am and made multiple stops around the north end of the lake between then and 12:30pm. It was a pleasant morning and view (10.41), but birds were rather scarce.

10.41

At my first stop, I picked up a Double-crested Cormorant, my only one for the county. Access points to the water were hard to find. I eventually found a trail (of a sort) that got me to a mud flat. I had success there with Golden-crowned Kinglet, Ruby-crowned Kinglet, Greater Yellowlegs, and a Red-tailed Hawk flying overhead (10.42). Overall, I added 17 species to reach 27 in the county – leaving a long way to go.

10.42

Despite the slow start on Armstrong County, I stuck to my plan to go to Westmoreland County in the afternoon for the 2 species I needed to finish it off. I went to Trout Run Reservoir, since multiple species I needed had been reported there.

It took longer than expected to get to the reservoir (over an hour). But it proved to be a great choice. I got my 2 species quickly, 22 Ring-necked Duck and 1 Hooded Merganser (10.43) plus 4 additional species, including a Greater Yellowlegs (too far to visually separate from Lesser, but it called when flying). On the way back to Armstrong County, I added a Rock Pigeon for a total of 72 for Westmoreland County.

Back in Armstrong County, I tried Crooked Creek Lake. In an hour, at two sites, I added 6 species. That put me just past half-way at 34 species. I tried one last site for the day, the Rosston Boat Launch on the Allegheny River. While I got a nice landscape photo in the early evening (10.44), birds were scarce, and I added zero new species.

+++

I opted to focus on Clarion County on October 26. I had a better chance to finish it than Armstrong County (51 vs. 34 species). As typical (except during the peak of migration) once I hit 50 species, progress was slow. Before lunch I added just 4 species, but they included Bald Eagle (adult pair), a group of Wild Turkey, and an American Kestrel.

I went to a game lands that looked promising. But there was one hunter there when I arrived, and another showed up. So, I decided not to walk around. The second hunter asked how the hunting was. I told him I was birdwatching, not hunting. He seemed to find that interesting and asked if I was looking for Snowy Owl. He said he had seen multiple Snowy Owls up on the hill, multiple years in a row, and that they had helped locate birds he was hunting (Pheasant and Grouse, I guessed). I doubted his Owl ID but did not say so – he was, after all, carrying a gun. There are few records (in eBird) of Snowy Owls in Pennsylvania as early as October and none west of Centre County.

After the game lands, I tried a small reserve (Beaver Creek Nature Area) with a bunch of ponds. I was hoping for migrating waterfowl. While eBird showed only spring, not fall, records, I gambled that lack of fall records resulted from too few birders rather than birds. The gamble did not pay off. I saw only Belted Kingfisher, Canada Goose, and Pied-billed Grebe, none were new.

From there I went to the one lake in the county (Kahle Lake). The weather was terrible, windy with rain that varied between light and heavy. But there were birds, including multiple waterfowl species. Plus, I flushed an American Pipit. I eventually left with 61 species.

I returned to the Game Lands (with hunters long gone), hoping to see raptors. The hunter I met mentioned several as regular. I was rewarded with a Cooper's Hawk. I also picked up Pine Siskin. I was at 63 species for Clarion County at that point, thus 4 to go.

On my way to the hotel in Armstrong County, after I was across the county border, I saw a bunch of Wild Turkey. I added that species to my Armstrong County list, reaching 35.

+++

On October 27, my first goal was to finish Clarion County. I decided to start at the Redbank Creek Park in New Bethlehem. Common Merganser had been reported a week earlier and I hoped they had not moved on yet. I got up early and arrived before dawn. I saw something with my binoculars coming toward me on the river that I thought could be a Common Merganser. It was hard to see, so I walked a bit closer and almost missed several of them, barely visible on the water. It was still before sunrise. I dialed the camera down to a 40th of a second to get a photo. It was still under exposed – but some editing made the ID clear, 13 Common Merganser. Most moved out of sight, but one stuck around and 10 minutes later I got a better photo (10.45-L).

I then decided to look for Green-winged Teal, so kept walking along the river. I was surprised by a Double-crested Cormorant (10.45-R).

That got me within 2. I kept looking and was hearing a variety of calls. One turned out to be a Winter Wren (#66).

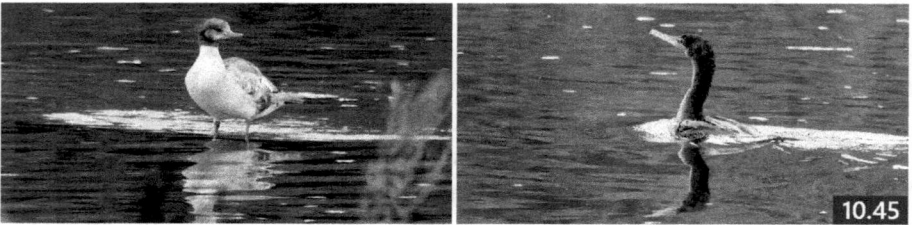

The Merlin App indicated Purple Finch. But I didn't hear it and couldn't find any, so did not report that. I did hear a call, once, that sounded like Evening Grosbeak. It would have been a great find, but I could not locate one, and was not certain, so did not report it either.

The final bird I got was a lone Green-winged Teal (#67), a female. I heard its soft "quack" call (like #4 in iBird Pro), clearly a Green-winged Teal rather than Blue-winged Teal (which would have been much less likely). I then saw it take off, further confirming it was a Teal.

It was 9:30am and I headed back to Armstrong County. First, I tried Armstrong Trail (North of Dam 8). I was quite surprised to find a group of Red-breasted Merganser (10.46-L). Checking eBird, they had been reported only once previously for the county in October (in 2009). These were also the first of the fall in Pennsylvania outside of Presque Isle in Erie County (eBird later showed them in Franklin County and Montgomery County that same day). I also found Wood Duck (10.46-R), Common Merganser, and three non-water species.

With three more stops (noon-5:00pm), I added 7 more species. That put me at only 48 species for Armstrong County.

+++

It would be a challenge to finish Armstrong County the next day before starting for home. I picked up Chinese carry-out for dinner. The "fortune" was interesting (10.47). I sent Fran the photo and added "the day didn't bring me enough birds, not sure what I gave the day."

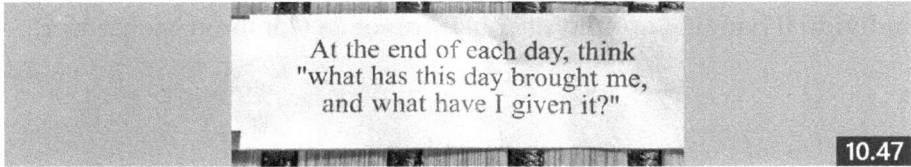

At the end of each day, think "what has this day brought me, and what have I given it?"

10.47

That evening, I sent the following text to Fran: *I've been looking over what's possible to see. Things look pretty grim. For example, number eight on the eBird Target list is Common Loon and there hasn't been one seen in the county in October since 2019. Part of it is lack of birders here. But it is also the time of year. The most likely species are relatively rare waterfowl that stop in for a day on a lake or pond or river, and then disappear. ... If I should succeed in reaching the 60s by 3:00pm, I'll probably book another night and try to finish. But that's not terribly likely. If I don't get that far I think I'll give up on the county, at least for now, and head home at that point.*

+++

I returned to Armstrong Trail – North of Dam 8 the next morning at 7:00am in the semi-dark (10.48-L), hoping for owls (Eastern Screech-Owl had been reported) but I had no luck. In 3 hours on the trail, shown on the map (10.48-M), I netted only 5 new species. These included a Brown Creeper and a Dark-eyed Junco (10.48-TR&BR) along with Common Grackle, Swamp Sparrow, and Yellow-bellied Sapsucker.

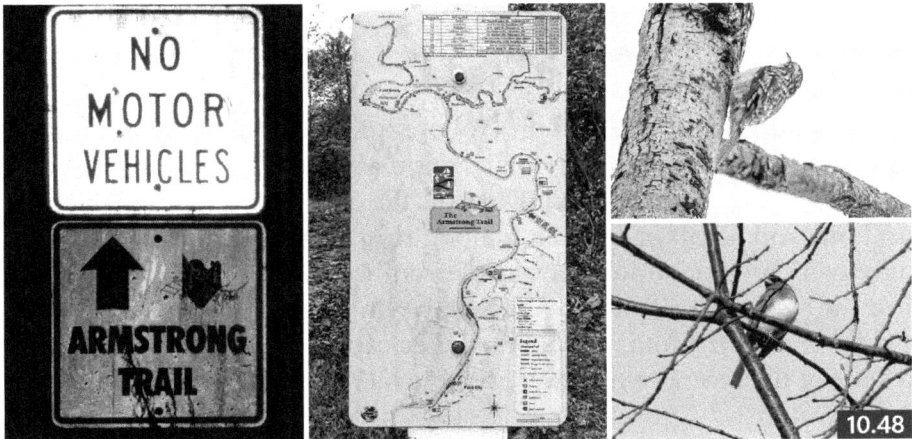

NO MOTOR VEHICLES

ARMSTRONG TRAIL

10.48

From there I moved to Keystone Lake (again), checking the mudflat (10.49-L) where I found a young buck (10.49-R) but few birds. In 50 min. I recorded only 11 species. One was new, Ring-necked Duck, a single individual hanging around near a group of 28 Common Merganser.

10.49

I then tried some nearby back roads. It was interesting to find multiple with "reefer" in the name. Reefer Hollow Rd. shown here (10.50) was not far from Reefer Cove Rd. I wondered whether the reference was to smoking *reefers* ... or to "one who reefs" (reducing sail area on a sailboat). Since I saw no sign of sailboats, and the only boats were for fishing, I'm guessing the former.

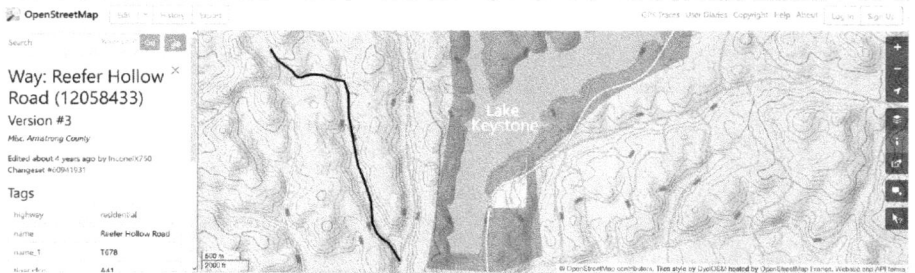

I did add a House Finch on Hollow Rd. (in the tiny community of Atwood – founded 1884, having its population peak of 191 in 1910, and dipping to 107 people today). That was the only new species with about an hour and a half of searching along rural roads. At that point, I was at only 55 species, so stuck to my plan and headed home. I would monitor the county in eBird in case enough winter waterfowl showed up to push me over the total. Keystone Lake is about 2 hours from home, so a spur of the moment trip was possible if enough species showed up.

+++

I spent two days at home, catching up on non-birding things, processing photos, and revising strategy. With October about to end, I was behind schedule. Recent outings brought home how quickly Pennsylvania species variety decreases as fall recedes. If I were to go to Italy for the ICA conference (I had not yet decided), my last possible birding day was December 14. If I opted not to travel to Italy, but do Christmas Bird Counts in Dare County, NC, my last possible day in Pennsylvania was December 17 (unless I did a trip back to PA between counts).

The next two weeks would be critical. My odds were not good, so I considered what to do if I ran out of time. A minimum target was birding in every county. But an intermediate target of 50 species in each county seemed doable. I started to consider that fallback option.

With all that in mind, I decided on a day trip for the final day in October. I opted for Lebanon County (with 4 species) and Lancaster County (with 47 species). A lot of good birds were seen in Lebanon County over the previous couple days. These included a Lesser Black-backed Gull, and several other water birds. There was also a Trumpeter Swan in adjacent Lancaster County about a week earlier, so I would be on the lookout for that.

+++

With my dwindling time in mind, I pulled out of the drive on October 31 at 6:09am; it was 54°F and raining. The forecast said rain would end by mid-morning. My plan was to spend most of the day in Lebanon County, but also try the most active site in Lancaster County, which was not much out of the way.

I had a good start to the day. I arrived at Memorial Lake a bit before 8:00am and spent about 2 ¾ hours around the lake. I left with 34 species in the county, including Downy Woodpecker, Dark-eyed Junco, Field Sparrow, and Northern Cardinal (10.51).

On, in, or flying over the water I also added Great Blue Heron, Pied-billed Grebe, Mallard, Double-crested Cormorant, Ring-necked Duck, Canada Goose, and a single Cackling Goose.

I next tried Middle Creek Wildlife Management Area (WMA) just into Lancaster County. By 2:00pm I had generated 5 lists in and around the WMA, netting 8 new species (reaching 55); among these were Northern Shoveler, American Black Duck, and Great Egret (10.52).

10.52

Returning to Lebanon County, I saw a sign for Calico Quilter's Inn. It turned out to be a place that hosts overnight quilting retreats. I sent Fran texts with a couple photos (10.53) because her work as a fabric artist usually results in quilted art.

10.53

I generated 4 more lists in Lebanon County that afternoon, yielding 11 new species, reaching 45 in the county. The best stops were roadside viewing of farm ponds with Green-winged Teal, Northern Pintail, and Northern Shoveler and some flooded farm fields with Least Sandpiper, Greater Yellowlegs, and Lesser Yellowlegs.

+++

October was finished, so it was time to check my map again (10.54). On the plus side, in 83% of the year I had visited 89% of the counties. On the minus side, I had completed just 76% of the counties. The western part of the state had been nearly completed, but I remained short in one western and one northern tier county. The eastern half of the state was where most of the gaps remained.

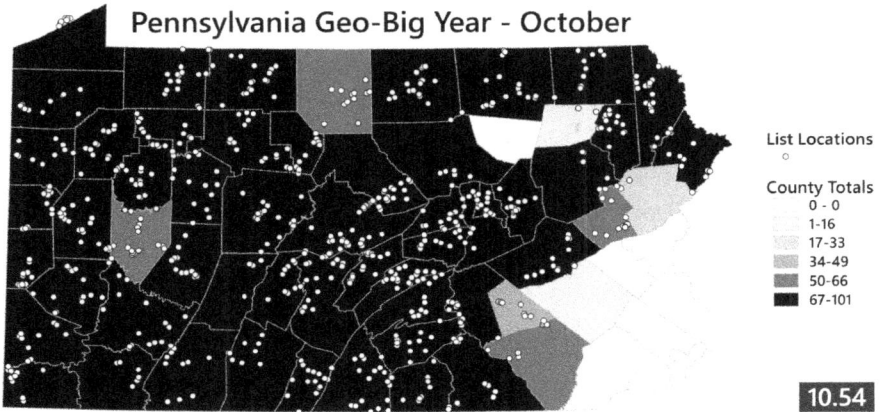

Pennsylvania Geo-Big Year - October

List Locations
County Totals
0 - 0
1-16
17-33
34-49
50-66
67-101

10.54

I was particularly worried about the two northern counties, Sullivan County (unvisited) and Wyoming County (with just 2 species). They are mostly rural, with few birders using eBird, and are likely to have fewer species at this time of year. With that in mind, I decided that my first trip for November would be to these two counties.

Beyond trip planning, I had multiple decisions to make or follow up on. One decision already made was that Fran and I would start our Social Security payments in January. I needed to call the local office sometime in the next week ... between trips ... to figure out the necessary steps. More directly related to my quest, I continued to wrestle with the decision about the ICA Conference in Italy. The pros and cons remained the same, but I still could not decide. The biggest factor continued to be COVID-19 risk. The most recent report, for the last week of October, indicated that one third of hospital admissions by COVID-19 patients locally had been vaccinated individuals. Thus, as time was running out to decide about booking a flight, the risk was clearly real, and I continued to find the decision to be a dilemma.

+++

Back to birding preparation for my first November trip, I read a great story about six guys on a quest to see 200 bird species in Connecticut on a single day in May. They followed the World Series of Birding rules that at least 95% of the species reported had to be identified by the full team. One thing that really struck me was the preparation they put into scouting sites ahead of time. It enabled them to predict the species possible at specific places and times (down to minutes) on their count day. I also noted their attention to pre-dawn and post-sunset birding. Particularly the number of pre-dawn species found was amazing.

A problem with following their strategies is that I was birding counties I had never been to. So, I could not scout ahead. Plus, birds call less in November or December than in May. Even if they did call, I don't have the bird call expertise that the guys in the story had.

+++++

NOVEMBER

On November 2, I headed off at 6:21am and 46°F, not bad ... for November. It was 66 miles on country roads to my first site, so it was 8:15am when I started a list at the Deer Lake/Loyalsock Rd. hotspot on Loyalsock Trail in Sullivan County — note Deer Lake (SW - dark highlight) and Hunter's Lake (NE) on OSM map below (11.01).

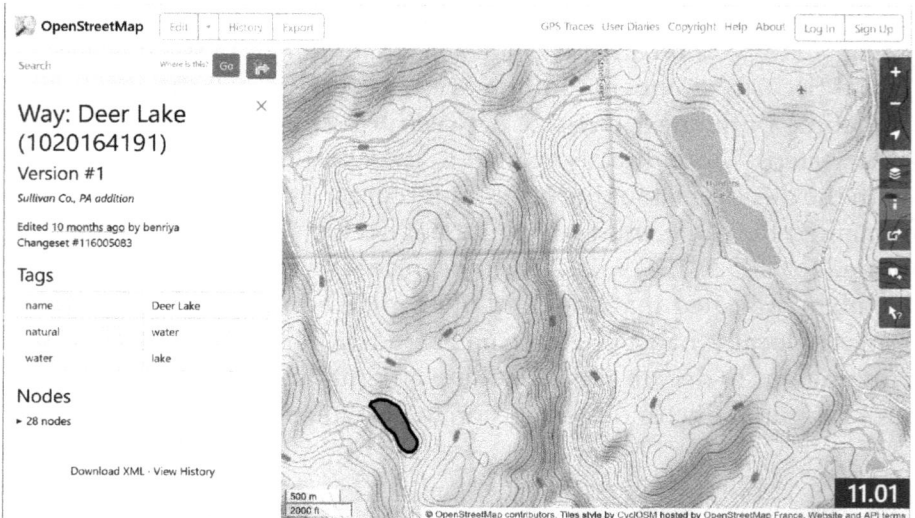

The day started slowly. I gradually picked up species, but birds were scarce. By 11:00am, after moving to Hunter's Lake, I had 24 species, including Pied-billed Grebe and Eastern Towhee (11.02).

The slow start was bad enough, but as I wrote this section in May, 2022, I realized my eBird Lesser Scaup photos were actually of Ring-necked Duck. For some reason, the eBird review did not prompt me about this, but also did not accept the report (no Lesser Scaup are listed for Sullivan County in November 2021). I fixed this error belatedly, which dropped my total for Sullivan County at the time to 23.

The slow day got slower. I added only 4 species by 2:00pm. This included zero for a stop at a State Park … the park name was prognostic about birds, but the landscape was impressive (11.03).

Given sparseness of birds, I paused to find *The Pavilion at the Park*, my accommodations, arriving at 2:30pm. It was tricky to figure out how to get in. All staff were apparently off helping with election day, manning the polls (Fran and I had voted earlier by mail). Everything about checking in was done via text. They sent me an access code that got me into the cottage. Since they had few guests, I was upgraded to a cottage with full kitchen, which looked great (11.04).

I went out to another site but saw only 5 individual birds, of 4 species: Ring-neck Duck (a pair of them), a Common Raven calling, an American Woodcock that I flushed, and an American Robin. At first, I thought I added 3 species in Sullivan County (all but the Robin). With the Lesser Scaup mistake mentioned above, that would have dropped to 2. But it turned out I was not in Sullivan County after all! I was just across the border in Wyoming County. With only 2 prior species there, all 4 species were new. Not for the first time, I wished Siri was smart enough to answer the question "what county am I in" – she still is not (as of July, 2022).

+++

Overall, the day was probably my least successful to that point. I ended up with only 27 species for Sullivan County and 6 for Wyoming County. Worse, when I checked the weather app the prediction was for 29°F overnight with snow showers! The next couple of nights, lows would be 26°F. I should have packed my snow pants.

After my extremely unproductive day, the 2021 67x67 quest appeared to be out of reach. Still, I was not completely ready to give up. I intended to get as many species as possible in both Sullivan and Wyoming counties, then focus on birding every county. I figured that I might finish all counties other than the four most challenging rural ones (Sullivan, Wyoming, Armstrong, and Potter) by mid-December. My fallback target was to spend at least one day birding each county, complete as many as possible, then finish the 67x67 quest next May when days were longer and migrants were passing through. While that alternative would not be a traditional "big year", I would spend fewer than 11 months in Pennsylvania during 2021 (due to trips to NC). So, I could still complete the quest within 12, non-consecutive months.

+++

November 3ʳᵈ continued with few birds. I started in Sullivan County at the State Game Lands 13--Splashdam Pond *hotspot*. It was not "hot" (in birds or temperature). I encountered a hazy sky and a cold trail with frosty, wet grass to walk through (11.05). In an hour and a half, walking 1.5 miles, I added just 2 species.

From the Sullivan County hotspot, I moved to Wyoming County. I progressed from 6 to 35 species there with 9 lists by the end of the day.

It was a poor bird photo day. My best two were of a Red-tailed Hawk flying and a pair of Sandhill Crane, the surprise species for the day (11.06).

An interesting but uncountable sighting was of a couple hybrid Geese at Lake Carey, probably Canada Goose-domestic Goose hybrid, the pinkish bill suggests domestic Graylag (11.07-L). Countable species seen there included Common Merganser and Ring-billed Gull (11.07-TR&BR).

+++

Back at my accommodations for the evening, my electric pot died. Fortunately, my room had been upgraded. I had a full kitchen and a couple pans, so I could boil water for my multiple cups of evening tea and do the same for morning tea, then coffee.

The day's poor progress convinced me that my best option was to pursue the idea to carry days missed in Pennsylvania during 2021 (probably about 30) into May 2022. For the rest of 2021, my revised plan was to bird every county, reach 67 in as many as I could, and try to hit at least 50 in the rest.

More immediately, I decided to split the next day between Sullivan and Wyoming Counties to work toward 50 in both. Many ordinary birds I was missing were seen around Lake Carey earlier in the day. So, I intended to start there the next morning to get Wyoming up to about 40. If/when I managed that, I planned to head back to Sullivan County for the rest of the day.

+++

I got a slow start on November 4th. On the drive to Lake Carey I had a House Sparrow (11.08-L) in Wyoming County. I then got started at Lake Carey about 8:00am and remained there until just after noon. The morning birding around the lake was less productive than I hoped, but I added 9 species, including Golden-crowned Kinglet, Brown Creeper, Belted Kingfisher, and (with photo) Yellow-bellied Sapsucker (11.08-M). I also got a photo of White-throated Sparrow (11.08-R), seen the day prior with no photo.

My slow pace at the lake was partly due to a problem at home. We had our old oil furnace replaced with a new heat pump + oil furnace backup. The oil furnace was supposed to kick in when the temperature was too low for the heat pump to cope. But it did not. I tried to switch to the oil furnace remotely. That did not work. So, Fran called the service folks. They sent someone out that morning, so I got back to birding. The technician who showed up found a mis-connected wire, fixed it (without breaking something else), and everything worked.

By 1:00pm, I had reached 46 species in Wyoming County. That surpassed my objective for the day, so I moved back to Sullivan County. Enroute, I stopped at a pond visible from the road. I saw 4 Bufflehead, which would not have been new for Sullivan County, but I then realized the pond and I were a couple hundred yards into Bradford County where I had no Bufflehead, pushing that total to 68 (thus one extra).

I generated 4 more eBird lists in Sullivan County that afternoon, but added only 3 new species, Common Grackle, Mallard, and Hermit Thrush. That left me at 32 for Sullivan County, below where I hoped to be. On return to the cottage, I checked the tiny park next-door. I was hoping for one last species, but neither saw nor heard a single bird.

+++

The trip, to that point, was disappointing. But I was determined to make the best of it. I decided to focus on Sullivan County in the morning, since I had the fewest species there.

+++

I packed up on the morning of November 5 and departed the cottage with the temperature at 27°F. It was going to be another cold start since I did not prepare for temperatures below freezing.

I headed to a hotspot a bit north; some farm fields. Several species I needed were reported there in prior Novembers — Sandhill Crane once, a year before. Since I had seen the latter nearby in Wyoming County, I hoped for a flyby. I had no luck with Cranes, but did pick up American Black Duck, Carolina Wren, and Red-winged Blackbird.

I spent the whole morning in Sullivan County, posting lists from 3 additional spots, reaching 45 species, including a Red-shouldered Hawk flying over farm fields. The landscape there was quite attractive, with some fall colors remaining (11.09).

11.09

At that point, I decided to move to Wyoming County to see what I could add before heading home. I made 4 stops, but added only 3 species: American Wigeon, Mute Swan, and Green-winged Teal (11.10). The first two were on a private pond visible from the road and the latter at a big pond / wetland with a ton of waterfowl. In that pond, most were so far away they were hard to identify. I was certain that there were a lot of Ring-neck Ducks, I put down 50 but probably underestimated. There were probably other species beyond the Green-winged Teal, but none I could see clearly enough. I hoped that some photos might show what I had missed, but I had no luck when I reviewed them.

Wyoming and Sullivan Counties had been hard work, and the work was not done. But it was my best day of the trip. I ended up at 48 species for Wyoming County and 46 for Sullivan County. I was within striking distance of 50 in each, but a long way from 67.

My route home followed Pennsylvania 118W, a route that I could not recall ever being on before. I had a 42 mile stretch of decent road with the speed limit mostly at 55 and little traffic. So, I made good time. The trees on the ridges were still showing a lot of color, making it a pleasant end to the day and the trip.

+++

I spent two days at home. I did grocery shopping, processed photos, and planned the next trip. I settled on a 4-night trip to the southeast focusing on Berks, Lehigh, Northampton, and Monroe Counties. The start would be a little slow. I needed to stop in Lewistown to get 10,000-mile service on my Toyota Venza on the way. Once done, I would head to Northampton County where I had booked a hotel.

Beyond the quest, I continued to agonize over the ICA Conference. I was leaning toward going. I booked a cancelable hotel. I also booked a flight. It was a good deal for business class (something I had never booked, but desirable for space in light of COVID-19 risk). The itinerary was State College to Washington DC to Boston to Munich to Florence. Return was better: Florence to Frankfurt to DC to home.

But … I did not sleep well. I woke up worrying about COVID-19 and other issues of traveling in early December. The thought of the very long, many stop trip, wearing a mask all the time, and then sitting (masked) in paper sessions (rather than birding) was not very attractive. If the Conference was sometime in 2022, and COVID-19 risk was lower, I would have definitely done the trip.

At any rate, I decided to cancel the flight while it was still possible (United allows 24 hours). I kept the hotel in case I reconsidered, which I might if I could find a less complicated flight. Going through Boston in December seemed like a particularly bad idea once I considered it – I guess that was why they had a great deal on business class tickets. So, the decision was (still) to put off the decision. Back to birds.

+++

On November 8, I had to time departure to match my Toyota service appointment in Lewistown. I arrived at 8:00am when they opened. But it was 9:30am by the time I was on the road again and 11:00am by the time I arrived at Lake Ontelaunee in Berks County.

I generated 2 lists from the lake, adding 15 species. I then went looking for a Cattle Egret that had been seen. I had no luck. By 2:00pm, I had added 4 more species, to reach 43. My only good photo to that point was a Golden-crowned Kinglet showing off its crown (11.11). I decided to check in at the hotel.

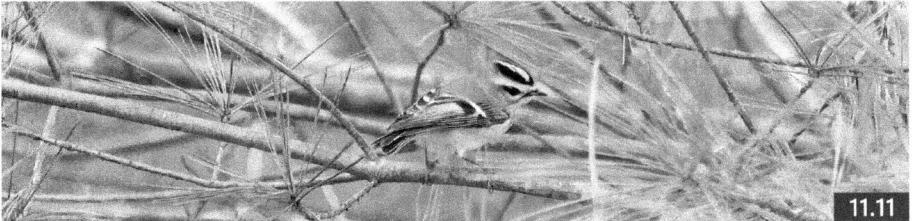
11.11

After checking in, I drove to Rodale Park in Lehigh County where I picked up 11 common species, including American Robin apparently listening for prey, Slate-colored Dark-eyed Junco, and male Northern Cardinal (11.12). My American Robin photo prompted me to look up information to confirm or counter my assumption that the Robin was listening for prey. I found a confirmation on the BirdNote blog (Written by Bob Sundstrom):

https://www.birdnote.org/listen/shows/does-robin-hear-its-worm.

After Rodale Park, I stopped at two ponds where I added some water birds. At the Knocks Rd. Retention Ponds (right in the middle of a group of highways) I found Mallard, Northern Shoveler, and Canada Goose. Then at Dorney Pond (next to a big Water Park amusement site) I added Mute Swan, Gadwall, and American Black Duck (11.13).

By the time I decided to head to the hotel to make dinner, I was at 19 species for Lehigh County. While I had only spent two hours in the county, the pace was rather slow for a previously unvisited county in which everything seen was new.

+++

With days getting shorter, I fixed dinner at the hotel before 6:00pm. I then spent time planning the next day's strategy. I decided to focus on Monroe County where I had 30 species (from July, plus a Great Blue Heron in September). Based on eBird alerts for the prior week, it looked like I had an outside shot to finish the county in one long day.

+++

I started the morning heading to Cherry Valley National Wildlife Refuge (NWR). It was difficult to locate. The refuge appeared to be fragmented and/or very long. I confirmed this later by checking an online map; later, I generated an OSM map (11.14-L). Once I determined where sections were, I visited the headquarters track later in the day (11.14-R); it is the small rectangle in the NE corner of the main map.

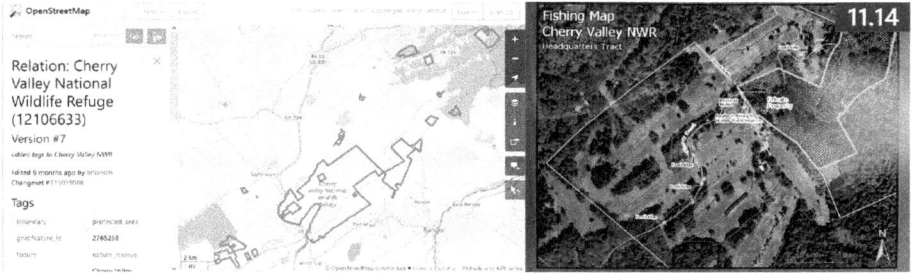

Due to uncertainty about NWR access points, I started on nearby rural roads. By 8:00am I progressed from 31 to 42 species for Monroe; additions included Northern Mockingbird, White-throated Sparrow, Dark-eyed Junco, Hooded Merganser, and Wood Duck (11.15).

I ran into a local birder who gave me a few pointers on recent sightings. I stopped at 4 additional sites during the morning, picking up 1-3 species at each to reach 51 species by about 11:30am. At that point, I finally found my way to the headquarters track for the Cherry Run NWR. There, I walked a quite long loop, picking up a Common Raven plus several other forest birds. By 1:40pm I was at 58 species.

I checked eBird and picked Gouldsboro State Park to the north as my next stop. It was a 40-minute drive, but I was seeking waterfowl that were less likely elsewhere. I found Belted Kingfisher, Bufflehead, Pied-billed Grebe, and Ring-necked Duck (11.16-L). Next, I checked a casino resort where Killdeer had been seen and I found 6 (11.16-ML). I moved to Pocono Summit Lake, picking up Gadwall and Ruddy Duck (11.16-MR). It was close to sunset, and I thought I was at 66 species. I went to a site where House Sparrow had been seen. But it was too dark (11.16-R). I headed for the hotel after 10 minutes of trying.

+++

When I reviewed photos that evening, I realized what I thought were two Cackling Geese (at Weir Lake) were not. The bill, head, and bodies were smaller than nearby Canada Geese (like a Cackling Goose). But, the foreheads were not steep enough and bills not stubby enough. I revised my ID to Canada Goose (small ones). That meant I was at 65, so House Sparrow would not have been number 67 anyway.

After reviewing my status, I decided to focus on Northampton County the next day. I would be starting at zero. While I had managed 67 species in one day with Mercer (where the 67 included 3 already seen), I still had not done 0-to-67 in one day. At this time of year it was unlikely … still, I would start early and see how close I could get.

+++

My first stop on November 10 was the St. Luke's Hospital Anderson Campus Complex. They have a large pond with a walkway around it and I was expecting waterfowl based on prior reports. The first thing I noticed, before birds, were some stunning sculptures around the pond (donated by artist Susan Opie). They included larger-than-life (human size) insects (11.17).

The site also included three of Susan Opie's human-related sculptures. One is a blind person with a guide dog, one a pair of old ice skates, and one a roller skater in motion (11.18). My photos of her art are included here by permission of the artist.

Beyond the sculptures, it proved to be a great birding site. I arrived at 6:30am and spent 2.5 hours walking 1.6 miles. On waterfowl, I had only Mallard and Canada Goose. But I found many other species on the walking path around the edge of adjacent farm fields (11.19).

The highlight on that walk was a Merlin eating breakfast (11.20). The 3rd photo was taken first, before the meal was found.

Other species included American Robin, female Purple Finch, male Eastern Bluebird, Northern Mockingbird, all in bushes or trees, plus Herring Gull and Red-tailed Hawk overhead (11.21). I also had a group of Lesser Black-backed Gull flying and a Yellow-bellied Sapsucker. I reported 32 species overall.

After the early success, I tried a couple of retention ponds that seemed from eBird to be the real hotspots this time of year. At one in front of Lehigh Hospital ... my hospital birding day ... I added a Great Blue Heron, Killdeer, and Greater Yellowlegs (11.22); the latter was hanging around rather late in the year.

I then tried a lake at a quarry, but I could not find a vantage point. Checking eBird again, I saw a report of American Pipit and Savannah Sparrow at the Lehigh Hospital Pond. I returned. I met a local birder (Dave DeReamus) who helped me find the Savannah Sparrow (11.23-R). We also saw the American Pipit (11.23-L). Dave then pointed out a Peregrine Falcon just visible on a tall electrical tower (11.23-MT&MB).

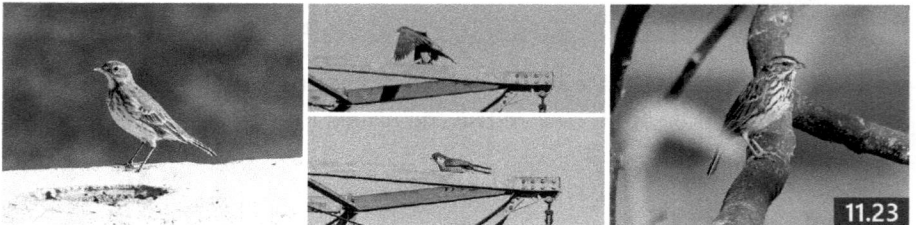

I mentioned my trouble finding a quarry vantage point to Dave. He said he was heading there next, and I was welcome to follow along, which I did. The best vantage point had marginal, distant views of the water, around trees and bushes. Still, we ended up having a great time there; I had several new species. While photos were poor-to-marginal due to the setting, I added Snow Goose, Double-crested Cormorant, Pied-billed Grebe, Ruddy Duck, Bufflehead, Ring-necked Duck, and Green-winged Teal. I was at 53 species when we left the quarry.

Dave led me to one more spot, the Bushkill/Penn Pump Park/ Bush-kill Creek Waterfowl Observation Area. He was confident I could add Wood Duck, which I did (11.24-M) along with Common Merganser and another Snow Goose (11.24-L&R).

Dave departed about 3:45pm. I was at 55 species. I checked eBird and picked Housenick Memorial Park/Archibald Johnson Conservation Area as a last stop. Hairy Woodpecker, Downy Woodpecker, and Northern Flicker had been reported. I added all 3, reaching 58 species. Starting the day at zero, it was my best county start since spring.

+++

That evening, I got Chinese takeout. It was among the best I had found, but also the smallest portion. Still, I decided to stretch it for two nights. I got another interesting "fortune" (11.25). I guess in terms of birding, this could mean that weather events might bring unusual birds to an area, but also might prompt all birds to stay out of sight.

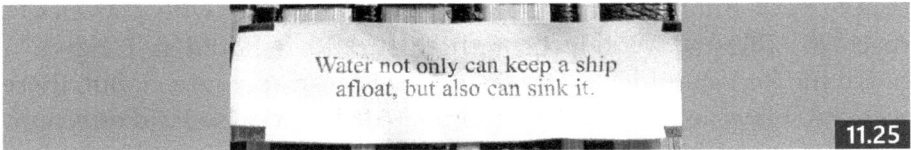

Water not only can keep a ship afloat, but also can sink it.

After dinner, I planned the next day, opting to work on Northampton County (with 58) and Monroe County (with 65) first. If they did not take too long, I thought I would probably head to Bucks County, where I had zero, to get a start there.

+++

On Nov. 11, I left the hotel at 6:00am precisely. It was 38°F, so a bit cooler than the prior two days. But it was supposed to go to 62°F again, so not bad. I headed for Lake Minsi, looking for Mute Swan, American Coot, and Gadwall (seen there the day before). I arrived and started my first eBird list at 6:49am.

I spent about an hour and a half trying spots on both sides of the lake. I found Mute Swan quickly. They were across the lake from me, so I drove around to get a photo and to figure out smaller waterfowl I saw moving through some reeds. I got the Mute Swan photo (11.26-L) but was unable to get a good look at the other birds, which moved to where I had just been. I returned to the first spot and saw American Coot (11.26-M). I also added Common Grackle and Belted Kingfisher.

Despite spending a lot of time scanning movement on the water, I never found Gadwall. But, as I was about to get in the car, I saw a House Sparrow on what I assumed to be a Bluebird Box (11.26-R). That put me at 63 species for Northampton County. I was feeling confident about finishing both Northampton and Monroe Counties early so I could move on to Bucks County.

My confidence was a bit misplaced. I went back to the Cherry Valley Blakeslee Rd. hotspot in Monroe County where I had success two days prior. A few species I was missing had been reported over the past couple days. But it took me about an hour to come up with 2 species to reach 67, Pileated Woodpecker first, then Red-shouldered Hawk. I heard the Red-shouldered Hawk and the Merlin app agreed. But, there were Blue Jays around, which can imitate the hawks, so I did not count it at first — until I then saw the hawk flying.

On my way back to Northampton County, I made a quick (7 min.) stop at Brodhead Creek Park. I found a Brown Creeper to raise my Monroe County total to 68. I managed one of my best Brown Creeper photos of the Geo-Big Year (11.27). They are quite hard to photograph since they are in constant motion and blend into their background.

11.27

After that short stop, I got back to Northampton County and tried the Lehigh Hospital retention pond again, hoping for a White-crowned Sparrow reported there that morning. I had no luck. I then tried Woodland Hills Preserve, still in Northampton County on the way toward Bucks County. I was there longer than planned, 3.5 hours, walking 4+ miles and finally adding Field Sparrow, that I had searched for since arriving, for number 67. I also got two "spares," a fly-over Ring-billed Gull and a Winter Wren near the end of my long loop walk.

I left the preserve at 3:45pm, driving south to Nockamixon State Park in Bucks County. On the way, I saw a Belted Kingfisher to start Bucks County. By sunset (11.28) my Bucks County list was at 9.

11.28

+++

Back at the hotel I debated strategy (with myself). I had 9 species in Bucks County and 19 in Lehigh County. I was unlikely to finish either before starting home the next day. And, rain was predicted. Ruling out Carbon County where I had 53 species, as too far away for an early start, I decided to try for water birds in Bucks County; they tolerate rain and were more practical to view from the car if rain was constant.

+++

The November 12 prediction was accurate. It was raining when I left the hotel at 6:25am and when I arrived at Lake Towhee County Park a bit before 7:00am. And, rain did not let up, as evident in this photo from inside the car just before 9:00am (11.29).

The was no chance for photos, and limited opportunity to be out of the car. But I added 18 species (including Bald Eagle, Pied-billed Grebe, American Black Duck, and Mute Swan) to get to 27 by about 9:30am. At that point, after checking the weather and eBird for good sites, I tried driving out of the rain by heading west to Lehigh County.

When I got to Lehigh County, rain continued. So, I drove farther west, to the Trexler Nature Preserve. It was a big place with multiple access points and varied habitat, and the rain had stopped. The route to the first access point followed roads that were part of a "covered bridge trail" and took me through one covered bridge, shown here (11.30).

After adding American Crow and Rock Pigeon enroute, I started birding at the Trexler Nature Preserve just before 11:00am. I walked a nice trail (11.31-L) along a stream (11.31-R) and added 12 species.

Species seen there included Turkey Vulture, Song Sparrow, Hairy Woodpecker, and Red-bellied Woodpecker (11.32) plus Black Vulture overhead and Common Merganser in the stream.

While the first stop was great, the next at the North Range of the Preserve was an even more impressive landscape. A map, with a You-Are-Here mark, showed the location of this site in the context of the overall Preserve, which covered 1108 acres (11.33-TL). My photos of the lone tree on a hill (11.33-TR) and the panoramic 180° view (11.33-B) together reminded me of scenes from my time in Colorado rather than of a location in Pennsylvania.

In addition to the interesting landscape, I had some success with birds. I added 8 species, including Eastern Bluebird, Red-headed Woodpecker, and White-crowned Sparrow (11.34).

A 20 min. stop at Lesser Lake added nothing new. I headed home with both Northampton and Monroe Counties completed, 41 species in Lehigh County, and 27 species in Bucks County. It was a good but not spectacular trip.

+++

At that point, 5 unvisited counties remained, 53 were complete, and 4 of the uncompleted ones were at 50 or more. My focus now was to maximize the chance of reaching 50 species in all counties while also hitting 67 in as many as possible prior to potential trips to Italy for the ICA Conference and/or North Carolina for Christmas Bird Counts. If I decided against Italy and picked up the pace enough to put the original 67x67 target in sight in 2021, I would skip the Christmas Counts (or travel back between them).

I continued to vacillate about the ICA Conference. I came somewhat close to booking a direct flight between Newark and Rome to minimize time in airports (by driving 3.5-4 hours to Newark). With that option, I'd take a train from Rome to Florence. Some of those trains had an "executive class" with spectacular looking seats in an uncrowded cabin – thus less risky for COVID-19 (particularly with the strict mask policy on public transport in Italy). It seemed worth the extra $50 each way. I needed to decide soon, but (again) did not.

My next step would be a day trip to Lebanon and Lancaster Counties, with 45 and 55 species, respectively. A day trip should get me to the 50 species fallback target for Lebanon County and perhaps the primary target for Lancaster County. I planned to follow this with a 3-night trip to the Southeast part of the state.

+++

November 14 started with a good omen – a Great Horned Owl heard at home just before 6:00am. It was number 102 for my home county –

way behind my usual Centre County total due to time on the road. The year before I was at 220 species for the county at this point. I was a bit surprised to see that my Pennsylvania State Year List was 4 species short of my Centre County total on the same date in 2020. This was a consequence of doing a Geo-Big Year focused on birding everywhere rather than targeting rarities.

Still, a Great Horned Owl was a great start to the day. I left for Lebanon County early enough for a nice sunrise. The temperature was 41°F in Centre County but only 36°F in Lebanon County with an expected high in the 40s. At least there was no prediction of snow.

I started at Memorial Lake at 7:51am. With 3 lists in 1.5 hours, I added just 4 species. One was Hooded Merganser (11.35-L) to reach the intermediate target of 50 species. But I decided to try adding a couple more before switching to Lancaster County. I moved to Snitz Creek Park where Marsh Wren had been reported. With the help of a local birder, I managed to find it, hear it repeatedly, and see it in brief glimpses that were never long enough to get the camera focused. A Swamp Sparrow and a Winter Wren were more cooperative (11.35-M&R).

That put me at 53 species for Lebanon County. Due to time spent unsuccessfully to get a photo of the Marsh Wren, it was nearly 11:30am when I moved on to Lancaster County. I headed for Middle Creek WMA, a site with varied habitat 30 min. away.

I posted 4 lists from spots in the WMA. I had decent success with waterfowl, adding Ring-necked Duck, Ruddy Duck, Bufflehead, Hooded Merganser, Northern Pintail, American Wigeon, Gadwall, and Tundra Swan, the only one I managed a photo of due to distance and lighting for others seen with the scope (11.36).

While it was a great day to visit Lancaster County for waterfowl, I was disappointed to find nothing else new. At about 3:30pm I was at 63 species. Given ever-earlier sunset and the scarcity of new species beyond those on the water, 4 new species before dark was unlikely. I opted against staying for owling and a drive home in the dark. So, I headed for home, figuring I could get the final 4 species on a subsequent trip to a nearby county.

+++

I continued vacillating about Italy. I (again) nearly booked the trip. I would drive to Newark on Wednesday, fly nonstop to arrive in Rome on Thursday, take a 2.5-hour one-stop train to Florence, and walk about 1.5 km to the hotel (24 hours door to door with no delays). I would then travel by train back to Rome on Saturday to fly home on Sunday – 48 hours of travel for two days in Italy (short to minimize impinging on the quest and/or Christmas counts). I ended up not booking again.

I was close to deciding against travel to Italy. While I wanted to receive the award in person and see colleagues from around the world, there was a fourth wave of COVID-19 ramping up in Europe. I would be uncomfortable around that many people due to COVID-19 concerns. Italy was probably safer than the U.S. due to smart public policy about masking and COVID-19 vaccination. But birding solo was safer yet since I had almost no interaction with others. I still did not cancel the hotel but planned on making a final decision over the coming weekend after my next trip.

As I took stock of progress toward my quest, I was confident I could reach 50 species in every county and thought I could reach the original target of 67 in 62 or 63 of them. There was still an outside chance to complete the original quest, but the odds were very small. The confluence of issues prompted words below.

Pandemic Retirement

Fall of the year,
Leaves – yellow, orange, red, and brown.
Fall of our lives,
The cycle is never ending and broken.

The pandemic comes in waves,
Here so often we have lost track.
Distant memories of social interaction,
The ease of conversing with anyone.

Public spaces have become frightening,
Travel used to be fun.
Does that restaurant have outdoor dining?
Whose world has it become?

Fall colors start fading,
The sky is perpetually gray.
A crow picks at roadkill,
The night hides the owl from prey.

Some places seem promising,
Others look glum.
Uncertain how far I'll get,
Or what I'll become.

Sunrise today is stunning,
Alone on the backroads.
A few birds heard singing,
And the list, it yet grows.

+++

It was 29° on November 16 as I left Boalsburg on my way to Carbon County. I faced a tedious 2.5-hour drive to my first stop. But that's the way it was as I tried to finish these far southeast counties. I got started at Hickory Run State Park at 9:34am. There was a dusting of snow on the ground, and it remained cold. I got a great photo of a Yellow-bellied Sapsucker (11.37-L). But nearly an hour of birding netted me zero new species. I moved on to Beltsville State Park where, between 11:00am and 2:30pm, I added only 3 more species (Ruddy Duck, Ring-billed Gull, Pileated Woodpecker). My only decent photos were of species I already had for the county, a Brown Creeper and an Eastern Bluebird (11.37-M&R).

I made four other stops during the day. Birds were scarce. In about an hour along rural roads I had added just 3 species. I then drove to Mauch Chunk Lake Park where several species I was missing were reported. I picked up just Bufflehead and Bald Eagle before the 4:43pm sunset (11.38).

+++

I ended the day with 61 species for Carbon County. Shorter days were impeding progress (particularly day 1 of a trip starting with a long drive). At my hotel in Allentown, I found I botched the booking (again); my reservation was for the next week. They had no suite (what I'd booked), but they did have a room with mini-fridge and microwave. I also forgot my (new) hotpot (to boil water for tea and coffee). I'd have to make do with the microwave.

I needed 6 species for Carbon County to hit 67. It would be a challenge. In eBird the prior week, exactly 6 species I needed were seen in the county. Sparrows and waterfowl appeared to be my best chance, so I would target places to see those the next day.

+++

I headed out on November 17 with the temperature at 30°F. It was slightly warmer than predicted, but cold enough to ice up the car windows. I had to wait a few minutes with defrost at full blast – I found I had not transferred my ice scraper to the Venza.

Beltzville State Park opened at 8:00am (winter hours) – and they meant it. The evening before, the park ranger was driving around announcing that the gates were about to close. Since I was too early, I stopped at Perryville Dam where Mallard and American Black Duck were reported. I got Mallard and a House Sparrow (11.39-L), but no American Black Duck. So, I tried Phiefer's Ice Dam Park, but saw only species I already had (including Belted Kingfisher and White-throated Sparrow). In Beltzville State Park, once open, I was pleasantly surprised to find both American Tree Sparrow and Fox Sparrow, completing a Sparrow 'hat trick' (11.39-M&R). That put me at 65 species.

I was disappointed not to get waterfowl at the State Park. But I completed Carbon County earlier than I might've ever expected, by 10:15am. I did so by finding both American Black Duck and Ring-necked Duck at the Penn Forest Reservoir (a site with no access and very limited vantage points – but sufficient this day).

I moved to Lehigh County. Birding slowed. My first site, a Rail Trail, was a mistake; most of the trail was back in Carbon County. So, I moved on to the Jordan Creek Parkway. But there was little bird activity except for a very large number of American Robin and a photogenic Red-tailed Hawk, not new, but a nice pose so I include it (11.40).

I stopped at multiple other sites during the day, including the Bake Oven Knob Hawk Watch (I saw no hawks, nor other new species). I added just 8 species in Lehigh, to reach 49 that day. Not only did I miss the primary target, I was short of the fallback.

+++

That evening back at the hotel, I emailed my colleague Menno-Jan Kraak in The Netherlands to find out if he planned to attend the ICA Conference in Italy. As ICA Past-President, I assumed he would attend. His reply matched that assumption, with the caveat that changes in COVID-19 risk could change his plans. Menno-Jan's probable attendance prompted me to keep the option to attend the conference open a bit longer.

+++

On November 18, I got an early start, pulling out of the hotel in the dark at 6:14am. I decided to start back at the Fogelsville Quarry. I arrived about 25 minutes before sunrise. It should have been dawn, but it was overcast and foggy, thus quite dark.

I moved to a vantage point on the perimeter fence with the lake far below; I could see almost nothing and there was no dawn chorus – perhaps the fog prompted birds to sleep in. After about 30min. I was cold, so got back in the car and picked another site. I added zero species, plus needed to wait until the fog cleared to turn left onto the highway.

It proved to be a grueling day with new species ticked off slowly. My best site was back at Rodale Park with 6 new species. They included Fox Sparrow, Yellow-rumped Warbler, and a Golden-crowned Kinglet (11.41), the latter watching as I ate lunch.

My last stop was the Bake Oven Knob Hawk Watch, again no new raptors. I did see Red-tailed Hawk, but that was not new. Overall, I added just 9 species and ended the day at 58.

+++

Since I reached the fallback target for Lehigh County and species were so scarce, I decided to focus my last trip day in Bucks County. My primary goal for the day was to exceed 50 species there. Once done I would move on to Montgomery County before heading for home. I had not been in Montgomery, so stopping there would reduce the number of counties not visited at all and starting at zero meant that everything seen would be new.

+++

I got a reasonably early start on November 18, considering it was hotel check-out day. I managed to see the sunrise on my way to Nockamixon State Park and started my first list there at 6:55am. There were fewer waterfowl than I was hoping for, but I did add Bufflehead and Ring-necked Duck. I did as well on non-water birds, adding Eastern Bluebird and White-breasted Nuthatch (11.42-L&M). I moved to Peace Valley Park, adding Northern Mockingbird (11.42-R). I had reached 53 in Bucks County. I watched the water while eating lunch but added nothing further.

It was about 12:30pm when I left for Montgomery County. I spent most of my time at sites in Green Lake Park. I got several species on and around water bodies there, including Gadwall, Northern Shoveler, Common Merganser, as well as Belted Kingfisher. On leaving Montgomery County for home, I thought I was at 24 species. When I processed photos, I realized that the Wood Duck I had on a log with a row of Common Mergansers was missing from the list (11.43-L), thus I had 25. Other new species from sections of Green Lake Park included Hooded Merganser, Northern Shoveler, American Wigeon, Gadwall, and Bufflehead (11.43), clockwise from top right.

+++

During days at home, I generated a draft of my comments for the Carl Mannerfelt Gold Medal ceremony. I was still unsure whether I would give it in person or remotely. I also worked on plans for my next quest trips. My short-term goal was to start my last two unvisited counties. Philadelphia County and Delaware County. I booked a hotel near their shared border for a 3-night trip. My route would be through Lebanon County where I had 54, so I planned to stop there as well.

+++

I got a good start, reaching Lebanon County at 7:40am when I saw 6 Wild Turkey. My first stop was Memorial Lake State Park. It was cold, so I took only short walks. On the lake I saw only Canada Goose, Mallard, and a few Bufflehead, the only new species (11.44-L). On land, I found a Hairy Woodpecker and Fox Sparrow (11.44-ML&MR). I made an additional stop at Lion's Park, where I added Ruddy Duck (11.44-R). The Ruddy Duck got me within striking distance at 60 species.

I moved on to my main trip objectives, Delaware and Philadelphia Counties. My first stop (1:00pm) was the Philadelphia County end of the John Heinz NWR (11.45-L). I spent an hour and three-quarters doing a 2.5 mile walk. The walk was time consuming since construction prevented doing the normal loop around the impoundment (11.45-R).

I did find waterfowl, including a photogenic Northern Shoveler, Northern Pintail (with one stretching its wings), and several Mute Swan (11.46). Others included Pied-billed Grebe, Ruddy Duck, Ring-necked Duck, Mallard, American Wigeon, Gadwall, and Wood Duck.

My walk also yielded forest and marsh birds, including Red-bellied Woodpecker (that caught a bee or wasp), Carolina Wren, and Great Blue Heron (11.47). Other nice sightings were Belted Kingfisher and Golden-crowned Kinglet. I reached 31 species by 2:45pm.

I then moved to the Delaware County end of the NWR. Specifically, I birded at the Tinicum site (11.48). Birds were quiet, but I decided to walk a loop trail.

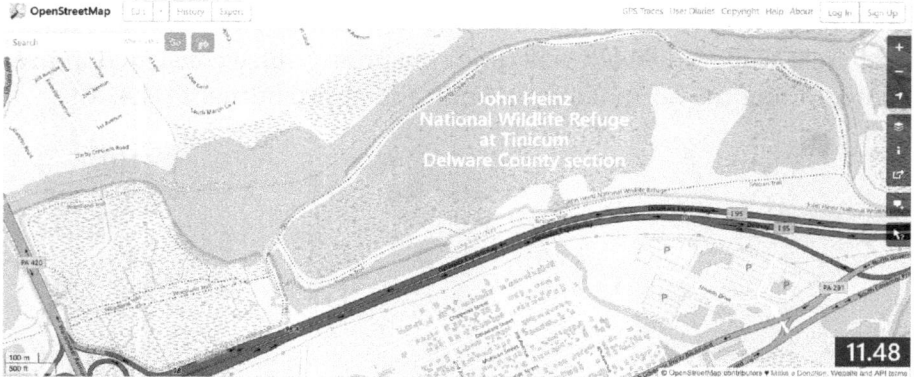

About 1/3 of the way around, I realized I could not complete the loop by dark. With no flashlight beyond my iPhone, and a low battery, I turned around and walked briskly back to the car. On that walk, I reached 20 species in Delaware County. The best photos were Mallard, Green-winged Teal, and Northern Pintail, all on the water (11.49).

+++

My November 23 goal was to finish Philadelphia County. I woke to 30°F with 12 mph winds. It would be tough. I returned to the John Heinz NWR, doing the 3.5 mile walk to the turnaround point. That was poor strategy. By the turn-around I had added only 7 species; 1 per half-mile. Many additions were water birds, including Bufflehead, American Coot, and Green-winged Teal (11.50).

The return trip was slightly better. I added 8 more species, reaching 46 for the county. These included Rusty Blackbird, Hermit Thrush, Brown Creeper, and Northern Flicker (11.51).

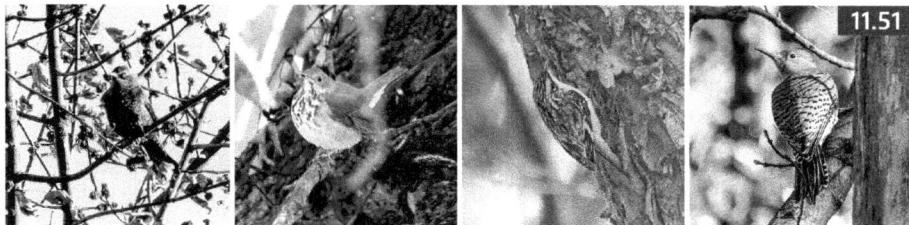

After 4.5 hours at the NWR, I headed to the city's north end, chasing Great Cormorant and Double-crested Cormorant, seen at Glen Foerd on the Delaware. On the way, I detoured to Bartram's Gardens adding 3 species, including a Yellow-bellied Sapsucker (11.52-L). I also got nice photos of Downy Woodpecker and Ruby-crowned Kinglet (11.52-M&R). A couple months later, Bartram's Gardens emailed, asking to include my Sapsucker photo on their new web site. Of course, I said yes.

I continued to Glen Foerd on the Delaware. It was very windy, but I saw both Great Cormorant and Double-crested Cormorant. The former was a year bird, not just for Pennsylvania, so, I include the distant photo (11.53). I missed a Great Black-backed Gull that had been reported but did add Laughing Gull and Bald Eagle.

I moved to a second site on the Delaware River. Another long, unproductive walk added zero species until seeing Dark-eyed Junco in the parking lot. I planned one more stop, another site with Great Black-backed Gull reported. But rush-hour on I-95 derailed the plan. I gave up and returned to the hotel with 55 species for the county.

+++

Back at the hotel, I considered options and decided to work on getting above 50 species in Delaware County the next day. I also checked the step count on my iPhone. I had 22,872 steps for the day. That was a lot of steps for 25 new species!

+++

November 24 again started at 30°F, but with a "feels like" of 24°F, due to wind. I focused on Delaware County, starting at Crum Reservoir where Common Goldeneye was seen. I got the Common Goldeneye, but thick fog meant blurry photos. I added 8 more species including Hooded Merganser. Dehaze cleaned that photo up enough (11.54-L). I returned later and got a clearer photo of the Common Goldeneye, at quite a distance (11.54-R).

11.54

I next tried a regional park/preserve. I found it to be under construction with no trespassing signs up. Around the edges I had a close (but safe) encounter with a Red Fox (11.55-L&M) and picked up 6 new species, including Downy Woodpecker (11.55-R).

11.55

From here I went to a local park and added 4 species. I then tried a nearby reservoir, but it was off-limits. I spent the rest of the morning at the Hildacy Farm Preserve, a very nice site where I walked nearly 2 miles. But I added just 4 species, including Chipping Sparrow, Field Sparrow, and Turkey Vulture (11.56).

When back at the Crum Creek Reservoir for a Common Goldeneye photo, a Mourning Dove got me to 44 species by lunchtime. I then headed to the Delaware River/Hog Island Rd. hotspot in Delaware County next to the airport. I spent about 40 min. listening for calls between planes taking off. Despite the noise, I had success on the Delaware River side of the road (including Herring Gull, Great Black-backed Gull, Ring-billed Gull, and Double-crested Cormorant). On the airport side, I added American Kestrel and Northern Mockingbird, the latter photo is paired below with one of a flight lifting off over the Mockingbird ... too close for my fixed lens (11.57).

That stop got me to 51 species in Delaware County. So, I stuck to my plan to attempt reaching 67 for Philadelphia County. The practical spot to try was back at the John Heinz NWR since it was only 15 minutes away. I spent the rest of the afternoon there with zero new species. That was quite disappointing.

+++

Back at the hotel, I considered options for Thanksgiving Day, the final day of my trip. Normally, Fran and I would be in NC to join Fran's family for Thanksgiving dinner at Owens' Restaurant in Nags Head. This year, COVID-19 concerns meant we would not eat out. So, we delayed travel to NC until mid-December (pending progress on my quest). I would use most of Thanksgiving Day for birding. We would have our Thanksgiving dinner (of duck) a day late at home in PA.

My trip so far was less successful than envisioned. I did pass 50 species in Philadelphia County (55) as well as Delaware County (51). But adding zero new species in Philadelphia County the prior afternoon gave me no confidence of reaching 67 for either county in one more day. Montgomery County (with 25) borders Philadelphia County. I decided to make that my Thanksgiving focus. If I reached 50 there, I would move to Chester County (with 1 from day one of the trip).

+++

I checked out at 6:30am. It was 38°F, the "warmest" morning so far on the trip, with a predicted high of 55°F. Traffic was light early on Thanksgiving morning. Skies were mostly clear with only a few cirrus clouds but looking rather red (making me think of the adage *red skies in the morning sailors take warning*).

My first Montgomery County stop was a waterfowl preserve. It was fenced off (they took "preserve" seriously) and it wasn't very big. But someone had built steps up to the fence to offer a vantage point on a marsh and pond. The highlight was a Tundra Swan (11.58). I also added an American Coot, a Cooper's Hawk flyover, and 8 additional new species to reach 35.

I moved to another preserve (Dixon Meadows – a former farm). At first, it looked inaccessible. Then, I found a path along one side. In a bit more than an hour, I added 5 species. Highlights were several Eastern Meadowlark, an American Kestrel, and Northern Mockingbird (2) doing what looked like a courting dance, territorial dispute, or perhaps a Thanksgiving Celebration (11.59).

From there I went to Fischer's Park, where several species I needed were reported in the previous few days. I added 9 species in about 1.5 hours. These included Great Blue Heron, Yellow-bellied Sapsucker, and Red-bellied Woodpecker (11.60).

That got me to 51 species by 11:30am. I ate lunch there and headed for Chester County. On the way pulling out of the parking lot I got Red-tailed Hawk and down the road I got a Black Vulture. So that put me at 53 for Montgomery County.

In Chester County I started at Wilson Farm Park, picking up 9 species including a Brown Creeper (11.61-L). I moved to Marsh Creek State Park, which has a lake. I added 9 more, including Great Blue Heron and House Finch (11.61-M&R), along with Ruddy Duck, Fox Sparrow, Mallard, and Belted Kingfisher. The highlight was a Rusty Blackbird that flew over calling.

I started home with 20 species in Chester County, and then added an American Kestrel (#21) on a wire while still in the county – nice to add them in two counties on the same day.

+++

All in all, I had some birds to be *thankful* for on Thanksgiving. I got over 50 species in two previously unvisited counties, pushed my total from 25 past 50 in Montgomery County, and made a start on my last previously unvisited county, Chester.

I had just 4 counties left with fewer than 50 species. My short-term goal was to exceed 50 in those by the end of November. Then I'd focus December on reaching 67 in as many remaining counties as I could. I nearly tried a day trip to Sullivan County (45) and Wyoming County (49) next. But after checking driving times, that were 2 hours or more to the closest sites in each, I decided an overnight would be better. So, I changed planned timing and opted for a day trip to Lebanon and Lancaster Counties, with 60 and 64 species, respectively, hoping to finish both in that one day.

While home, I finally made the decision not to attend the ICA Conference but needed to let the organizers know. Increases in COVID-19 incidence in the US and Europe plus news of a new COVID-19 strain in South Africa that could reach Europe soon had added to my concern. Plus, with increasing COVID-19 risk, many people I knew would probably skip the meeting as well.

+++

On November 27, I left the house at 6:04am, heading for Memorial Lake (again) in Lebanon County, just over an hour and a half away. Multiple species I needed had been reported recently. So, my odds of 7 species to finish at least Lebanon County were good.

Red sky in the morning, sailors take warning. It was a good thing I did not plan any sailing. Mimicking the red sky in the morning prediction, a highway sign warned of winter weather by evening. I could only hope that the bad weather arrived after I got home.

Birding started slowly. At Memorial Lake State Park, I did the 3-mile loop trail around the lake. That was a mistake. I had only 2 new species: White-crowned Sparrow and Chipping Sparrow.

From there I went to Ebenezer Lake (at Lion's Lake Park) and picked up Herring Gull, my only passable photo of a new species that morning (11.62). From there, I moved to Lebanon Valley College where reports were promising. I picked up Yellow-bellied Sapsucker. I then checked eBird and found a report of multiple species I needed at a local land-fill. I drove there and added both Great Black-backed Gull and Lesser Black-backed Gull along with a Black Vulture and a Common Raven. That got me to 69 species for Lebanon County.

After finishing Lebanon County, which I expected to be the harder one, I thought it would be easy to get 3 species to finish Lancaster County. But it wasn't to be. To avoid an extra hour and a half of driving, I went to Middle Creek Wildlife Management Area rather than further south where I was certain to get 3.

At Middle Creek, I got a group of Green-winged Teal quickly. I looked for Wood Duck, American Coot, Pied-billed Grebe, Mute Swan, and/or Snow Goose with no success. I then looked for non-water birds, including Pileated Woodpecker, Tufted Titmouse, Golden-crowned Kinglet, and Yellow-bellied Sapsucker. I was surprised and disappointed to find none (or other new species). I stayed at Middle Creek too long to head south, so tried a couple nearby spots before heading for home. The only interesting bird after the Green-winged Teal was an American Pipit, but I already had one from a previous trip. I quit for the day at 65 species, planning to try for the others on a trip to adjacent Chester County.

+++

I spent two days at home planning my next trip. I decided on the southeast to meet at least my fallback target in Chester County and Berks County (two of the four still below the 50 threshold). There were also adjacent counties I might push over the original 67 threshold. This time, as the year was running out, I opted for a 4-night trip. Looking back, if I had done more long trips, I would probably have achieved the original 67x67 quest easily and would have driven fewer miles. … If only I had a time machine!

+++

It was the last day of November. At 6:19am as I left, it was above freezing but snowing. I headed for Octoraro Reservoir (IBA) on the border between Lancaster and Chester Counties. The plan (hope) was to get my last 2 species for Lancaster County quickly, then move to the Chester side.

Lancaster County was nearly as easy as hoped. In 20 minutes, I picked up a Herring Gull and a Yellow-bellied Sapsucker (11.63-L). As I moved to the Chester County side of the Reservoir, I saw an unusual Goose. It turned out to be a domestic hybrid (11.63-M), but I then saw American Coot for number 68 for Lancaster (11.63-R).

While the plan went well for Lancaster County, it went awry in Chester County. The route I took netted an American Coot for Lancaster County but did not lead to the Chester side of the reservoir. I had to backtrack, and I never did find a good access point for the reservoir in Chester. Cell coverage was (again) terrible, so navigation apps were useless. I should've used my paper atlas ... but, even though my career had been focused on cartography, I forgot I had it with me!

I next headed to Hibernia Park. I found myself turning onto *Street Rd*. It caught my attention as one of the odd Street or Road names that gave my research group fits as we built Geographic Information Retrieval software to recognize place references in text, extract those references, and geolocate them. So, I snapped a couple photos (11.64).

On Street Rd. I added 3 species in 6 minutes of driving slowly for 2 miles (Red-tailed Hawk, American Crow, and Mourning Dove). All are common, but new none-the-less. I gradually added species during the morning, getting Chester County from 20 to 37. Among these were Tundra Swan, Ring-necked Duck, and Yellow-bellied Sapsucker in Hibernia County Park (11.65).

Slow progress continued in the afternoon. I stopped at Struble Lake, Marsh Creek State Park, and Exton Park and added only 8 species to reach 45 before heading to the hotel. While I ended up with no good photos of new species, I did get a nice one of Rusty Blackbird, the best photo of that species for the year (11.66).

Since I did not reach 50 in Chester County, I needed to spend more time there before moving to Berks County where I remained 20 short of the fallback target of 50.

+++

With the end of another month, it was time to generate a new map and assess progress, or lack of it. Since it was my first day of 5 on the road and I did not carry my laptop along, I was not able to generate the map until I returned home. But I insert it here at the end of the month that the map summarizes (11.67).

I had made considerable progress since October. There were no remaining blank (white) counties nor any below halfway to the primary target of 67. However, I fell short of the goal to reach the fallback target of 50 species in all counties before the end of November. I continued to have four counties under that threshold.

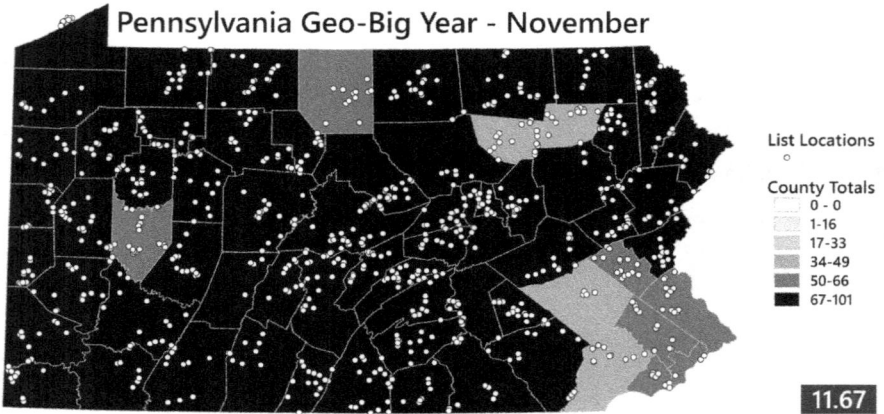

The most important goal for the rest of the trip was to reach 50 for both Chester and Berks Counties. I opted to focus on Berks the next day. I had fewer species there, so it seemed important to use the best birding hours early in the day for that.

+++++

DECEMBER

I got a late start on December 1, not the best harbinger. I arrived at my first stop in Berks County, Morgantown Lake at 7:29am. It was in an urban space, so perhaps not a great choice. I did pick up 3 species: Ring-necked Duck, Bufflehead, and (a photo managed) Ruddy Duck (12.01-L). I couldn't figure out how to access the next hotspot I tried, so wasted time. I moved to Union Meadows Park, picking up Eastern Bluebird enroute, then spent nearly 2 hours walking about 2 miles. I added 8 species to reach 49 for Berks County, these included Downy Woodpecker and Northern Cardinal (12.01-M&R).

I picked up number 50 at a quarry, American Black Duck, but views were distant. With additional days in the trip, I opted to continue in Berks County to push that total higher. I spent an hour at Blue Marsh Lake. I added a Merlin, which seemed to be taking a bath on the edge of the lake, and a Herring Gull (12.02).

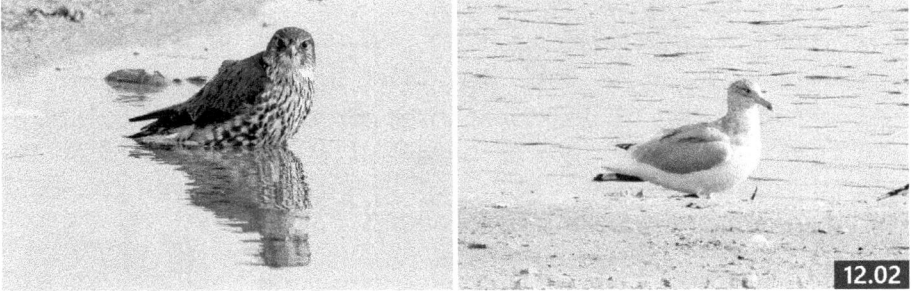

I next tried Lake Ontelaunee. The surrounding countryside, with multiple farms, was attractive (12.03-T). In an hour, I netted 2 additions – Winter Wren (12.03-BL) and Rusty Blackbird, seeing both male and female (12.03-BM&BR). I ended the day with 54 species in Berks County.

+++

Given the few species beyond 50 I added in Berks County, it would have been better to return to Chester County. All day I had felt slightly under the weather and hoped I did not have COVID-19. I had so little contact with others that seemed unlikely. However, even if it was a cold, I got it from someone. My symptoms were very slight, so I opted to decide in the morning whether to continue or truncate the trip.

On top of feeling ill, the fridge conspired against me. I had frozen beets and semi-frozen avocado with dinner. The potatoes were frozen too but the microwave fixed that. I turned the fridge thermostat down and hoped for the best with the remaining food.

Checking eBird, I saw a report of several species I needed at Struble Lake in Chester County. They included an Iceland Gull. That would be my first stop the next morning.

When I awoke on December 2, I still felt slightly unwell. The symptoms remained very mild cold-like ones. Since I was birding solo (thus rarely even encountering anyone outside), I posed minimal risk to others. But I decided that if I did not feel better as the day progressed, I would go out and buy a COVID-19 test kit.

+++

I began the day at Struble Lake in Chester County. My day's objective was to reach 50 species (from 45), then try for the primary target of 67. I ended up adding 6 species in less than two hours, reaching 51. I spent much of my time scoping hundreds of Ring-billed Gull, searching for the Iceland Gull – to no avail. The gulls kept moving and bunching up on sandbars, so I could easily have missed an Iceland Gull amongst them. I did add Herring Gull as well as a Common Loon.

My car said 47°F outside, but I was wishing I had not left my heavy winter coat at the hotel. I was wearing a lighter coat plus a raincoat. That was not quite enough. Despite the cold temperature, I generated 5 more Chester County eBird lists that day, one adding 3 species, one 2 species, three 1 species, and one 0 species (the latter from an hour at Binky Lee Preserve). Thus, progress was slow to none.

I had few decent photos. The best were waterfowl: an American Black Duck at Hibernia County Park plus a Gadwall and Northern Shoveler at Marsh Creek State Park (12.04). The last species of the day was Greater Scaup at Marsh Creek State Park (#59, well over the intermediate goal of 50, but far from the primary target of 67).

12.04

+++

I went to bed feeling pretty good, so thought whatever mild illness I had was gone. But I woke up (Dec. 3) with a slight sore throat. Whatever I had still lingered. I planned to buy a COVID-19 test that day just to be sure. My symptoms were very mild, so I continued as planned. My objective was to reach 67 in Chester County (8 needed), then move to either Montgomery or Berks depending on eBird reports.

+++

On December 3, the morning temperature was 44°F, with a high of 45°F. At least there was limited wind as I started out – and I brought all my coats along. I continued in Chester County.

My first stop was Atwater Quarry where I added Pied-billed Grebe and Common Merganser, but the vantage point was too distant for good photos. The nicest site was Exton Park where I did a pleasant loop walk and picked up 3 species, including a Merlin flying over. The best photos were of species I had already seen, Northern Flicker and Eastern Bluebird (12.05).

At my 5th site of the day, I finally got 66, 67, and 68: Lesser Scaup, Field Sparrow (12.06-L), and American Coot (12.06-R).

After finishing Chester County about 12:30pm, I headed back to Berks County. I spent about 2 hours at French Creek State Park, posting 3 lists. I picked up only 2 species, Hermit Thrush and Yellow-bellied Sapsucker. On return to the hotel, I stopped at a small reservoir I had tried before. There were hundreds of Ring-billed Gull, lots of Ring-necked Duck, several Ruddy Duck, and a few Bufflehead; nothing new. I finished the day with 56 in Berks County, thus I made almost no dent in the gap between the intermediate target of 50 and the primary one of 67.

+++

I was pleased to have reached the primary target of 67 in Chester County but discouraged about progress in Berks County where I still had 11 species to go. Given the morning and afternoon spent in Berks on this trip already, it was clear that reaching 67 the next day would be a challenge. My objective for check-out day (Dec. 4) was to finish Berks County early enough to make a stop at the waterfowl sanctuary in Montgomery County. Greater White-fronted Goose had been reported there.

When I woke the next morning, I still had mild cold-like symptoms. While I was congested and had a runny nose, I no longer felt achy, didn't have a sore throat, and was pretty sure I did not have a fever. I had tried to obtain an instant COVID-19 test kit the day prior, but they were unavailable in places I called to check. I decided to continue with the birding plan for the day, but then schedule a COVID-19 test at home if symptoms persisted.

+++

All in all, December 4 was discouraging. I started at 7:32am on a part of the Union Canal Trail. Two hours there walking about 2.25 miles netted only 2 new species (Red-winged Blackbird and Eastern Towhee). Next, 40min. at Lake Ontelaunee got me 1 more, Common Merganser. More than an hour at Kaercher Creek Park resulted in zero additions. About 2:45pm I made one last try at a site on the Schuylkill River Trail. The map-based trail sign recounting history was nice (12.07), and I saw some birds. But 50 min. and .8 miles netted zero new species. I ended with 59 species for Berks County. So, at the very least I got it well over 50. But adding only 22 species in nearly a full day was disappointing.

12.07

SCHUYLKILL RIVER TRAIL

"The Schuylkill was too thin to plow, too thick to drink"

What does the Schuylkill River have in commmon with your backyard barbecue?

The fading daylight I faced on the drive home is shown in photos below from the edge of the road, with the first at 4:03pm near the start of the journey and then part way there at 5:09pm (12.08).

12.08

+++

My 4-night trip did succeed in getting me over 50 in two of the four counties where I was short. I also reached the primary target of 67 in both Lancaster and Chester Counties. But, five days doing that removed all hope of completing the full quest in 2021, even if I skipped the Dare County, NC Christmas Bird Counts. So, my main objective became reaching 50 species in the two remaining counties. Once done, I'd reevaluate whether to attempt getting to 67 in more counties or leaving the rest for the coming May.

The next morning, I still had cold-like symptoms. I decided to get tested. I was able to schedule a test for Monday, December 6. I got the negative results on the 7th. I apparently had a common cold, something the COVID-19 and pneumonia vaccines did not help to fend off. I felt mostly OK, so I booked a night for the 8th in Laporte, Sullivan County.

I figured that Wyoming County would be easy. I had 49 species and eBird reports had shown 2-3 species I needed each day. Sullivan County seemed less easy. I thought I had 46 species (but only had 45, due to the Lesser Scaup error I had not yet discovered), it had few water bodies, and had few birders reporting in eBird. The Target Species list from eBird had only 17 species I needed EVER reported in the county for December, most of these reported only once or twice.

+++

On the morning of December 8, I still had cold symptoms, but the possibility of COVID-19 had been alleviated. The place I booked did not charge up front, so it might not cost if I felt worse and needed to cancel. I headed to Sullivan County, arriving at 8:40am. There was absolutely nothing on the lake at Ricketts Glen State Park and 30min. there turned up nothing but crows. I drove to Dushore, hoping for something on the small pond there. But it was frozen. I drove around hoping for House Finch or Northern Cardinal at feeders. I had no luck. I even searched for Rock Pigeon – grasping at straws. I struck out in Dushore.

I decided to move to Wyoming County to try finishing it. On the way, I did pick up Rock Pigeon for Sullivan County (12.09).

As I entered Wyoming County, I stopped at some feeders and heard a Hairy Woodpecker – number 50 for Wyoming County. I then went to the big pond where I'd seen Sandhill Crane. Initially, I saw nothing. But then five American Black Duck flew up, number 51 for Wyoming County. I headed back to Sullivan County.

Once there, I tried a game lands. There were no birds. I went to Splash Dam Pond, a place I tried on my last trip. No birds. I went to Laporte and walked a tiny park and a cemetery. Nothing but Blue Jays (not new). By then, I was feeling achy. I was near my accommodations but had not checked in. I texted the innkeeper that I needed to cancel due to illness. She was quite understanding, charging me nothing.

I still had daylight left and thought I was 3 species short. On the route home I went to Eagles Mere Lake. No birds. I then went to Hunters Lake. Nothing. I started for home disappointed with what I thought was 47 in Sullivan County, but was just 46.

+++

The cold that I came down with lingered. That plus windy, cold weather kept me home for several days. As I assessed the situation, I had two possible birding days left before leaving for NC in time for me to do the Kitty Hawk Christmas Count. I still thought I was at 47 species for Sullivan County and thought I had a marginal chance to hit 50 with a day trip. I considered being prepared to do an overnight, but I decided that the hotel options were inconvenient enough in relation to the best birding spots that I would do a second day trip if needed.

To prepare for the day trip, I checked eBird Target Species for Sullivan County again. Now (having seen Rock Pigeon), there were 16 species seen in the county at least once in some past December that I had yet to see. Given the sparse data (and likely sparse birds), I focused on identifying good habitat for species I had not seen, and on making sure I got an early start on the day.

+++

On December 13, I headed out at 6:07am, getting to a rural spot in the Muncy Valley at 7:54am. I spent an hour and a half there, walking up and down a couple roads listening to birds calling. It was a promising start to the day, with a Field Sparrow, then a Winter Wren – what I thought were numbers 48 and 49.

I moved on to a different location, still in the Valley area of the county. I parked along the roadside at what looked like a decent site. There were many sparrows and the Merlin app reported Northern Cardinal. I did not hear it or see it, so did not record it. I saw another couple Field Sparrow but also saw an American Tree Sparrow (what I believed was #50). I could not get focused on it with the camera, and then saw a Chipping Sparrow, which I did manage a photo of. I thought it was number 51, but it proved to be number 50 once I found and corrected my Lesser Scaup error.

I tried multiple other sites looking for that Northern Cardinal, the species I thought was most likely. But I never managed to find one. At

2:20pm it was getting quite breezy, thus anything new would be that much harder to find. Since I had reached 50 and thought I had one to spare (which turned out to be critical), I decided to call it a day and head for home.

Of the 3 new species, both Field Sparrow and Chipping Sparrow (12.10-L&R) were flagged as rare in eBird and neither were on the list of 16 target species! I also saw an adult Bald Eagle (12.10-M). It was not new, but the soaring flight represented the completion of my fallback goal of finding at least 50 species in every county!

+++

The International Cartographic Conference began in Florence, Italy the next day (Dec. 14). During the Opening Ceremony, I was presented (virtually) with the Carl Mannerfelt Gold Medal. I had sent a video acceptance, subsequently posted here: https://youtu.be/_cKxunoZjDk by the ICA. Back in Pennsylvania, I enjoyed seeing Tweets about the ceremony. One was from former Ph.D. student, now a faculty colleague at Penn State – Anthony Robinson (12.11-L). Another by Ken Fields had a photo showing my video being played on the screen (12.11-R).

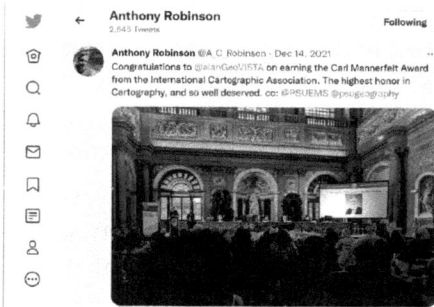

In a first for the organization, they awarded two Gold Medals in the same year, the other to Prof. em. Dr. Ulrich Freitag. Neither of us knew that the other would also be getting the award until the ceremony. On learning that, I was triply sorry to miss the Conference where I could have met up with long-time friends, congratulated Prof. Freitag who did attend, and enjoyed the spectacular venue where the Opening Ceremony happened.

+++

That day, I created a December map (12.12). While December was not over, I was resigned to the fact that I had no chance with 15 days left to finish the counties where I was over 50 but less than 67. As the map shows, I reached 50 species in every county, but had 10 counties left where I was short of 67. Six were in the Southeast where I might have managed to reach the target with a 15-day trip of 3 days/county. But even doing that (and missing all three Dare County, NC Christmas Bird Counts), there would have been four other particularly challenging counties left.

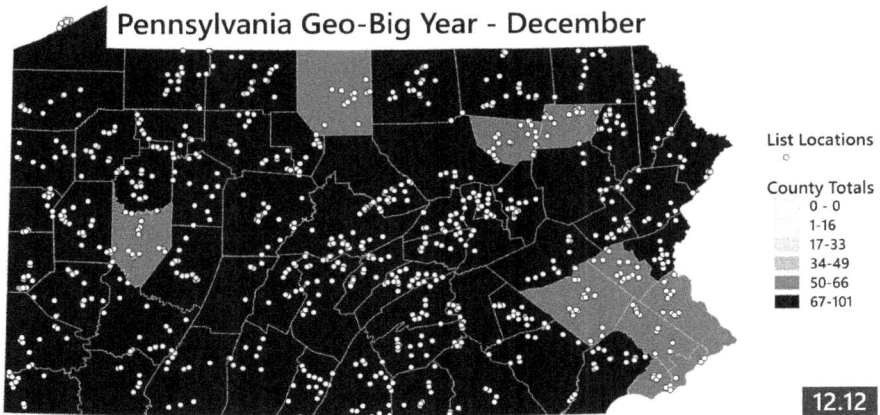

Pennsylvania Geo-Big Year - December

List Locations
○

County Totals
  0 - 0
  1-16
  17-33
  34-49
  50-66
  67-101

12.12

So, I put the quest on hold for 2021. As mentioned above, I had been out of Pennsylvania for about three weeks at that point. Thus, I had reached the fallback target in less than eleven months, and I decided to return to the now fragmented overall 67x67 quest using the month of May 2022 as the twelfth month in a disjointed year.

Fran and I left for North Carolina on Thursday December 16 so that I could do the Kitty Hawk Christmas Count on December 18, with my territory including our NC house.

+++

Between doing the Kitty Hawk Count and the Bodie Light Count (on December 28), I generated the 4th Quarter, thus year-end, graph of my Geo-Big Year quest (12.13). It is a good illustration of the effort of the year as well as the disappointment of getting quite close but not reaching the original goal.

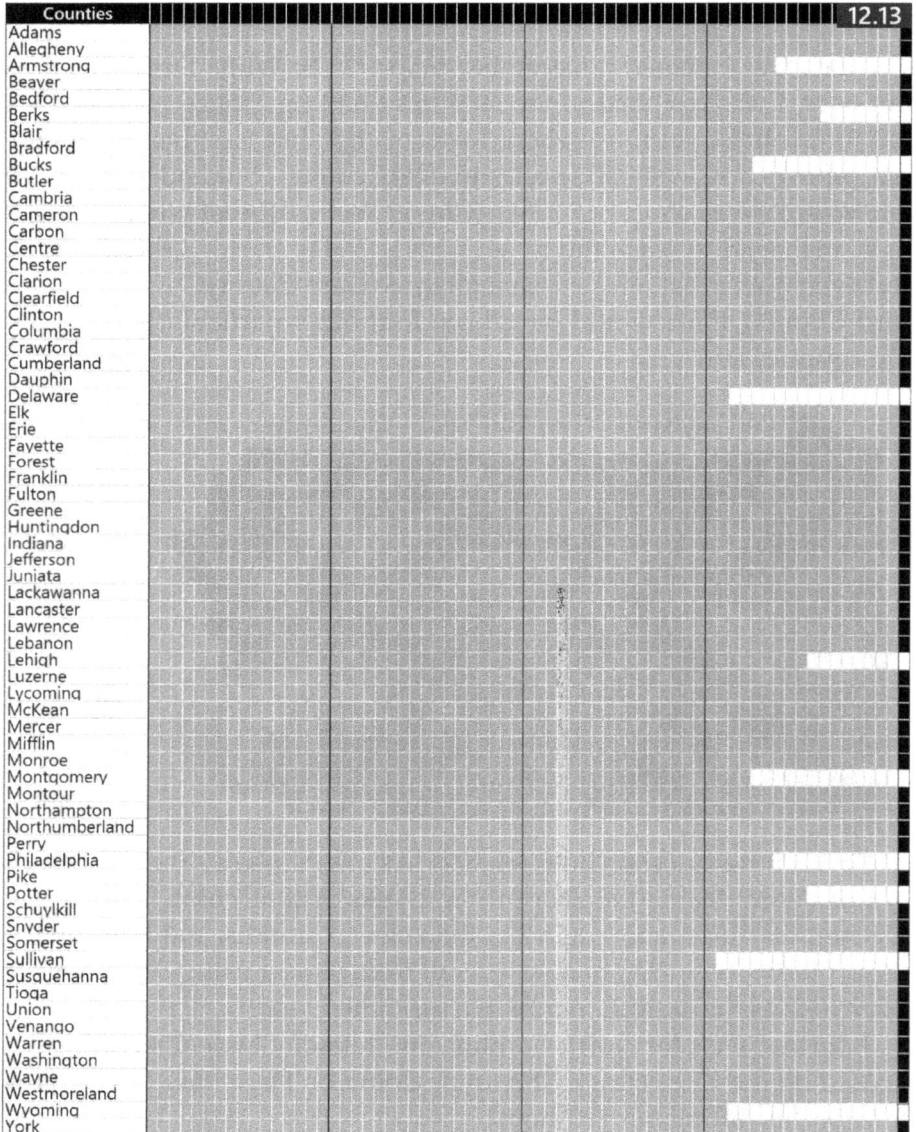

12.13

Reflections on the Quest

Winter brings a pause
Recalling all those misses
Promise comes in spring

Big Years sound exciting, after all they are called "Big" … and they have been the stuff of books and movies.

Many birders have a competitive streak – some much more than others (as evident in The Big Year movie!). Those birders may be motivated primarily by the competition that Big Years can involve. For others, like me, who are only mildly competitive (as in liking to be in the top 10 for year-lists in the two counties I spend my time in), the first Big Year thoughts may be of the plethora of birds to be encountered and/or simply of the *chase*. I now wonder how many birders among those who contemplate a Big Year, particularly those who have done (or started) one, thought ahead about the hours on the road, nights in boring hotel rooms, time standing out in the cold or heat or rain on days/nights when few birds are in sight. For anyone contemplating a second Big Year (like me), those latter factors are likely to be a key consideration.

Despite the miles of driving, varied weather, breakfasts in hotel rooms (often fresh berries plus either Bob's Red Mill Classic Oatmeal or Greek Yogurt), and evening hotel room microwave leftovers from home, the year was both fun and exciting. I experienced parts of Pennsylvania I had never been to nor would have visited if not for my quest. I birded many State Parks, Nature Preserves, County Parks, City Parks,

Game Lands, Wetlands, Wildlife Management Areas, cemeteries, and even some county dumps.

Some photos in chapters above capture the flavor of the mostly rural places in Pennsylvania that I experienced. Looking back, I wish I had been more systematic about photos of places as well as of birds. I particularly enjoyed encountering historical sites and outdoor art. As a Geographer, I appreciated the tremendous landscape variation encountered. Beyond the birds, I (usually) enjoyed the solitude offered by solo birding, particularly in seldom birded locations where I saw nobody else all day.

As I visited sites, I collected brochures and maps – particularly maps, of course. Most were paper versions, some were digital. To reflect the range and distribution of these sites, I generated a mosaic map of Pennsylvania (Re.01) with images of maps/guides superimposed at the approximate geographic locations of the places they reflect.

While there were many positives about pursuing the quest, one disappointment was the dearth of lifers seen during the year. Among the 1,629 eBird lists I posted, I had only two lifers, the Hoary Redpoll in a State College neighborhood and the Upland Sandpiper in Crawford County. I did add 17 species to my Pennsylvania Life List, including the surprising Roseate Spoonbill.

The biggest disappointment of the year was my Pennsylvania Year List. A consequence of the "Geo" Big Year was that I had to limit time spent in key hotspots and seldom took the opportunity to chase rarities, even county rarities at home. As a result, my 2021 Pennsylvania Year List was 2 fewer species than my 2020 Centre County Year List!

Reflecting on my Year List result now, I can see that it represents the same trade-off that birders who participate in Breeding Bird Surveys make. You see/hear many individuals for the species that frequent the places you are focused on, while missing the chance to see/hear other species elsewhere. I saw common species frequently, Canada Goose, American Robin, and Blue Jay in every county. I recorded 28 species in single counties (listed in the online supplement by county), but only a few of them were particularly rare for Pennsylvania.

In addition to the impact on my Year List, another (not surprising) consequence of my Geo-Big Year was that I walked alot. I sometimes walked too much in areas where I saw few new species – those loop trails that sound so attractive from a hiking perspective are often not the best choice for birding. While many walks were less productive for birds than hoped, I got great exercise. On the 189 days for which I posted eBird lists for somewhere in Pennsylvania other than home, I averaged over 12,000 steps/day (based on my iPhone). Unlike many who gained weight during the pandemic year, I lost 16 pounds, reaching a weight I had not seen since grad school in 1979.

To explore my walking, I extracted all the step data from my iPhone and generated a couple of summary graphs (Re.02). Both depict steps/day on my 189 birding days in 2021. The first (Re.02-L) is a histogram of my step/day distribution, binned by ranges of steps/day. The small number of days with fewer than 10,000 steps are grouped in the leftmost bin and each successive bin depicts increasing numbers of steps/day in 2,500-step increments up to the maximum of 25,000-27,500 steps. The distribution is clearly skewed, with only 32 days having fewer than 10,000 steps, the 12,500-15,000 steps/day range being most common, and a long tail extending to one day with 26,537 steps.

The second graph (Re.02-R) depicts mean number of steps per birding day grouped by month (for the 189 days I went out birding). Mean for each month ranges from 7,674 steps/day in February to 14,425 steps/day in September, respectively. I had a moderately active start near home (considering winter weather) with about 10,000 steps per day in January. Walking took a hit in February with even colder weather and more time spent in the car getting to nearby counties (and observing the small amounts of open water in big reservoirs from inside the warm car). Plus, this was a busy month at work with teaching and other responsibilities. My walking ramped up from then through September as better weather (and more birds) were the norm. Walking decreased a bit in the last three months of the year as weather became worse and birds scarcer – the latter prompting me to drive more from one site to another seeking different habitats. Walking in spring might have resembled that during fall, if not for the fact I was still working and clearing out my office at Penn State. That caused me to do more part-day trips with as many hours driving as walking.

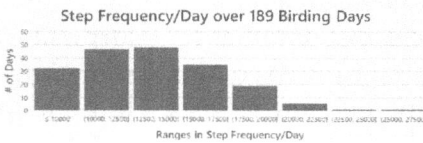

Hindsight is 20-20, or at least that is how the saying goes. In this case, I think it is accurate. Given what I know now, I am sure I could manage the 67x67 Geo-Big Year birding quest within a calendar year. I would make three changes to my strategy. *First*, I would be more proactive during spring migration. I would adopt a geographic south-to-north strategy, in spring, for where to bird when, and the reverse in fall. I would also spend a lot more time in the field during migration weeks, at the time when species are most diverse. The fact that I was still teaching during the spring, had other work responsibilities, and was coping with sorting through 36 years of "stuff" in my office got in the way. *Second*, I would do fewer but longer trips. I spent too much time going to and from distant counties. *Third*, I would make sure to visit the most remote counties, where fewer other birders post sightings, during the peaks of migration when postings by others are not needed.

Beyond the above, the pandemic meant that almost all my birding was done solo. While (as I have mentioned multiple times) I do enjoy solo birding, I also enjoy birding with others, and 2021 offered little opportunity to do that. In addition to the social engagement with like-minded folks, birding in unfamiliar locations with local birders is often more successful since locals know where to bird when.

I probably will not repeat my Pennsylvania Geo-Big Year. I will settle for finishing the 67x67 quest in May 2022 (see Epilog below). But I am thinking ahead to a quest in 2023. The two likely options are my original goal of doing a U.S. Geo-Big Year by state or focusing on North Carolina (if cross-U.S. travel seems impractical due to continuing COVID-19, gas prices, or simply climate change implications).

North Carolina does pose a compelling challenge. Is a 100x100 Geo-Big Year doable? … Only time will tell (Re.03).

Re.03

Source: https://gisgeography.com/

Epilog – filling the gaps

12 months to a year
36 days in OBX
May to fill the gap

Fran and I returned from the Outer Banks on April 26, 2022, so I could prepare for my May blitz. I ended 2021 with 10 Pennsylvania counties at 50 or more but under 67. Given prior slow progress in these counties, I wanted to start quickly at the beginning of May. While spring migration should offer many species missing in late fall, I did not want to come up short again through overconfidence.

Based on Cornell Lab of Ornithology models, Pennsylvania spring migration would peak May 6 along a northwest-southeast transect from Erie to Philadelphia. Counties where I was under 67 included one just southwest of that line (Armstrong-55), three northeast of the line (Potter-58, Sullivan-50, and Wyoming-51), and six in the southeast straddling the line (Lehigh-58, Bucks-52, Berks-59, Montgomery-53, Delaware-51, and Philadelphia-56).

I decided to do Potter County first and Armstrong County second, even though the projected migration line might dictate the opposite. Since Armstrong County was slightly further away and had a few more species needed, I thought it might require an overnight. So, I opted for a Potter County daytrip first. I meant to start on May 1. But I had a small car mishap with a curb. I thought a tire was damaged. Plus, I had after-effects of my second vaccine booster. May 1 was spent recovering from the booster and doing a careful examination of the tire, which turned out to be OK.

+++

On May 2, I was up early, at 5:30am. I got breakfast, walked our dog Skoti, and was out the door toward Potter County about 6:30am. Potter County had been a challenge due to the sparsity of posts in eBird and what seemed to be limited habitat variation. It is mostly rural with rugged and forested terrain.

When I checked eBird alerts, I found 21 species I had not seen. So, I was moderately hopeful that 9 new species was practical in a day trip. My intention was to start at Ole Bull State Park. The plan (unless I got 9 quickly there) was to then move on to Galeton Lake (in Galeton) where several waterfowl I needed had shown up.

The route I took to Potter County was a real flashback. I turned onto Hyner Run Road, which took me right past Hyner View State Park (Ep.01-L). That's the place I first flew my hang glider off a real cliff, in 1994 (I think). On that day, I flew back-and-forth along the ridge above the river a couple times and then negotiated over the trees and across the river to the landing field below. That was my closest to knowing what it feels like to be a bird. I had better luck than another guy trying the same thing that day; he crossed the river too low and ended up "landing" in a tree and needed to be rescued.

The route I took (State Route 120, to Hyner Mountain Road, to State Route 44) entered Potter County along the edge of Susquehannock State Forest. The fog of early morning had cleared when I reached the Pine Hill Summit (Ep.01-R). I decided to stop at spots along the road while birds might be calling.

Starting at 8:23am, I generated three lists while walking along forest roads. On one road, a pickup truck with guys in camouflage stopped. In rural Pennsylvania, that always makes me a bit nervous. The driver initially asked what I was looking for, perhaps thinking I was scouting something they wanted to shoot. When I told him I was trying to get a Yellow-bellied Sapsucker photo, he seemed interested and commented on other birds in the area, including Pileated Woodpecker (already on my county list).

They moved on and I got my photo (Ep.02-L). Shortly after, while trying for a photo of Blackburnian Warbler (which did not cooperate), I saw a porcupine in a tree, so took a photo (Ep.02-R). The Blackburnian Warbler was one of 6 new species that included Yellow Warbler and Black-and-white Warbler.

Ep.02

Given my progress and habitat similarity to where I was, I skipped Ole Bull State Park and moved on to Galeton Lake. There, I quickly added Common Grackle, Barn Swallow, and then number 67 - Solitary Sandpiper (Ep.03). I went on to add several more, including Yellow Warbler, Tree Swallow, and Northern Rough-winged Swallow to reach 72 species by 10:35am. I ate early lunch by the lake. While doing so I saw some Yellowlegs and after moving a bit closer was able to identify both Greater Yellowlegs and Lesser Yellowlegs to reach 74 species for the county.

Ep.03

That was, by far, one of the best days of birding I'd had in Pennsylvania since the peak of fall Migration. I left for home having blown past my target – before noon! For once in a long while, I would get home in time to process photos the same day.

+++

After dealing with photos and checking the weather, I opted to do another day trip the next day (May 3) to Armstrong County. While Armstrong County is farther in miles than Potter County, travel time turned out to be about the same, at two hours. My 2021 total for Armstrong was 55, thus I would have a bit more to do to reach my target, but it seemed doable after the prior day's success.

The nearest eBird hotspot in Armstrong County was Keystone Lake where I'd birded a couple times before. It had fewer recent sightings for species I needed than some sites, but some were reported, and the habitat was promising. I planned to try a rails-to-trail site or a state park after that, depending on eBird reports.

+++

On May 3, I was out the door at 6:30am. On the way out of town, I swung by the post office to drop my primary ballot in the mail. That allowed nearly 2 weeks to go the few miles from State College to Bellefonte. Even with today's postal service, I figured that would be sufficient – I eventually got confirmation it was.

I arrived at Keystone Lake at 8:38am. Birding was good. As in Potter County, locals were curious about why I was walking along a rural road with binoculars and camera. First, a local Pennsylvania woodsman (based on his camouflage hat, pickup truck, and gun rack) stopped to chat. After finding out my home was near Penn State and I had worked there, he asked if I knew a friend of his named Wagner. His now retired friend (who I did not know) had been Vice President for Business & Operations. The woodsman seemed happy that an "outsider" appreciated his county enough to travel there to bird.

As I walked further along the roadside, I also had a young woman stop to ask about what I was doing. She was interested in my search for birds. While she was not a birder, she clearly appreciated birds. Next, the first guy came back and stopped again – he liked to talk. This time he mentioned a friend who lived near Axeman (in Centre County) and the fact that he'd been to my County multiple times for fishing. I learned that this friend was quite a woodcarver. It was nice to talk to someone for a change, but I think I may have missed a warbler that called a couple times but had stopped before I could listen carefully.

Even if I missed a bird, I added species steadily throughout the morning. By 11:00am I had reached 65 species. Some good additions were Common Loon, Yellow Warbler, and multiple Baltimore Oriole (Ep.04). I also had Bonaparte's Gull, Spotted Sandpiper, Ovenbird, and American Redstart (#65).

Ep.04

I decided to head to a different location to try to find the remaining two. The plan was to eat lunch at a rails-to-trail access point and bird there. But, on my way, I encountered my last two. They were a Brown-headed Cowbird (Ep.05-L) for 66 and a Field Sparrow for 67. The Merlin app had been signaling Field Sparrows repeatedly. But I never heard them (I assume it was keying in on a call rather than song), so I had not recorded any. This time I heard two singing very clearly.

Since I had reached 67, I decided not to go to the rails-to-trails site, which would have taken me 25 min. further from home. But it was still early so I opted to look for a few extras before heading home. I drove slowly and heard several birds making a lot of noise. There were clearly some American Robin, but something else too. It was either Gray Catbird, Northern Mockingbird, or Brown Thrasher; I was not initially sure which. I had the first two on my list, but not the third. I stopped, turned off the car, and listened carefully. Ultimately a Brown Thrasher came out into the open (Ep.05-R).

There were still a bunch of birds chattering, so I stayed by the side of the road and listened. I heard what sounded like Chipping Sparrow (which I had on my list). I looked for it to be sure. It was perched on an old-style television antenna – something that is not seen much anymore. Also there, to my surprise, was a Ruby-throated Hummingbird. It was a male (Ep.05-M).

Ep.05

At that point, I still had not had lunch. I drove around to the other side of the lake where I knew there was a parking lot. I ate lunch watching for an Osprey. That would've made an even 70. No luck on that, so I finished up lunch and headed for home at 12:30pm with 69 species for Armstrong County.

+++

I was making great progress on my May 2022 "epilogue" to the 2021 Geo-Big Year. In two daytrips, I easily finished two counties. I was less confident about Sullivan and Wyoming Counties. They are small, not heavily birded (thus not much help from eBird), have limited habitat variation, and had been the most challenging during the late fall when I was trying to reach my fallback target of 50. For these reasons, I opted to try them next, leaving the six counties of the southeast to last.

Optimistically, if I could finish Sullivan County (the closest to home) before lunch, as I had managed with the previous two counties, I might finish both on a one day trip. If not, I would do a follow up day trip. My optimism was perhaps just that, since I was starting with 50 and 51 species from 2021. Maybe birding on *Cinco de Mayo* would bring me luck!. Since I was only cautiously optimistic, I decided to take stuff for an overnight, if necessary, as an alternative to a second day trip.

+++

To have a shot at completing both counties in the same day, I got out of the house at 5:30am. I would be seeing my first sunrise for a couple of weeks. I got to Sullivan County about 7:30am. I stopped along the roadside immediately after passing the signs for Ricketts Glen and the County Boundary (Ep.06-L&M) – the sign for Wyoming County was seen a bit later in the day (Ep.06-R).

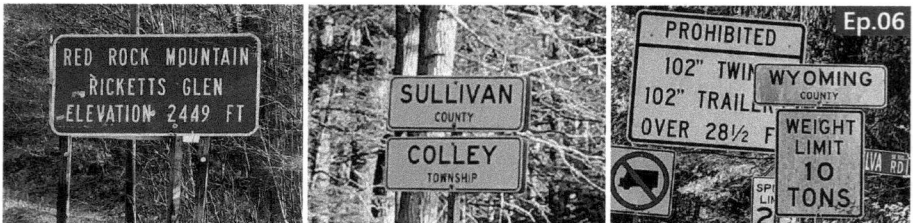

As soon as I stopped, I heard Ovenbird; I also picked up a Nashville Warbler (reaching 52 species). I went on to Ricketts Glen State Park and added 8 more species in the campground (reaching 60 species). These included Blue-headed Vireo, Black-throated Green Warbler, American Redstart, and Tree Swallow (Ep.07).

Ep.07

From there, I drove to the northern part of the state park and spent about 40 minutes at the Hayfield hotspot. I added an additional 8 species there, reaching 68 by 9:00am! These included Black-and-white Warbler, Yellow Warbler, Gray Catbird, and Eastern Kingbird (Ep.08).

Ep.08

At that point, I did not know I had surpassed the target since there was no cell coverage. I could neither submit my lists nor check to see which species I was missing (I had not thought to print a list of those out). I finally found a spot at the top of the hill where I had a marginal cell signal. It was sufficient to upload my lists. Once I knew I was over the top, I figured out that the Eastern Kingbird had been number 67. Then, I set a route to Wyoming County that would get me into the county as quickly as possible. On the way there, I added Broad-winged Hawk for Sullivan County (#69).

Just inside the Wyoming County boundary, see sign shown above (Ep.06-R), I started a list that added 5 species including Black-throated Blue Warbler and Blue-headed Vireo (Ep.09-L&M). I then stopped at a bunch of locations along a back road passing through some game lands and picked up new species at each stop. Again, I didn't know what my total was because there was no cell signal. I could not find a cell signal until nearly 1:00pm. When I did, I found that I had reached 67 for Wyoming County with Least Flycatcher (Ep.09-R).

Ep.09

I decided to make one more stop at the wetlands where I had found Sandhill Crane in the fall, since it did not seem out-of-the-way for the route home. Due to some road construction, it ended up being a bit out of the way, but not very much. On the drive there I picked up an Osprey (Ep.10-L). I then did quite well at the wetland adding 8 species including Baltimore Oriole and Wood Duck (Ep.10-M&R).

Ep.10

Overall, I had an extremely successful day, finishing two counties and starting home before 2:00pm.

+++

I have been a birder since 1991, so I expect spring migration to be great. But my extreme difference in success over efforts in the late fall was beyond my expectations. In Wyoming County, it had taken me parts of 5 days in November and December to manage 51 species on my county list. Now, in less than half of one day I added 25 new species to blow past my target of 67 to reach 76. Success in Sullivan County as well as Potter and Armstrong Counties had been similar.

I still had six counties to complete, but they were clustered in the southeast. Based on my May success to that point, I was optimistic that, having finished two adjacent counties in one daytrip, I could do six clustered counties on a three-day trip. I stayed at home for a couple days due to a forecast for a lot of rain. I booked two nights (May 8 and 9) in Pottstown Pennsylvania. Pottstown is in Montgomery County, but nearly at the geographic center of the six counties left to finish.

Staying home had worse implications than lack of progress on my quest. While working at my desk processing pictures from the last outing, my binocular strap caught on a chair arm, pulling the binoculars off the counter and onto the tile floor. At first glance they looked fine. The rubber armoring did its job. But they apparently fell right on one of the strap loops. Even though it is metal, it broke right off (Ep.11).

Ep.11

While the binoculars remained functional optically, they could not be attached to a neck strap or harness. I had owned the binoculars for 16 years. I checked with Swarovski about repairs. They replied quickly that the damage was fixable (for $150), but it would take 4-8 weeks. I had heard many stories over the years about Swarovski doing free repairs for almost anything (until they recently changed to a 10-year warranty). But that apparently does not extend to dropping the optics onto a tile floor. The cost was reasonable but sending the binoculars off for repair would mean being without my good binoculars for the rest of May and beyond. The second-best binoculars in the house, were my old Nikon 8x32 Premier SE pair from 1998. They became Fran's when I got my Swarovski pair. Optically they are pretty good. But they are not waterproof, they don't transmit as much light (so less clear in the early morning or late evening), and we lost the eyepiece cover long ago, thus they are doubly challenging in the rain.

After thinking about it for a day, I drove to the Lost Creek Shoe Shop to buy new binoculars. Despite status as the top place for optics in Central Pennsylvania (as noted earlier), being an Amish shop, they do not have a phone. Thus, I could not call them to check stock (other than by leaving a message at a nearby business that helps them out; then waiting a day for a reply). The 45-minute drive there was easier.

It was pouring rain on the drive, with flood warnings. The shop's entrance had standing water when I arrived, but it was passable. I went in intending to buy a new pair of the Swarovski EL 8.5x42 binoculars that I had. The newer version has slightly better optics, and I planned to pass my old ones to Fran once they came back from repair (I had decided to spring for another $250 to replace optics that were scratched as well). The grandson of Aden who owns the shop got out a pair of binoculars for me to look at, which I did. He encouraged me to go on the back porch to give them a try. They have the perfect spot for testing optics. Among other things, we saw 7 White-crowned Sparrows.

While trying the ELs, the grandson asked if I had ever tried the new NLs. I said I'd only read about them. Not surprisingly (since they list for about $800 more), I was encouraged to try the NLs. I somewhat foolishly agreed. Not long after, I left as the proud owner of a new pair of Swarovski 8x40 NLs.

Reviews I had read suggested that the NLs have a tiny optical improvement over the ELs. But, I could not sense that. The big differences, however, are that the NLs have a wider field of view, they have a slightly less flat image, and they have a very different shape to the body. For me, the wider field of view turned out to be noticeable (since I wear glasses) and a slightly more adjustable eye cup position was noticeable too. Most important was that the shape and balance worked great in my hands. Given that I am now 70 years old, when I reach the end of a long day of birding, I have noticed that holding the binoculars steady is harder than it used to be. The NLs seemed particularly easy to keep steady. The Lost Creek Shoe Shop has quite good prices because their overhead is so low. Thus the price was better than in other retail outlets and the difference in price from the Els was a bit less. Still, this was an expense I had not anticipated. After having bought a new Swarovski scope back in February, I figured I was now one of the top customers at the Lost Creek Shoe Shop to that point in 2022!

+++

On May 8, I got out the driveway at 6:31am toward my first stop in Berks County. I arrived at the Green Hills Preserve about 9:00am. I spent a bit over 2 hours there, walking nearly 3 miles. As in the past – I should have learned – I made the mistake of doing a loop trail. I could've reached 67 with a much shorter walk. Instead, starting at 59, I ended up with 74 species for the county. Additions included American Kestrel, Tree Swallow, Field Sparrow, Wood Thrush, Chestnut-sided

Warbler, and Common Yellowthroat (Ep.12). Blue-winged Warbler was number 67, but I could not get a good photo of that one.

Ep.12

I decided to move to the Rodale Park in Lehigh County I had visited before. I spent 2.5 hours there, generating 4 eBird lists. My first new species were a Killdeer and a Solitary Sandpiper in a shallow pond just outside the Park. Over the time there, I gradually picked up species, ultimately reaching 70 for the county. These included House Wren, Baltimore Oriole, Gray Catbird, and Indigo Bunting (Ep.13).

Ep.13

The most spectacular was number 67, a Great-horned Owl and its large fledgling (Ep.14).

Ep.14

Having finished Lehigh County at 2:45pm, I moved to Bucks County where I needed 15 species. Just after I entered Bucks County I added an American Kestrel perched on a pole. At Lake Towhee Park I took another loop trail (seems like I never learn). At least this loop was shorter than several I'd done (less than a mile). I added species steadily as I walked. By the end, I was at 66 species, thus one to go. Nice additions included Fish Crow (just heard), Ruby-throated Hummingbird, Black Vulture, and Veery.

I moved to a different section of the park and walked around the edges of a big clearing. I found an American Redstart (Ep.15-L) for number 67, then added Black-and-white Warbler for 68. Except for the American Redstart, I had marginal success with photos of anything else new but did get nice shots of Eastern Bluebird and Red-winged Blackbird (Ep.15-M&R).

Since it was only about 4:30pm when I completed Bucks County, my third for the day, I decided to try Montgomery County to see how far I could get toward the 14 I needed there.

I started at White's Mill Preserve at 5:01pm. The Preserve is about 100 acres and not very developed. This time, I did a short out and back path rather than a loop – because there were no loop choices rather than because I had finally learned. In three-quarters of an hour, I added 8 new species that included a Blue-gray Gnatcatcher and a Northern Rough-winged Swallow.

From there, I made a quick stop at Unami Creek IBA where I picked up Louisiana Waterthrush. Next, I went to Green Lake Park, picking up House Finch and Common Grackle, enroute. It was 6:38pm and I needed 3 more species. It seemed unlikely I could manage that, but I opted to try. I was glad I did. I added Chipping Sparrow (Ep.16-L), then Spotted Sandpiper, and then Gray Catbird (Ep.16-R) for number 67. After the Catbird, I found a Warbling Vireo and then a Yellow Warbler (Ep.16-M) to raise the total to 69 before heading to the hotel.

Ep.16

+++

That was a spectacular day. Starting from home, I managed to finish 4 of the 6 remaining counties. Being at the peak of spring migration was clearly ideal. In addition, I had developed better strategies for finding species quickly, with mostly shorter stops to cover multiple kinds of habitat quickly. I also spent less time on photos than during the primary 2021 quest.

As I got close to finishing the third county earlier in the day, I realized that I probably did not need two hotel nights, so I called and canceled my second night. I figured that if my pace slowed and I needed another night I could book it then.

The plan for the second day was obviously to focus on my final two counties: Philadelphia and Delaware. Since the John Heinz NWR spans the county boundary, that was the logical place to go.

+++

I was out of the parking lot at 6:19am. That was later than I was hoping but not too bad. Google Maps estimated 0:50-1:10 travel time to get from the hotel to the Delaware County part of the NWR in Monday morning traffic. Traffic turned out being average and I got started at 7:15am.

I did a small loop trail on the Delaware County side of the NWR and added 18 species by 8:25am. The first was Gray Catbird (Ep.17-L). Others included Yellow Warbler, Northern Parula, Common Yellowthroat, and Warbling Vireo. I approached the target with Wood Duck (Ep.17-M), added Black-and-white Warbler, and then for number 67, Spotted Sandpiper (Ep.17-R) – my standby to close out counties. I was at 69 species (the last had been a Brown-headed Cowbird) when I drove to the Philadelphia County access point for the NWR. Things were looking good to head home without another night.

Ep.17

On the Philadelphia side of the NWR, I did a loop starting at 9:00am. I added species quickly. By about 10:30am I had far exceeded my target. In the first part of the walk out in the open, along the impoundment, thnew species included Yellow Warbler (I seemed to be seeing them everywhere) Great Egret, and Osprey (Ep.18).

Ep.18

As I continued, a Baltimore Oriole provided a great photo opportunity as it worked on some flowers in a tree (Ep.19-L), a Gray Catbird (Ep.19-M) was also quite photogenic, but too close to get completely in the frame, and then I found number 67, a Black-and-white Warbler calling as it worked a tree (Ep.19-R).

Ep.19

As I completed the loop, I continued to add species. One of the last was Northern Rough-winged Swallow (Ep.20-L), number 74. When I got back to the car, I added a final species, White-crowned Sparrow for number 75. It was listed as rare, and fortunately I got a halfway decent photo that I could post with my list (Ep.20-R). I ate lunch in the car with no further species showing up. When done, I started for home, **my quest finally completed**, after an incredible two days!

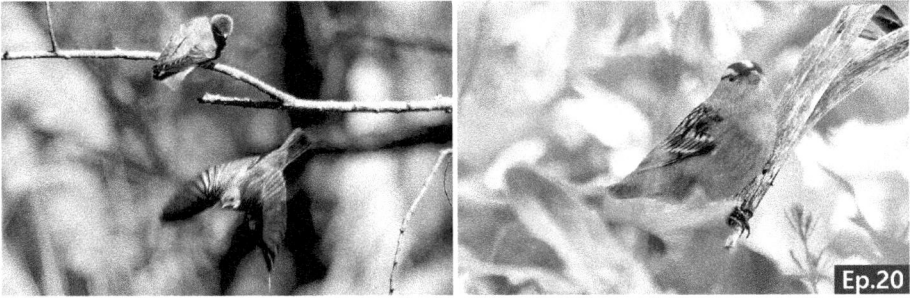

+++

In mid-December 2021 when I settled for my fallback plan to find 50 or more species in every Pennsylvania County, it was a bittersweet conclusion to an eventful year. I was happy to have experienced birding in every PA county and to meet the 50 species target in time to do Christmas Bird Counts in Dare County, NC. Not surprisingly, however, it was a big disappointment to fall short of the original 67x67 goal for the Geo-Big Year.

When I came up with the plan to continue in May 2022, to fill in the 10 counties for which I reached 50 but not 67, it felt like the result would be a bit contrived. But I am extremely glad I decided to follow through with the idea.

Finishing all 10 counties in just five days of birding was exhilarating. As I write this on the first day of summer, 2022, I am ready to go birding. I encourage you, the reader, to get out and do the same!

+++++

Figure Credits

"by author" below refers to photos by Alan M. MacEachren

Page	Figure	Image and credits / permissions
5	In.01	Map of Pennsylvania eBird hotspots. Data that underlie the map are from eBird, an online database of bird distribution and abundance. Source: eBird, Cornell Lab of Ornithology, Ithaca, New York: http://www.ebird.org. (data provided 4/28, 2022).
6	In.02	Screen capture of eBird bar chart. Image provided by eBird (www.ebird.org) and created 2/10/2022.
7	In.03	Photo (by author) of eBird mobile app on author's phone. iPhone screen image provided by eBird (www.ebird.org) and created 1/29/2022.
17	01.08	January progress map. List location data provided by eBird (www.ebird.org) and downloaded 1/31/2021.
27	02.08	February progress map. List location data provided by eBird (www.ebird.org) and downloaded 2/28/2021.
50	03.31	March progress map. List location data provided by eBird (www.ebird.org) and downloaded 3/31/2021.
66	04.15	April progress map. List location data provided by eBird (www.ebird.org) and downloaded 4/30/2021.
76	05.09	A split photo set of a Gnome Village All photos (by the author) included here with permission of the Gnome Home creator, Steve Hoke.
85	05.24	An OpenStreetMap screen capture for the Quehanna Wild Area with the area boundary in black. OpenStreetMap cartography is licensed under the Creative Commons Attribution-ShareAlike 2.0 license (CC-BY-SA). The basemap design uses the Tile Style by CyclOSM, hosted by OpenStreetMap France. See: http://www.openstreetmap.org/copyright.
101	05.47	Map Plaque showing the Susquehanna River Watershed. Photo (by author) included courtesy of Shikellamy State Park, DCNR Bureau of State Parks.
102	05.50	May progress map. List location data provided by eBird (www.ebird.org) and downloaded 6/1/2021.
115	06.19	An OpenStreetMap screen capture for the Meyersdale, PA region showing the Great Allegheny Passage Trail as a broad gray transparent line passing through Keystone, Glade City, Meyersdale, and Salisbury Junction OpenStreetMap cartography is licensed under the Creative Commons Attribution-ShareAlike 2.0 license (CC-BY-SA). The basemap design uses Tiles courtesy of Andy Allan. See: http://www.openstreetmap.org/copyright.
128	06.38	Historical marker detailing The Pennsylvania Canal (at Wildwood Park). Photo (by author) included with permission of Dauphin County Parks and Recreation.
129	06.39	(left panel) Art in the Park installation at Wildwood Park "It's Just a Phase". Photo (by author) included with permission of the artist, Kristin Ziegler.
132	06.44	June progress map. List location data provided by eBird (www.ebird.org) and downloaded 6/30/2021.
140	07.06	Screen capture of sonogram generated from the author's audio recording, using the Merlin app from the Cornell Lab of Ornithology. Image provided by eBird (www.ebird.org) and created 3/2/2022.

144	07.14	(left panel) The Thomas Darling Nature Preserve sign. Photo (by author) included with permission from The Nature Conservancy.
147	07.18	(left panel) Art in the Park installation Wildwood Park called Lotus on the Land. Photo (by author) included with permission of the artist Lorayn McPoyle.
148	07.20	Section of an eBird bar graph. Image provided by eBird (www.ebird.org) and created 3/10/2022.
151	07.22	Map of Todd Nature Reserve at entrance. Photo (by author) included with permission of the Audubon Society of Western Pennsylvania, Todd Nature Reserve.
163	07.40	July progress map. List location data provided by eBird (www.ebird.org) and downloaded 7/31/2021.
167	08.07	(top left panel) A train engine bike rack. Photo (by author) included with permission of Michael Les from the Seneca Highlands Career & Technical Ctr Welding Class; (bottom panel) Mural created by artist Angela Cornelius. Photo (by author) included with permission from the artist.
170	08.10	(left panel) Photo of the National Park Service, North Country National Scenic Trail panel posted at a trail access point in McKean County, PA for the trail that runs from Vermont to North Dakota. Photo (by author) included with permission of the North Country Trail Association.
177	08.20	Two USDA Forest Service signs posted on Allegheny National Forest land, both are site maps depicting trail systems. Photos of signs (by auhor) included courtesy of the USDA Forest Service.
190	08.44	(left panel) A commemorative plaque highlighting a donation from the James M. and Margret V. Stine Foundation that supported construction of a pedestrian bridge and walkway at Sweet Arrow Lake in Schuylkill County. Photo (by author) included with permission from Schuylkill County Parks and Recreation.
194	08.52	August Progress map. List location data provided by eBird (www.ebird.org) and downloaded 8/31/2021.
197	09.06	Wildflower Reserve Map and Trail descriptions from Racoon Creek State Park brochure (rev. 11/04/20). Photos (by author) included Courtesy Pennsylvania State Parks.
208	09.19	Section of an eBird bar graph. Image provided by eBird (www.ebird.org) and created 4/10/2022.
233	09.58	September progress map. List location data provided by eBird (www.ebird.org) and downloaded 9/30/2021.
239	10.03	(left panel) Photo of Clarion Loop Trail Map. Photo (by author) included with permission of Pennsylvania Great Outdoors Visitors Bureau, see www.clariontrails.com for downloadable map.
241	10.09	(right panel) An OpenStreetMap screen capture for the Oil Creek State Park section that contains the Blood Farm Interpretive Trail. Labels on the map for the trail and for Oil Creek have been added to the screen capture post-capture. OpenStreetMap cartography is licensed under the Creative Commons Attribution-ShareAlike 2.0 license (CC-BY-SA). The basemap design uses Tiles courtesy of Andy Allan. See: http://www.openstreet-map.org/copyright.
247	10.18	A creative land/seascape at the base of the bridge by Brandi Bee. Photo (by author) included with permission of the artist.

249	10.20	A map at the Wingfield Pines Conservation Area. Photo (by author) included courtesy of Allegheny Land Trust. www.alleghenylandtrust.org.
253	10.28	Portion of a historical map of North Huntingdon Township from Beer's Atlas of Westmoreland County, 1867. Open source, retrieved from http://usgwarchives.net/maps/pa/county/westmo/1867/nhunting.jpg.
267	10.48	(middle panel) photo of trail map on post just north of Lock & Dam 8 provided by Armstrong Trails. The map can be viewed and downloaded from: https://armstrongtrails.org/trail-map/.
268	10.50	An OpenStreetMap screen capture showing Reefer Hollow Road. OpenStreetMap cartography is licensed under the Creative Commons Attribution-ShareAlike 2.0 license (CC-BY-SA). The basemap uses the Tiles style by CyclOSM hosted by OpenStreetmap France. See: http://www.openstreetmap.org/copyright.
271	10.54	October progress map. List location data provided by eBird (www.ebird.org) and downloaded 10/31/2021.
272	11.01	An OpenStreetMap screen capture showing Deer Lake and Hunter's Lake, Sullivan County. OpenStreetMap cartography is licensed under the Creative Commons Attribution-ShareAlike 2.0 license (CC-BY-SA). The basemap uses the Tiles style by CyclOSM hosted by OpenStreetmap France. See: http://www.openstreetmap.org/copyright.
281	11.14	(left panel) An OpenStreetMap screen capture showing Cherry Valley NWR. OpenStreetMap cartography is licensed under the Creative Commons Attribution-ShareAlike 2.0 license (CC-BY-SA). The basemap design is the default OpenStreetMap design. See: http://www.openstreetmap.org/copyright.
282	11.17	Two large sculptures by Susan Opie. Photos (by author) included with permission of the artist.
283	11.18	Three large sculptures by Susan Opie. Photos (by author) included with permission of the artist.
289	11.33	Sign for Trexler Nature Preserve (top left image). Photo (by author) included with permission of Lehigh County Parks.
299	11.45	(left panel) An OpenStreetMap screen capture, John Heinz National Wildlife Refuge area. OpenStreetMap cartography is licensed under the Creative Commons Attribution-ShareAlike 2.0 license (CC-BY-SA). The basemap design is the default OpenStreetMap design. See: http://www.openstreetmap.org/copyright. (right panel - photo of a trail repair warning sign, taken 11/22/22 at the John Heinz National Wildlife Refuge impoundment trail).
300	11.48	An OpenStreetMap screen capture for the Delaware County portion of the John Heinz National Wildlife Refuge area. OpenStreetMap cartography is licensed under the Creative Commons Attribution-ShareAlike 2.0 license (CC-BY-SA). The basemap design is the default OpenStreetMap design. See: http://www.openstreetmap.org/copyright.
310	11.67	November progress map. List location data provided by eBird (www.ebird.org) and downloaded 12/5/2021.
315	12.07	Historical sign at Kernsville Dam Recreation Area. Photo (by author) included with permission of the Schuylkill River Greenways National Heritage Area.
319	12.12	December progress map. List location data provided by eBird (www.ebird.org) and downloaded 12/15/2021.

That was so much fun
Can't every month be May
Birds singing again

www.ingramcontent.com/pod-product-compliance
Lightning Source LLC
Chambersburg PA
CBHW062115020426
42335CB00013B/970